Technology, Teaching and Learning

Issues in the
Integration of Technology

Barrie R.C. Barrell, Editor

Detselig Enterprises Ltd.

Calgary, Alberta, Canada

© 2001 Detselig Enterprises Ltd.

National Library of Canada Cataloguing in Publication Data

Main entry under title:

Technology, teaching and learning

Includes bibliographic references.

ISBN 1-55059-217-3

1. Educational technology. 2. Internet in education. 3. Computer-assisted instruction. I. Barrell, Barrie R.C. (Barrie Robert Christopher).

LB1028.3.T45   2001   371.33   C2001-911469-9

Detselig Enterprises Ltd.

210-1220 Kensington Rd. N.W., Calgary, AB T2N 3P5

Telephone: (403) 283-0900/Fax: (403) 283-6947

E-mail: temeron@telusplanet.net

www.temerondetselig.com

All rights reserved. No part of this book may be reproduced in any form or by any means without permission in writing from the publisher.

We acknowledge the financial support of the Government of Canada through the Book Publishing Industry Development Program (BPIDP) for our publishing activities.

1-55050-217-3

SAN 115-0324

Printed in Canada

Table of Contents

Contributors 5
Foreword – John Willinsky 13
Introduction – Tangled in the Net.
Barrie R.C. Barrell 17

Part I – Issues and Perspectives

1. The Stewardship of the Intellect: Classroom Life, Educational Innovation and Technology. Pat Clifford & Sharon Friesen 29
2. Singing Up the Country: Multiple Readings of a Middle School Writing Classroom as (Cyber)text. Rob Cohen 43
3. Factors Affecting the Adoption and Use of Instructional Devices. George H. Buck 61
4. The Hand-Made's Tail: A Novel Approach to Educational Technology. Michele Jacobsen & Ricki Goldman 83
5. Object Lessons: Critical Visions of Educational Technology. Suzanne de Castell, Mary Bryson & Jennifer Jenson. 113

Part II – Case Studies and Classroom Uses of ICT

6. Tearing Down the Walls: New Literacies and New Horizons in the Elementary School. Heather Lotherington, Mary Leigh Morbey, Colette Granger & Lara Doan 129
7. Lessons Learned: Three Case Studies of ICT in Teaching and Their Implications for Practice. Herbert H. Wideman & Ronald D. Owston 163
8. Integrating Robotics into a Grade 2 Classroom: Making Space for Robert. Mary M. Cameron & Barrie R.C. Barrell 183
9. Virtual Schooling: Integrating Schooling into Technology. William J. Hunter & Rosina Smith 197

PART III – TECHNOLOGY LEADERSHIP AND TEACHER EDUCATION

10. THE MANY FACES OF ICT LEADERSHIP FOR DIGITAL TECHNOLOGY AND CANADIAN PEDAGOGY. DIANNE YEE 221

11. INVERTED HOLLYWOOD: THE PITCH FOR e-KNOWLEDGE MEETS PRE-SERVICE TEACHER EDUCATION. LISA KORTEWEG 239

12. COMPUTERS IN HUMANITIES EDUCATION: FIVE TEACHERS EXAMINE THE ISSUES. JIM GREENLAW, NATASHA BOUDREAU, JILL BURRY, MARILYN MACLEAN & MARY ANN MURRIN 261

13. ISSUES OF EDUCATIONAL USES OF THE INTERNET: A CASE STUDY OF MATHEMATICS PRE-SERVICE TEACHERS. JUDY M. ISEKE-BARNES 281

14. CLASSROOM MANAGEMENT IN THE NETWORKED CLASSROOM: NEW PROBLEMS AND POSSIBILITIES. ELIZABETH MURPHY & THÉRÈSE LAFERRIÈRE 305

Contributors

Barrie R.C. Barrell is Associate Professor of Secondary English Education, Memorial University of Newfoundland. His previous book *Advocating Change: Contemporary Issues in Subject English* brought together two dozen Canadian scholars to discuss the transformation taking place in Canadian English language arts education brought about by the inclusion of technology, media, viewing, and other ways of communicating and representing knowledge. Informing his university work are experiences in elementary, middle and secondary schools in remote, rural and urban settings in Canada and the United States. He has recently completed a year as Visiting Scholar at the University of Calgary.

Natasha Boudreau is an elementary French teacher in Ontario.

Mary Bryson teaches in the Department of Educational Psychology at the University of British Columbia. Her primary interest is in technology and marginality. For 1998-1999, Mary was appointed "UBC Scholar-in-Residence" at UBC's Centre for Research in Women's Studies. She and Suzanne de Castell were co-recipients of the Pioneer in New Technologies and Media award, presented by Women in the Spotlight/Wired Woman Society. They have written collaboratively on theoretical treatments of gender and technology, and equity in education, culminating in *Radical In<ter>ventions*, 1997, SUNY Press.

George H. Buck's interest in technology, history, human learning and curricular change dates from an early age. After working as an Industrial Arts teacher for several years, he studied the technological history of public transportation in Edmonton and the factors leading to changes in this area for his M.Ed. degree. His doctoral work in Educational Psychology was concerned with the development of instructional devices and the factors that led to some succeeding and to others failing. Other research has been concerned with the use of computers for instruction, the design of school architecture and its influence on learning and curriculum, and the development and role of railways in the growth of Western Canada. Currently, he is an Associate Professor of Secondary Education, and an Adjunct professor of Educational Psychology at the University of Alberta.

Jill Burry is a Grade 5 and 6 teacher who is currently working in Prince Edward Island after teaching for many years in Newfoundland.

6 Contributors

Mary M. Cameron is a consultant for Rocky View School Division, Alberta. Working with the Coalition of Innovative Schools and division-wide ICT integration, she was the technology administrator and a classroom teacher at Banded Peak School in Bragg Creek, Alberta. She holds undergraduate and graduate degrees from the University of Prince Edward Island and Memorial University of Newfoundland. At Banded Peak School she pushed the limits of technology integration and helped parents understand the possibilities of constructivist pedagogy when combined with innovative uses of digital technologies. Her classes in robotics have been enjoyed by grade 2s and have drawn the attention of Sony Japan and SMART Technologies.

Pat Clifford is co-founder and President of the Galileo Educational Network. Pat has an extensive teaching background that includes Grades 1 to 12, university undergraduate and graduate classes, and a wide range of teacher in-service topics related to curriculum, school improvement and leadership. For the past nine years she has worked in teaching and research partnership with Sharon Friesen. She and Sharon are co-recipients of numerous awards for both research and teaching practice: 1999 The Alberta Teachers' Association Educational Research Award; 1999 Prime Minister's Award for Teaching Excellence; 1998 Aoki Award for educational research; 1996 ASCD Celebrating Educational Successes in Alberta award; 1994 National Institute Award for Technology Integration; 1991 Alberta Excellence in Teaching finalist. Most recently, her work has centred on essential issues in the effective integration of technology.

Rob Cohen is a middle school English teacher creating a state-of-the-art hypertext authoring enrichment program for the middle school in Franklin Lakes, New Jersey. He has been a consultant to school districts throughout New Jersey with regard to classroom technology infusion and standards based curriculum alignment. He holds an MA in Writing from William Paterson College and is currently working toward his Ed.D. in English Education at Teachers College, Columbia University.

Suzanne de Castell teaches in the Faculty of Education at Simon Fraser University. Her primary interests are in media and epistemology. See Mary Bryson bio for more detail.

Lara Doan is a doctoral student in the Graduate program in Language, Culture, and Teaching at York University in Toronto. With a focus on social equity and pedagogies of possibility, Doan's research concerns the role of new information technologies and on-line pedagogies in teacher education.

Sharon Friesen is co-founder of The Galileo Network. Sharon's experience as a teacher includes kindergarten, elementary, and junior high grades. She has been in demand as a consultant for a wide range of teacher in-service topics related to curriculum and school improvement. Her sessions have included leadership in curriculum development, school reform, mathematics reform, effective technology integration, school improvement planning, and professional development. She has also assisted schools to assess their technology requirements to enhance teaching and learning environments. She has experience as a systems analyst and a web developer. See Pat Clifford bio for more detail.

Ricki Goldman is Professor of Information Science at the New Jersey Institute of Technology, examining the role of learning systems from a qualitative research perspective. A pioneer in New Media learning and research environments since her tenure at the MIT Media Lab as a doctoral student, Goldman has designed award-winning video ethnographic research tools and methods to understand children's knowledge construction in computationally-rich learning environments. This work is described in detail in her book, *Points of Viewing Children's Thinking: A Digital Ethnographer's Journey* (Lawrence Erlbaum Associates, 1998). As Associate Professor of Education within the Faculty of Education at the UBC, Goldman established a research lab, MERLin, devoted to the design and use of digital video data analysis tools. Her software, WebConstellations, took First Prize in Canada's National Centers of Excellence in Telelearning Annual Meeting in 1998.

Colette Granger is a doctoral candidate in the Faculty of Education at York University. Her work takes a multidisciplinary approach to questions of teaching and learning. She has participated in several projects concerning ICT implementation in schools, and is particularly interested in the ways in which new technologies trouble traditional notions of pedagogy.

Jim Greenlaw is an Associate Professor in the Education Department at St. Francis Xavier University in Nova Scotia. His recent publications include the book, *English Language Arts and Reading on the Internet: A Resource for K-12 Teachers* (2001).

Bill Hunter has served as Director of the Educational Technology Unit and Head of the Department of Teacher Education and Supervision at the University of Calgary. At present, he is the Academic Coordinator for the Distance Delivery Unit in the Graduate Division of Educational Research and Coordinator of the Educational Technology graduate area at the University of Calgary. He has recently completed service as the editor of the *Canadian Journal of Education*. He recently completed a study of virtual school web pages. Bill was once a high school English teacher and has taught for university departments of mathematics, nursing, psychology and home economics. He has conducted research on moral reasoning, on the uses of computers in teaching and learning and on a variety of measurement issues and problems. He recently published a chapter on case-based teaching arising from his experience as the coach of a University of Calgary team.

Judy M. Iseke-Barnes is a faculty member in the Department of Sociology and Equity Studies in Education, Ontario Institute for Studies in Education of the University of Toronto. She teaches courses in Aboriginal and Indigenous studies in education, equity issues in school and society, mathematics education, computer science and cultural narratives in cyberspace. She has been a classroom teacher of mathematics and computer science. She has conducted and continues to conduct studies in regard to the Internet, which are focused upon pre-service and in-service teachers and in broader educational contexts. Her research activities have also engaged groups of Aboriginal educators in interactions on the Internet in a Canada-wide study of Aboriginal pedagogy and the Internet.

Jennifer Jenson has recently accepted a position in the Faculty of Education at York University in Toronto.

Michele Jacobsen is an assistant professor specializing in educational technology in the Faculty of Education at the University of Calgary. She teaches about software design in the Graduate Division of Educational Research and about integrating technology in the Division of Teacher Preparation. Her current research explores a range of issues to do with integrating technology into K-20 teaching and learning, such as professional development, network design and capacity building, along with other projects on leveraging educational partnerships, employing web-based psychological and educational research methods, and electronic publishing. She is currently a co-review editor for the

International Electronic Journal for Leadership in Learning, and on the editorial team of the *EGallery*, an electronic publication of exemplary student scholarship.

Lisa Korteweg is a continuing contract teacher with the Richmond School District (Vancouver, BC) where she teaches in the Late French Immersion program. She is also a doctoral candidate at the Centre for the Study of Curriculum and Instruction, University of British Columbia. She became interested in the social and pedagogical aspects of technologies during her masters' thesis research of the Science World exhibit, Mind Games. Her doctoral thesis examines the relationship of technologies, public knowledge and teacher professional development through the work of the research consortium, the Public Knowledge Project. Lisa has been a researcher with UBC's Public Knowledge Project since its inception.

Thérèse Laferrière is full professor at Laval University where she teaches classroom organization and management in regular and networked classrooms. Her theoretical perspectives are grounded in group psychology and socio-constructivism. She supervises student teachers in classrooms where every student has a laptop, and engages in collaborative project-based learning. She conducts collaborative research with teachers working in K-12 networked classrooms. In her own teaching, she uses information and communication technologies, and design learning activities in telecollaborative environments. She is the leader of Educating Educators, within the TeleLearning Network of Centres of Excellence (Canada).

Heather Lotherington is Associate Professor of Multilingual Education at York University. She has taught at universities in Canada, England, Australia, and Fiji, and has international research experience in second language and bilingual education, particularly with regard to multiliteracies. She is currently involved in interdisciplinary research on new media, teacher innovation and literacy in schools in Toronto.

Marilyn MacLean is an elementary and middle school teacher-librarian in Prince Edward Island.

Mary Leigh Morbey is Associate Professor of Culture and Technology in the York University Faculty of Graduate Studies and Faculty of Education. She is a trained art historian who spent 15 years of academic life chairing two university undergraduate Departments of

Art and Art History. Her research, writing and teaching are situated at the intersection of culture, information technology, and education, both theory and practice. In recent years, Mary Leigh's research has focussed on an investigation of barriers to computing and in particular relation to the digital arts. Her current research interests centre on computing innovation and education, and the colonization by First World computing ideologies of less affluent populations and the Third World which she is exploring through a research study of computer employment in the State Hermitage Museum, St. Petersburg, Russia.

Elizabeth Murphy serves as Assistant Professor in the Faculty of Education at Memorial University of Newfoundland, where she provides instruction and conducts research into the use of web-based technologies for instructional purposes. She has taught French, Mathematics and Social Studies in various grades from K-12 and most recently served as a principal of a junior high school. Her current areas of research include using computer-mediated communication to provide teachers with opportunities to reflect on their practices with technology. As well, she is interested in barriers to the adoption of new and emerging technologies by educators.

Mary Ann Murrin has recently returned to Nova Scotia after teaching high school English for many years in Nunavut.

Ronald Owston is Professor of Education and founding director of the Centre for the Study of Computers in Education at York University in Toronto. In 2000 he was appointed co-director of York's faculty research and development centre, the Office of Technology Enhanced Learning (oTEL). His article "The World Wide Web: A technology to enhance teaching and learning" was published in *Educational Researcher* in 1997; it is widely cited internationally as one of the first academic analyses of the contribution of the Web to education. In 1998 he co-authored *The Learning Highway: Smart Students and the Internet* (Key Porter), and published *Making the Link: Teacher Professional Development on the Internet* with Heinemann. Currently, Ron Owston is a lead researcher in the Second International Technology in Education Study, Module 2 (SITES-M2) that is examining innovative pedagogical practices using technology in some 30 countries.

Rosina Smith has 18 years' experience as a teacher in the K-12 context. She has served as consultant and Acting Director of the Centre for Gifted Education at the University of Calgary. She was awarded the

2000 post-doctoral fellowship from the Galileo Educational Network at the University of Calgary. Her areas of research include educational technology as well as gifted and talented education. She has extensive experience in professional development for teachers in the Province of Alberta relative to her areas of expertise. Presently, she serves as a consultant at the Galileo Educational Network and will continue to teach sessionally at the University of Calgary in the area of Educational Technology.

Herb Wideman is Senior Researcher at the Institute for Research on Learning Technologies at York University. His research interests include the study of ICT implementation processes and their effects on teacher and student practice; and the exploration of ICT's potential for supporting and facilitating authentic, student-driven learning.

John Willinsky is Pacific Press Professor of Literacy and Technology at the University of British Columbia and has recently published *Learning to Divide the World* and *Technologies of Knowing*.

Dianne Yee has worked in Saskatchewan and Alberta as a classroom teacher, counselor, resource teacher, principal, and sessional instructor. Currently she is the teaching principal of County Central High School in Vulcan, Alberta – a grade 7 to 12 school located southeast of Calgary. As a result of being principal of a technology project school in Saskatchewan, she has a passion for working with information and communication technology (ICT) as a teaching and learning tool. In addition to leadership and educational technology, she is also very interested in special needs students, counseling, and middle schools.

DEDICATION

Dedicated to the thousands who lost their lives in the
September 11, 2001, attack on the World Trade Center.
May we learn from their sacrifice;
May their souls find comfort.

FOREWORD

JOHN WILLINSKY

Foreword, forearmed? For what exactly? For facing the question, in the case of this book, of what we have with this new digital, multimedia, information technology. Could we really be on the verge of a new era, culturally, educationally? The contributors to this collection come at this pressing question of the immediate present and near future, not with sweeping generalizations or prophetic pronouncements, but far more cautiously and curiously. They work from the intimations that can only be drawn from what students and teachers, as well as the contributors themselves, are making of these new tools. They recognize that the principal issue in integrating technology into the classroom may well be perspective.

Where do we stand to get a close-up on the new, without letting what has always been critically important to our teaching and learning fall out of focus? How can we possibly get a grip on the significance of a technology that wraps our lives as tightly and completely as yesterday's newspaper once wrapped our fish and chips? Gaining insight into this ubiquitous newness is all about *points of viewing*, in my friend Ricki Goldman's memorable phrase, and this book's very plurality of perspectives may be our best hope of catching sight of both what is happening and what that happening can mean.

In driving forward into digitally charted territories, my own perspectival tendencies are to keep an eye or two on the rear-view mirror, much as Marshall McLuhan warned was inevitable in moving into the future. I keep looking back, hoping to catch sight of a past that is not yet gone. I do so knowing that the very first lesson history teaches us, before all else, is that gaining a perspective on the immediate present is near impossible. Why? For no other reason than we are living inside it, and all the more so in the case of a technology that is constantly at our fingertips and in our ears. We can no more step out of it than Archimedes could step away from the earth to demonstrate how he could, if he had place to stand and a lever long enough, leverage this very planet as easily as a hi-tech start-up could once leverage itself into the economic stratosphere not so very long ago. (But perhaps the better Archimedean analogy lies with the bathtub, as we puzzle over how much is displaced by this new technology that we might know what it truly is, until we end up streaking down the streets of Palo Alto shrieking "Eureka" at having discovered, as the contributors herein have, how to test the true metal of this purportedly golden opportunity.)

We cannot hope, then, to know if these new information and communication technologies will turn out to be Gutenberg-like in their epoch-making capacity, anymore than Gutenberg could sense that his invention would award him a galaxy within the history of communications. No Bill Gates this Johann Gutenberg, in terms of market-share recognition, and the inventive German goldsmith died in relative obscurity, even as his commonplace claim as singular inventor of print has fallen into question, as a result, naturally, of a computer analysis of his fonts. What we can see from here, looking back to the 15th-century, is that his invention of moveable typefaces did not produce a sudden transformation of the literate world. Gutenberg sent out his printed biblical pages to be hand decorated in the traditional manner of the illuminated manuscript, and the new technology, at least initially, reproduced the old world of literacy. It certainly increased the number of Bibles and papal Indulgences, but it was all more of the same for more of the same people. At least initially.

Within two or three generations, we can now see, nothing was quite the same. The change did not spout from the technology, itself, like the noxious oxides of industrial waste that were to change the very blue of the sky. The changes wrought by the printing press came from those who were driven by vision, imagination and moral purpose to use this new print technology for something more that Bibles and Indulgences. They envisioned a vast educational project that included putting print into many more people's hands, creating, in effect, a public that was to form around this very spread of literate exchange. These writers and printers are the ones who found that print was critical to imagining the possibilities of democracy and public education, in what Raymond Williams called the long revolution, and it is a revolution that is only clearly visible now, centuries later.

These visionaries were driven by something other than the way it sped up production and communication, something other than the neat way it could lay out a page, even as they were not dismayed by the loss of the beautiful and idiosyncratic illumination running along the margins. (One can imagine those who could afford illuminated manuscripts predicting that these new-fangled printed books would never replace the illuminated manuscript, as if anyone would want such dull, mechanically produced things.)

Well, some people saw that with the printing press more was at stake than the look and feel of a book. Whether one thinks of Wiliam Tyndale's first English translation of the Bible, or Thomas Paine's politically explosive *Rights of Man*, or Mary Wolstonecraft's *Vindication of the Rights of Women*; whether one considers the spread of newspapers and broadsides, the common schools and the public libraries, there is little question that writers and readers found the printing press a machine for thinking and learning that went well beyond what it had originally been intended for. People's lives and human history were altered by this technology. This was a technology that was absorbed on a global and daily basis. In large and small acts of literacy and learning, this technology could well be said to improve the way people lived, loved, worked and cared for one another. It raised their very expectations for such things. It was also used to threaten their very existence.

So, the forward-looking question for a book such as this is not whether we can know that this new digitally based technology is critical to learning or to the future – we cannot – it is that we must test and exhaust its possibilities for realizing something more, something better. This is why we must invest this technology with the same ideals and hopes than have long driven our aspirations for a better world, knowing that we can never be sure that we are on the right path. Yet if we cannot be sure, we can still make educated, and carefully worked out, guesses. We can still follow inclinations and intimations, still learn lessons from attending closely, as the contributors to this book attend, to the current place of technology in education. And we can judge, in each case, whether the lessons are about the ideals of learning and teaching, about extending what we have always wanted from the collective pursuit of knowledge and understanding.

It is not that the technology is simply a tool, as we so often hear. It is that we cannot be sure of what we, as educators, can build with such tools, once we turn our minds to it. Nor can we be sure of what others will build, if it is left up to those who do not know education as we know it. Certainly, our first efforts to work with this technology in education are bound to look much like what came before. It may just mean more, faster, as the printing press did, and as technology appears to be doing for scholarship at this point.

So we have to ask ourselves what might we now do, how can we push ahead with this new technology to make something more of education s promise? How can we possibly test this new technology to see if it might serve greater ends, if ever so incrementally. We must risk seeming naïve, knowing that playing out our hopes is the only way to break through the inertia. No sure bets in this work; certainly no guaranteed test-score increases. But then, no experimentation, no education, to borrow a Deweyism. For the learning comes of testing the variations.

At the risk of turning this into more of a manifesto than a preface – more of an onward than a foreword – let me conclude this book's opening with a call for two strands of action which are well supported by what follows. We need to push the technology optimistically, hopefully, into what we have always wanted of education. We need to see how it can extend the intellectually engaged and democratic aspects of education as a right of all, for the good of all, on a global basis. Yet in doing so, we still need that critical pause, the careful analysis, the difficult moment of puzzling over the shortfalls and lost hopes. Any path forward can end up threatening those ideals, itself a lesson all too easily drawn from the 20th century – and so we must remain vigilant, while encouraging the experimentation, the constant speculation.

To make a bumper sticker of Exhaust the Possibilities that sits over the tail pipe is too close to a bad pun (though it does serve as a reminder of another liberating technology that overshot the mark). Yet what we have to learn through this book on the educational uses of digital technologies is that this brave new world, which seems to lie before us like a land of dreams, as Matthew Arnold wrote of his own old world, so various, so beautiful, so new, calls for, in equal measure, a testing of whether these machines can carry us some small distance beyond the darkling plain, and an ability to say no at times, when the machines fall short of what it means to be educated in any sense by which we can happily, proudly abide.

INTRODUCTION
TANGLED IN THE NET
BARRIE R.C. BARRELL

When it comes to the integration of technology into our schools, you can create it, you can legislate it, you can order it, you can supply it, you can give it standards, and you can write outcomes for it. But the bottom line is that if it is going to happen in substantial ways, it is classroom teachers who will make it happen.

        Jacqueline Goodlore, Washington, DC teacher, 2000 AERA Conference, New Orleans, LA

This book is about the integration of technology into teaching, learning and school culture. It is aimed at those wishing to build communities of learners in an age where digital technologies are reshaping the way schooling is undertaken and practiced. It is a resource for both pre-service and experienced teachers faced with national, provincial and territorial demands to graduate technologically competent and literate students. In Canada, the Western Canadian Protocol for Collaboration in Basic Education, the Atlantic Provinces Education Foundation and other large policy setting constituencies all require teachers to integrate technology directly into classroom practice. In Alberta, the government has gone so far as to mandate its universities to graduate technologically literate teachers; Imperial Oil Canada has backed up this mandate by donating a million dollars to the University of Calgary's Faculty of Education to specifically study technology integration. Bishop's University in Quebec, Memorial University in Newfoundland and other Canadian institutions now require pre-service teachers to take computer applications and resource courses as part of their undergraduate teacher preparation programs. Some school boards, such as Rocky View School Division in southern Alberta, have created consultant positions aimed directly at supporting teachers as they go about integrating technology into practice. This kind of government, university, business, curricula and school district support is a firm indication that information and communications technology (ICT) will play an increasing role in shaping classroom discourse, organization and structure. It can be assumed that as new and emerging technologies become widely available and more easily adaptable to praxis, the very nature of both teaching and learning will undergo fundamental and systemic change. Thus a text that looks at some of the critical issues surrounding the uses of digital technology in classroom and offers thoughtful reflection on what is appropriate and what needs to be avoided as we reshape schooling should be helpful.

Canadian life has been transformed by recent technological advancements. The very structure and nature of how we work, research, communicate, shop, bank and spend our leisure time has shifted within a continuously evolving digital revolution. However, this revolution has been somewhat slow to affect teaching and learning. In many ways classrooms look much as they did at the turn of the last century. Architects have been slow to offer alternative plans to accommodate constructivist teaching styles, to serve the active and engaged movement of students, or to consider the infrastructure needed to house the new technologies. Ergonomically friendly workstations that fulfill the requirements of growing children are not generally available. Building materials capable of capturing the noise of 30 or more verbally interacting students are rarely installed on walls or ceilings. However, despite the structural limitations of older buildings and limited architectural planning and imagination, digital technologies have arrived in full force in most Canadian and US schools. Indeed, as a millennium has clicked over, it is the very *absence* of computers, Internet and Intranet connections in classrooms that now draw the attention of students and parents.

It is generally understood that all stakeholders want to see technology used for emancipatory, democratic and creative purposes and not for the control of students or the surveillance of their records, attendance, dress, homework, movements or parking habits. Further, it should be understood by all concerned that technology integration means moving well beyond electronic workbooks and tutorials, PowerPoint presentations of recycled lecture notes, or keyboarding skill and drill exercises.

A fundamental and engaging question raised by authors in this book is what will it mean and what will it take to be considered literate in the coming decades? What are the most effective and interesting ways to integrate technology into teaching and learning in light of society's growing reliance and interdependence on digital technologies? Budgetary considerations, the limited technical skills of some teachers and professors, and the limited availability of models of best pedagogical practice aside, schools are in the midst of systemic and evolving change.

Stand-alone computers first appeared in the schools I taught in on the desks of the school secretaries (these were probably preceded by their arrival in the board office). In the early 1980s my own school-based professional development, like that of so many others, was situated around learning programming skills rather than content-related instruction or uses. Computers were used to learn about computers, not about ecology or mathematics or social studies. In the early 1990s using computers as a tool for learning content emerged, but this was generally for drill and practice in elementary schools. High schools controlled the location of technology and its uses by building labs aimed specifically at 'computer education.' In the mid- and late-1990s, schools were given massive governmental ICT support. This support came from provincial politicians like New Brunswick's Frank McKenna, Alberta's Ralph Klein, and Ontario's Mike Harris. They, together with federal politicians, drew lines directly between the economic well being of the nation, the building of electronic infrastructures capable of supporting expanding digital requirements, business and the education of people capable of functioning in digital environments. Thus, briefly then, in the mid to late 1990s, new curriculum initiatives came down from department and ministries of education, monies for the purchase of educational software and hardware were allocated and schools where wired to receive access to the World Wide Web. These events caught most teachers and school administrators off guard and left them scrabbling for professional development in their use.

For those who quickly grasped the educational possibilities of the bundled applications that came with most ICT hardware, new opportunities for problem solving were conceived, expanded textual engagements seen, deeper student investigations of interdisciplinary subjects visualized and the collection and management of large student gathered databases conceptualized. These pedagogical visionaries saw the possibility to publish directly from classrooms to the world and for students to communicate nationally and internationally with all kinds of people, interest groups and organizations. Opportunities to bring about a dramatic change in traditional teaching styles and learning practices were envisioned. Students now had direct access to new sources of information from both the arts and sciences and with it the opportunity to do more authentic and connected work. Electronic portfolios were seen as ways to extend traditional assessment practices. Class web sites were a way of showing student work and informing parents and guardians of upcoming classroom events. Many teachers saw the growth and alignment of constructivist teaching principles with ICT applications as a way to make schools more exciting places to be and to work.

Computers, as cultural artifacts, are shaping our culture, expanding our communication capacities, increasing our ability to mold texts, and, in turn, are challenging the way we think. Student compositions suddenly are able to move beyond printcentric text constructions to multiple layered constructs that incorporate visual, sound, graphic, iconographic and/or musical components. Both conservative and progressive notions of literacy have been forced to rapidly expand; students now are expected to read the world and represent their learning(s) in multiple ways, constructions and forms. Some classroom teachers, it can now be said, routinely use the Internet to prepare classroom materials, access research and best practice literature, download teaching materials, complete administrative tasks and/or email colleagues (U.S. Department of Education, 2000).

As Clifford and Friesen envision in their chapter, those trying to seamlessly integrate technology into educational practices see possibilities for profound pedagogical change and a revitalizing of the way students engage with the world and schooling. They have a vision in which students have greater control over their own learning. This student controlled learning is supported by a growing number of electronic resources being built in various educational constituencies (universities, museums, art galleries, national theatre companies, scientific establishments, libraries, government space agencies, etc.). ICT, when joined together with inquiry-based learning practices and constructivist theory, becomes a potent force in the education of students faced with a shifting world order, the realities of economic globalization, environmental erosion and the doubling of knowledge in ever shorter periods of time. Given the quality and the availability of resources now accessible to classrooms, teachers have the opportunity to ask much larger social, artistic, scientific and ethical questions of the nation's students. They have the online resources to foster deeper thinking about current affairs and social problems, about timeless human questions, possibilities and quests.

The digital revolution, as MIT's Michael Dertouzos (2001) points out, is an unfinished revolution. Schools are just beginning to play catch-up. Given our knowledge about multiple intelligences (Gardener, 1999; 2001), sophisticated applications can now be brought into the service of the varied learning styles of young scholars. ICT, together with new consortia curriculum document initiatives, offer ways for teachers to break the stranglehold industrial models of education and assembly line notions of schooling have maintained over many educational jurisdictions.

What must be remembered in the mix is that ICT is not new to students. Most have had some experience surfing the Net, can handle keyboard and mouse, have played computer games, have used infrared technologies to direct CD players, TVs, and VCRs or can handle a cellular telephone with the two fisted dexterity gained from experience with digital game controls. As Tapscott (1998) and as Cohen details in his chapter, the young in much of the industrialized world no longer "see" digital technology; they simply wear it, watch it, play it or communicate through it.

This is a generation of students already versed in a great deal of knowledge about technology and who is quite capable of back filling in the skills needed to operate older technologies. Given the chance, this generation is quite willing to jump around and learn various skills to get done what they deem essential to their digital engagements, investigations and quests. Any linear conception of technological skill acquisition is challenged time and time again by the quality of the work produced in the nation's schools. Teachers need to see themselves as partners with students in the integration of technology.

The possibilities of creating visual compositions have dramatically increased with the arrival of digital cameras. Students can shoot hundreds of images now that film and developing costs have been dissolved. Videographic representations and multimedia compositions will challenge teachers brought up in a print-centered world or whose skills come from the editing and evaluating of print texts and grammars. In the humanities, where knowledge does not so much accumulate, but shift and expand as cultural events and artifacts get contested and reshaped, traditional ways of engagement can be challenged by students using hypermedia and hypertext constructions. The new curriculum documents give teachers little choice but to re-examine their own understanding and critical responses to visual texts and representations of information and knowledge. The 'reading' of some television information and news channels demand that speech, print, graphic displays and video clips be attended to simultaneously. Similarly, student compositions can be expected to incorporate various media to represent their engagements with the world.

Canadian English language arts teachers are mandated to teach and assess "other ways of representing" knowledge and information (see Barrell, 2000, Ch. 4 or any territorial or provincial ELA curriculum document). Though this new ELA strand might include puppetry, the greater use of school bulletin boards or flow charts, the framers of the new documents have a much broader conception of "other ways of representing" knowledge and information. The documents demand opportunities be given to students to engage with digital applications. For the student whose expressive forte extends into music, video or computer graphics and whose 'reading' habits extend well beyond print texts, the new curriculum documents demand new textual engagements and opportunities be afforded.

An example comes from my own work with pre-service teachers engaging in a study of *The Shipping News*. Together with my colleague Roberta Hammett (in press), we asked our students to construct web pages depicting their engagement with the text. The 265 web pages were posted to a collective web site (http://134.153.160.118/educ4142/index.html) as an example of how technology could be integrated into a novel study. But then students at Penn State University found the site, created their own digital engagements with *The Shipping News* and linked up their pages to ours. Students at Norway's Oslo University College also found the site, did the same kind of work, and linked into our original site. Thus the work done in Canada suddenly had connections to students in Europe and the United States. Each of the three constituencies brought a different perspective that enhanced and expanded the original work with the text. Each gained from reading an 'outside' perspective. Each gained from viewing and listening to the explications of others engaged in the same work.

Importantly, we need to be reminded that in this example the work done was not at all about technology. Rather, it is about what the technology enables people to do and share. In this example, technology is shown to sit in the background providing the canvas upon which we can create, communicate and represent our engagement. It acts as an example of future possibilities where student gathered data is linked to the research of social and natural scientists. Electronically linked and published projects give students a sense of reality, a sense of the importance of getting the science right or that their work is not just practice for or simulation of work to be done as adults. Given the opportunity, I believe young students would choose to do real historical research, engage in earth science that was connected to ongoing university projects, and make observations connected with the work of astronomers or anthropologists or ornithologists.

Obviously the real utility of computers and the true value of the information revolution lies ahead. As computer storage capacities increase and the gigabyte costs dramatically fall, the odds increase that we have moved out and away from the industrial age and into an electronic age. The implications for education are enormous. Computers still need to become simpler to operate, more 'user friendly', more opaque. The new instructional practices and methodologies that ICT allow us to construct and implement for the revitalization of schooling are only now starting to emerge.

We are on the cusp of a new era in education that can allow for the revitalization of some literary forms and the introduction of new genres. Much of what gets written disappears into the ether as delete buttons are pushed. ICQ discussions often disappear after discussions take place. What will literary works look like when three or four or five authors come together to 'write' into the same electronic compositional spaces? Such forms will challenge certain ideologies; they might draw more inspiration from jazz jam sessions than past print experiences. The grammar of HTML can be more exacting than print; how and when will it be taught to students? Email has few rules and differing conventions and seems to have more in common with speech than writing; does its use get taught and how will it be evaluated? Or will its requirements get subsumed into day to day life, much as elocution or telephone etiquette lessons did in the past? Technology affords opportunities to dismantle claustrophobic disciplinary structures and to truly engage the rhetoric of interdisciplinarity. Lip service does not have to be paid to "holistic education" or "integrated learning" anymore. In a real radical sense it is time to ask, as Faigley does, "what it means to slip the prosthetic arm of technology onto the deconstructed self and to ask what lies at the threshold of this joining" (Faigley, 1998, p. 83).

Recently revised provincial and territorial curriculum documents, with their incorporation and interweaving of technological outcomes, challenge traditional classroom practices and insist upon systemic structural change. These documents relocate the types of skills, knowledge and educational encounters students are required to have if they are to successfully make their way in the digital age. As Clifford and Friesen explain in their chapter, technology is the catalyst for bringing about educational reform. As access to computers and the Internet has grown, research interests have focused on the specific purposes to which these new technologies are put. In conjunction with the wise teacher, the inventive use of ICT offers challenges to instructional theory. It opens possibilities for deep probing and questioning of discipline and subject knowledge and it provides the power, when put in the hands of young people, to do purposeful and meaningful work – work that can be put on line and challenge or add to existing knowledge.

Deborah Brandt (1990) has said that literate knowledge – that is knowing how to read and write – "is a knowledge embodied in the doing" (p. 193). ICT increases the possibilities for "doing" so many more things. Technology has disrupted the way we read, construct and make meaning. The characteristics of texts have been transformed. With this transformation comes a requirement to understand and to use information and communication technologies to engage the world in more purposeful ways. Science and technology can lay claim to getting us into the environmental mess that now surrounds us. The depletion of resources is affecting geopolitical regions and governance. However, it is my belief that electronically interconnected science and technology efforts can be used to help mend the earth and revitalize the human quest for emancipation and inclusive democratic principles and solutions. This kind of work can only rely on a creative and imaginative group of investigators who bring diverse experiences and a broad range of skills and insights to bear on specific problems. Those working in various school systems need to help the process by creating opportunities that prepare students for such work.

What are the instructional philosophies and pedagogies that will guide these initiatives? What articulations of curricular engagements through the use of technology are being worked through, encouraged and envisioned by curricula leaders? How will technology enhance the radically new curriculum documents in Canada? What exemplars of best practice do we have in this country? And, finally, what can we learn from efforts that go wrong and do not meet intended objectives?

The contributors to this book offer a perspective on these and other issues in teaching and learning with technology. Gathered together in these pages is the work of over two dozen professors, teachers, consultants and principals. Represented here is their recent research and theoretical findings. The text is divided into three sections. The first section clarifies recent issues and perspectives on technology. It opens with the chapter titled, "The Stewardship of the Intellect: Classroom Life, Educational Innovation and Technology" by Pat Clifford and Sharon Friesen of the Galileo Educational Network located in the Faculty of Education at the University of Calgary. This chapter reminds us that the integration of technology is "first and foremost a matter of educational reform." This simple reminder resounds throughout the chapters that follow, for to integrate technology into educational practice is to cause a rethinking of the entire way we go about schooling. Clifford and Friesen give us an overview of what schools need to be mindful of and what they need to be doing with computers. Next, Rob Cohen moves us inside an affluent middle school and presents us with the view of what it is like to be working with kids who are on the upside of the digital divide. He is challenged to rethink his practice by his students and gives us an important glimpse inside the digitally constructed worlds of teenagers who have easy access to computers both in and outside of school.

George Buck's chapter follows with an historical examination of the continued resistance to the use of various technologies as they have come into use in schools. He allows us to build on prior success and to avoid past mistakes that have lead to the deployment and then abandonment "of technology in a cyclical manner." Michele Jacobsen and Ricki Goldman give us a perspective on the nature of shifting power relations when technology is introduced into learning communities. Together they ask what kinds of "multi-visions of society" do we have and "how do we chose what technologies to develop and use to meet those visions?" Importantly, they also ask, "who is in control of designing and implementing technologies?" They use Margaret Atwood's novel *The Handmaid's Tale* as the platform for launching into this thoughtful discussion.

Suzanne de Castell, Mary Bryson and Jennifer Jenson, in their chapter "Object Lessons: Critical Visions of Educational Technology," lay down the foundation for their supportive work with students and teachers in British Columbia. They call for an educational theory of technology that would examine the assumptions, purposes and values situated around the integration of education and technology. Such a theory of technology "would offer material grounding to a rethinking of educational epistemology." Hence, they argue that "to learn from our tools, we have also to study them, as well as the context of their intended use." Investigations need to include the commercialization of aspects of schooling. Together the authors challenge educational uses of technology to do traditional things and call for a rethinking of technological pedagogy.

The second section of the book looks at two school-based case studies, a classroom use of ICT and aspects of virtual schooling in Alberta. The research of Heather Lotherington, Leigh Morbey, Colette Granger and Lara Doan at the Centre for the Study of Computers in Education, York University, details an examination of two "inner city" elementary schools in metropolitan Toronto that are significantly contributing to innovations in ICT pedagogy. "Tearing Down Walls: New Literacies and New Horizons in the Elementary School" reports on a study which is part of a much larger international study of educational technology. The researchers triangulated observations at two school-based research sites and revealed the creative ways technology is being used to meet a provincially defined agenda. The team offers markers for best practices that echo much of Yee's work later in this text.

Herbert Wideman and Ronald Owston at York University's Institute for Research on Learning Technologies report there are successful innovations in the uses of ICT, but that there are also failures. "Lessons Learned: Three Case Studies of ICT in Teaching and Their Implications for Practice," offers practicing teachers a way to "separate the wheat from the chaff" and details uses of ICT that are far from successful. Mary Cameron and Barrie Barrell reveal a view of ICT integration from inside a primary classroom. Here a classroom teacher and a university professor give their textured inside accounts of the work done by children in a grade 2 constructivist classroom nestled in the foothills of the Rockies.

Bill Hunter and Rosina Smith clarify issues surrounding the evolutionary state of virtual schooling. They write about the integration of schooling into technology and offer a perspective on an alternative education delivery method that takes into account the views of teachers, parents and students.

The last section of the book addresses issues in ICT leadership and in teacher education. In her chapter, "The Many Faces of ICT Leadership for Digital Technology and Canadian Pedagogy," Dianne Yee reports her research into what principals, specialist teachers and classroom teachers can do to foster the appropriate use of ICT in their schools. Through her examination of ICT-enriched schools in Canada, New Zealand and the United States, she offers a sound perspective backed up by detailed observations.

Lisa Korteweg's chapter makes an analysis of the Public Knowledge Project at the University of British Columbia and its position as an online education resource. Here materials relevant to the integration of technology are electronically housed and delivered to pre-service teachers, teachers and the general public. In a real sense it is an online community of inquiry.

Jim Greenlaw's chapter demonstrates the types of conversations practicing teachers have around adjusting their pedagogical practices to the digital age. In an on-line graduate course, they struggle to incorporate new resources into their teaching. Judy Iseke-Barnes reports her research on work done with pre-service mathematics teachers in a teacher education program. Finally, Elizabeth Murphy and Thérèse Laferrière take a look at classroom management issues in the connected classroom.

The intended aim of this collective research is the reform of education, the improvement of pedagogical theory and the presentation of alternatives ways of proceeding based on an examination of what is being attempted by educators and researchers of good will.

REFERENCES

Barrell, B. and R. Hammett (eds.) (2000). *Advocating Change: Contemporary Issues in Subject English*. Toronto: Irwin Publishing.

Barrell, B. and R. Hammett (In press). "A Critique of a Critical Social Literacy Project: Newfoundlanders Confront *The Shipping News.*" *Interchange.*

Brandt, D. (1990). "Literacy and Knowledge." In Lunsford, A., H. Moglen, J. Slevin, eds. *The Right to Literacy.* New York: MLA, 189-96.

Gardner, H. (1999). *The Disciplined Mind: Beyond Facts and Standardized Tests, the K-12 Education That Every Child Deserves.* Penguin.

Gardner, H. (2001). "Can Technology Exploit Our Many Ways of Knowing?" In David T. Gordon, (ed). *The Digital Classroom: How Technology is Changing the Way We Teach and Learn.* Cambridge, MA: The Harvard Educational Letter.

U.S. Department of Education (2000). National Center for Education Statistics. *Teachers Tools for the 21st Century: A Report on Teachers' Use of Technology.* NCES 2000-102 by Becky Smerdon, Stephanie Cronen, Lawrence Lanahan, Jennifer Anderson, Nicholas Iannotti, January Angeles. Washington, DC.

Part I

Issues and Perspectives

Chapter 1

The Stewardship of the Intellect

Classroom Life, Educational Innovation and Technology

Pat Clifford and Sharon Friesen

Introduction

The history of computers in schools is, in some ways, curiously brief. There was no World Wide Web prior to 1995, and many teachers working with Pentiums today still remember when floppy disks were floppy and dot matrix printers were as good as it got. In another sense, however, computers have been with us for decades. And while teachers couldn't network our Apple IIEs, we could word process, program, use paint programs and spreadsheets. Almost 20 years ago, government policy (at least in Alberta) provided funding for computers in schools. It feels as if "forever ago" has passed in the blink of an eye, and yet it also feels as if fundamental questions about what these machines are good for remain in some sense as unsettled now as they were two decades ago.

Public and political interest in the elusive promise that technology will somehow sharpen Canada's global, competitive advantage gathers, at its extremes, around sharply different perspectives. Enthusiasts see, if not salvation, then at least inherent charm in the boxes, and urge schools and teachers to get with it, to get *on* with it. Get the kids on line, producing multimedia, using animation software and simulations and touch sensitive screens and scanners and digital video editing and home pages and file sharing and...well, you get the picture. Alarmists pull as hard in the opposite direction. They pit computer use against normal childhood development, fear predation and exploitation, and wonder what on earth schools are doing by marching ten year olds off to computer labs to learn to keyboard on Pentium IIIs.

The debates are lively and instructive – not so much for the particulars advanced by either side as for the on-going need to step back just a bit and lift those particulars into larger contexts. In this chapter we ask this: how can teachers create classroom environments in which digital technologies enhance rather than diminish learning? Thus, while we will certainly deal with dead-practical matters such as classroom configurations and software applications, we will do this by keeping our eye sharply focused on the fact that designing classroom environments for the effective integration of technology is first and foremost a matter of educational reform. It is only with *this* context that what we have to say about wires and boxes makes any sense at all.

THE STEWARDSHIP OF THE INTELLECT

The felicitous phrase "stewardship of the intellect" comes from *Out of Our Minds: Anti-Intellectualism and Talent Development in American Schooling*, a 1995 book that doesn't have a thing to do with technology. It is a difficult and impassioned look at the ways in which American schools could better serve all students (including the gifted students whose concerns are closest to the hearts of the authors). Schools, they argue, ought to be about the life of the mind. They should foster intellectual habits of thought, meaning-making and discourse in all students, rich and poor, gifted and severely ordinary. Intellect, in this light, is not just braininess, and is certainly not the conditioned right answer giving that passes in too much of the public mind as "achievement." More broadly defined, intellect "represents the complexity of understanding, critique, and imagination of which the human mind is capable...Intellect [has] to do with what passes between minds and generations of humans...[through] explicit, negotiated meaningfulness" (Howley, Howley and Pendarvis, 1995, 4).

For us, this means that schools ought to be about developing everyone's talents and gifts (for who among us comes gift-less to school?). A good teacher respects and cultivates the dispositions that all children bring with them when they first walk through our doors: imagination, curiosity, persistence and the drive to know how the world works. Good teachers respect and cultivate the ability of all children to think – with their words, their drawings, their bodies, their hearts. Good teaching helps children and youth engage with, and understand, difficult matters. A good teacher helps students uncover things that have been hidden, and brings to life brand new questions, ideas and abilities. A good teacher makes school an intellectually exciting place to be, a place where learning is fun even when it is hard, perhaps especially *when* it is hard, and frustrating, and challenging. There is a passion and generosity about good teaching that drives fine teachers to extend the very best of themselves in the service of learning. And schools, as institutions, should be charged with stewardship that

> *comprehends the need for humans to take pleasure in their work and to care for the human artifact. Stewardship also comprehends care for generations past and generations to come. This sort of stewardship is a commitment due students from teachers, children from parents, and the world at large from the people within it (Howley, Howley and Pendarvis, 1995, 185).*

In the years since we first began to work with the Apple IIEs that came into schools in such large numbers in the early 1980s, the two of us have struggled to understand how technology can help schools and teachers move toward a vision like this. The early years of educational technology were heady and full of promise. Then everything seemed to fizzle. Except for a few sites energized by the talent and drive of individual teachers and administrators, schools didn't make much headway in bringing computers into the life of classrooms energized by the genuine pleasure teachers and students alike might take in their work. As disappointing as that fizzle has been, we think that the picture has begun to clear enough to allow us see what went wrong:

- Too often, schools set up computer labs. Computer classrooms became just like most other classrooms. Rows of machines, often facing the teacher at the front of the room, replaced rows of desks facing forward – only now they were tethered by miles of cable to one spot. Computing became an event into which students were time tabled, whether or not those time slots made any sense at all in terms of the actual work with which students were engaged.

- Teachers thought about applications and software in the same way they thought about worksheets, textbooks, tests and course delivery. It has been difficult for most of us to understand that while computers *can* do the old and familiar things at the speed of light, they *shouldn't* be used that way. There are far better things to do with information and communications technologies.

- A new breed of technology gatekeepers grew up. Knowing that they needed technical support to use computers effectively, teachers often gave a great deal of power to the computer teacher, the on-site "techie" or a district specialist without knowing it. Expertise and confidence gathered around relatively few people in schools. What this small number said or thought was possible or desirable too often drove educational decisions.

- On the one hand, technology was dismissed as trivial. Playing games or going on the Internet were offered as diversions or rewards for "getting your (real) work done."
- On the other hand, technology was offered as a new savior. Enthusiasts made grand claims about how computers would revolutionize schools in the blink of an eye. And while no part of our world outside schools has actually remained untouched by the new technologies, people seriously underestimated the power of the institution of schooling to protect and perpetuate itself in both policy and practice. Grandiose expectations that went nowhere only served to increase the cynicism of many sensible teachers.
- Teachers became increasingly out of touch with how their students actually use computers in their lives outside school. While many teachers struggle to figure out how to use PowerPoint or a spreadsheet, large numbers of their students are exploring the worlds of synchronous and asynchronous communications, playing interactive games, making their own digital movies, creating animations and navigating through toy universes. Too often students keep quiet about this engagement when they come to school. They expect that the equipment they find in their classrooms and labs will be less powerful than the machines they have in their bedrooms, and that their teachers will know less than their own network of peers and family.

In short, it has **become** very difficult for most of us to see what is in front of us, and to decide what to do with it. Now, this is not to cast any blame at all– not on teachers as a group, and certainly not on all the individuals who have struggled over the years to understand these powerful new technologies. In a way, we are all in exactly the same position as we were when cars first started rolling off the assembly line. The early automobiles were called "horseless carriages," and in that lovely phrase we can see a perfectly sane and understandable turn of mind. People first come to terms with what is new by casting it in the light of the familiar. Henry Ford made carriages that could still move, only now without a horse. That much was very clear, but the four legs and the tail still offered the essential frame of reference for this new vehicle. For a while, we got distracted by trying to find the best place for buggy whip holders on the new machines instead of figuring out what they could do so differently that a whip became irrelevant. Many people laughed as cars broke down or slid into the ditch, and detractors trotted by comfortably. "Get a horse," they sneered, secure in the certainties of their own locomotion.

In schools, some of these secure certainties center on unquestioned assumptions about

- the effectiveness of teacher-directed, highly controlled environments in which learners' next steps are determined in advance by teachers' planning or by commercial software packages.
- the character of good work
- the relationship between school and the rest of the world

We think these assumptions are good candidates for the educational four-legs-and-a-tail framework that currently shapes much discourse about educational technology. These are very complex issues, and it is tempting to theorize in lofty, abstract terms about them and leave it to you to figure out what to *do* with all that talk. But since automobile manufacturers actually had to make decisions about those buggy whips, we think it is also helpful to roll up our sleeves and restate these issues in more practical terms: where should we put computers in our buildings, and what should students be doing with them?

WHERE SHOULD WE PUT COMPUTERS IN OUR BUILDINGS?

The short answer to that question is, not in labs. Like all short answers, it is only mainly true, but as a general rule, labs are poor solutions to the issues that technology use in schools present. Sometimes, in specialized situations, labs work. In high schools and junior high schools, there can be a role for production-quality work with high-end computers in which a lab is clearly the best solution. If your students are producing the school yearbook, publishing for the community, doing sophisticated media production and the like, you will probably need computer labs that function like studios and real shops. You will need teachers with greater expertise to create powerful learning environments in which students can produce the appropriate quality of work.

For all other uses of computers, labs are likely a poor choice. We hesitate to put the matter this baldly, given how common they are in schools, and how difficult it can be to find the money to retrofit existing buildings. But we still see so many examples of brand new buildings constructed with labs that we think the problem is more one of old thinking than of practical necessity. When teachers, architects and computer specialists are married to the idea of a lab, they are probably also deeply committed to at least two fundamental assumptions, and probably more.

Assumption #1: All students need to be doing the same thing at the same time. Creative teachers whose schools have labs often find ways around booking schedules by sending students down to the lab to see if there are a couple of free machines they could use, or they post signs on their classroom door letting others know when the computers at the back of their room are available for others to use if they need them. They negotiate with the computer teacher to let students work on their *Shakespeare For Dummies* presentation as part of their Information Processing class or they wangle donations so they can have a few more computers available. These kinds of teachers are already comfortable with the idea that there can be many different things happening at the same time and they are amazingly effective at finding ways around The Lab Schedule. However, the fact is, these teachers are usually frustrated with labs, and they'd be just as happy not to have to use their creativity to get around obstacles. When people ask for labs, chances are they see a teacher bringing an entire class down at the same time every week to do something with computers—rather than seeing students turning to a computer if and when that is the tool they need at the moment to address the work at hand.

Assumption #2: Computers are the point. Too often, we make the assumption that "computer literacy" means being able to make the hardware and software work. It's like saying that being a good writer means having keyboarding skills or good penmanship. While you cannot write anything without some kind of instrument, the mastery of the instrument is only a small part of what writing is actually all about.

Mastery of a tool should always be in service of a bigger goal. For a long time, we assumed that skill building had to come before use. To this end, students were taught to keyboard before they got to compose any kind of digital text. They were taught to use draw and paint tools long before they were asked to draw and paint anything that actually mattered to them. Labs were used for practice, not for real work, in the belief that once the foundations were properly laid down, teachers and students would then know what to do with them.

So how should we be thinking about computer use, if not in labs? Let's start with the ideal. Students should have anytime, anywhere access to the learning tools they need. People don't think in the abstract; they think about *something*. They don't use computers in the abstract, either; they use computers to do *things*. In principle, the work students are doing should guide their decisions about which technology tools they need. Scheduled access to machines should *never* determine what they get to think about.

In practice, this means we have to look at having enough computers available in classrooms that students can turn to them when they need them. Our favorite current configurations involve throwing out individual desks and bringing in tables (or having millwork constructed to the purpose, if the purse is large enough) so that students can work in pods of 4, 6 or 8, with a ratio of no more than 4 students per computer. At the moment, schools are constrained by the unwieldy size of CPUs and monitors. The amount of space they take up and the difficulty of wiring classrooms in such a way that students have easy access to computer workspaces (including the virtual workspace created by a network) when they need it needs to be overcome. But that is only a temporary constraint, and it should not draw our attention away from the fundamental principle of ubiquitous access for all.

Increasingly, schools are turning to laptops and wireless solutions, and the accelerating power and sophistication of personal digital assistants (PDAs) mean that our current images of what a computer *is* will change. The time is not long in coming when we will tell young people stories of how big and cumbersome a desktop computer used to be, in the way we now tell young whipper snappers about how machines with less computing power than a calculator used to take up entire rooms and required their own air conditioners while key punch operators were sweltering in the summer heat. We are reasonably confident, however, in holding to another principle: while all children require easy access to technology, we should not be looking at one computer for every child until we can get our heads around the nature of collaborative work. At the moment, it would be very easy to think of a computer like a textbook: every kid needs one to do their own work all by themselves. And that's not what computers are best for.

Thus, while it is essential to have computers in classrooms in sufficient numbers that students can use them easily, it is also helpful to have clusters of computers or common work areas that are easily accessible so that students can connect with their network, get on line quickly and put their heads together effectively. There are times when groups of students need to huddle together around a machine as they share emerging solutions and ideas. Libraries are natural places for this, especially because they encourage an ease of use between books, digital resources, art resources and music collections. In some schools, wide corridor space has been designed or renovated to permit nooks of computers. Placed in public areas of the building, such spaces have network connections. They are easy to supervise and comfortable to use. They can combine with comfortable chairs or large working tables to encourage conferencing, shared reading or design and text building. Sometimes walls between classrooms are knocked out to facilitate team teaching. The space in between is suddenly freed up for a digital workspace available to two groups of students, not just one. Found space where cloakrooms used to be can also be made to fit the accessibility bill.

When we think of ubiquitous access as a principle, it is also important to think of peripherals. Students should have easy access to digital cameras, scanners, color as well as black and white printers. No desktop machines should come into buildings without sound cards, microphones and headsets. Network architecture should operate on the assumption that students will be doing many different things from many different places – and then teaching assumptions should ensure that this happens.

WHAT SHOULD STUDENTS BE DOING WITH COMPUTERS?

New technologies should never be about pouring old wine into new bottles. If we are to take the stewardship of the intellect seriously as an educational charge, students must be given the opportunity to "think different" each time they pick up a digital tool. How *can* they use technology to think? In a general sense, technology allows students to do things at a level of complexity and sophistication impossible without a computer. It permits them to move with ease and confidence in real and virtual worlds where things change. It allows them to create, not simply consume and reproduce knowledge. In somewhat more detail, here are some of the ways in which teachers could be working with digital tools and in digital environments.

Simulations, microworlds and games involve posing new problems, creating rules and analyzing consequences. Sometimes people call these toy universes, but they have very serious uses in the world. Simulations are an important part of the education of doctors, engineers, pilots, astronauts, police officers and architects. Creating and working in simulated environments requires systems thinking. You have to know more than isolated pieces of information. You have to know how things connect and interact with each other. And you have to know how they *feel*. Simulations work only when they are emotionally and intellectually engaging. As an extreme example, fighter pilots are trained on programs that cultivate feelings of genuine terror when the plane is about to crash. In the absence of such real terror in a simulated cockpit, the learning does not stick. Good teachers have always understood the power of the imagination to draw students into world upon world. They have always resisted the emotionally deadened – and deadening – climate of so much schooling. They have always danced with ideas. There is a widespread public fear that children who use computers are forgetting how to play, and given the unimaginative use to which computers are put in so many classrooms, there is a solid basis for that fear. But if we remember what we have always known about the power of the virtual world of ideas and the imagination, we can live up to the possibility of enhancing, not diminishing, the full life of the mind.

Spreadsheets are a standard feature of any integrated software package, and have been for decades, but they are shockingly underutilized in classrooms. They are good for exploring relationships between variables and properties, forecasting, reckoning probabilities and sharing data on line. The most common use for spreadsheets is data in the form of numbers, and that has caused too many teachers to think of them only in terms of mathematics curricula. But think for a moment of the use scientists make of statistical data. There is a world of powerful information readily available to students in both the physical and social sciences. A pedagogical use of spreadsheets would allow students to concentrate on analysis and interpretation – that is, on real thinking – rather than on performing repetitive calculations, setting up tables or making charts. Thinking *with* data rather than simply practicing the use of the software application lets students try out strategies, revise hypotheses and ask and receive instant feedback to the powerful question, 'What if?' And ironically, learning to use the software within the culture of meaningful use ensures that students actually will learn and remember how to set up tables, enter formulae and create charts.

Databases are good for helping students to organize and search for all sorts of information: text, pictures, sounds, videos, references to other sources that contain more information. Databases allow students to create knowledge by working with information, not just memorizing it. By using databases, they can look for commonalities and differences among groups or classes of things, analyze relationships, identify and interpret trends and patterns, test and refine hypotheses and organize and share information. For databases to be really powerful intellectual tools, students need to be involved in every aspect of their construction. They need to debate and determine the categories, or fields, decide what data will count and to collect effectively to populate the categories. All of this involves coming to terms with fundamental structures and ideas in the topic or discipline under study.

Multimedia authoring tools permit students to visualize meaning, imagine and create multifaceted texts and compose in non-linear ways. People use all their senses for thinking, but in school we often restrict students to reading, writing and listening. Multimedia authoring tools let students create by using many of their other senses. They can include their own music, video clips, voices, art work and animations. This permits a more complex and richly textured exploration using images, sounds, animation and text. Composing and reading multimedia text shifts understanding from left-brain linearity and sequence to right-brain comprehension of the *gestalt*, the whole image. Functional literacy that permits us to build up the meaning of a line of written text from letters, syllables and words is not adequate to the literacy of pattern recognition that lets us identify the face of a friend in a crowd or the cry of our own particular child. Since the ascendancy of print literacy, illustrations have generally been afterthoughts, and there have been few technologies that require us to read text, see a picture and hear a sound at the same time in order to both create and interpret meaning. Multimedia has changed all that – and schools need to awaken to the need for both teachers and students to develop complex new literacies.

Hypermedia are relative newcomers on the digital scene. They are good for composing media texts where ideas are related in nonlinear ways. Traditional text is organized with beginnings, middles and endings. Words move from left to right and top to bottom across the page. Hypermedia change that. Authors create links between ideas that readers can follow if they wish. Navigation tools and structures are as much a part of the "meaning" as the words on the page. Composing with such tools and structures means learning established fundamental relationships between elements that are far more richly textured and complex than the traditional page-turning navigational structure of books. Links between pictures, sounds and words create a fluid environment in which each reader's experience is determined by what he or she does in a place of possibilities created by an author with an entirely new palette at her command.

Students should be using **synchronous and asynchronous communications** for chatting with others in real time, videoconferencing, sending email, participating in discussion forums, and forming and managing collaborative working groups. Communication technologies permit students to experience diverse perspectives and points of view. They can provide parallel working environments for students who want to share information and get ideas from one another. We see this commonly in key pal exchanges, for example. In addition, however, communication technologies can also permit students to work collaboratively with others across time and space to create new designs and constructions that none of them could have built in isolation.

People in the world outside schools are telling teachers how important it is that students learn how to work in teams both to pose and to solve problems in ill-defined environments. Of course, that is not what school has traditionally been charged to do. Traditionally, we have been required to transmit information and identify information leakage through tests and assignments. Curriculum guides, textbooks and the teacher worksheets have generally set problems; good students learn to mastered the information and algorithms needed to find correct answers. Faced with communications technologies that put masses of information at the fingertips of even the most inexperienced, schools must come to terms yet again with the bald fact that we can no longer be in the business of controlling and dispensing information from one isolated individual to another. The same good teachers who understand the power of the imagination have always known that meaning is created in dialogue. When people talk, debate, defend, argue, prove and play with ideas together, they create new understandings. We can do that face-to-face, and now we can use both synchronous and asynchronous communications to extend that way of working across time and space. People can share documents they have created by themselves. They can edit, make notes and send attachments back and forth. They can publish findings instantly, contribute to global data banks, gain access to world class libraries and museums, and view and download remote data. But the new technologies permit even more than that. They allow people to collaborate in real time in common working environments, share one another's desktops, set up on-line meetings and teleconference from multiple locations.

Imagine, then, schools in which students are regularly asked and assisted to

- explore complex and changing relationships
- bring multiple perspectives to bear on meaningful problems
- open communication and information channels to peers and to experts
- draw upon dynamic and rich data sets
- publish their own work to contribute to the knowledge of the world
- play with ideas
- design and construct things
- control their learning environment

We think that's the kind of school that comes much closer to nurturing the active life of active minds. And that's what we think technology is good for.

References

Howley, Craig B., Howley, Aimee & Pendarvis, Edwina D. (1995). *Out of Our Minds: Anti-Intellectualism and Talent Development in American Schooling*. New York: Teachers College Press.

Norton, P. and Wiberg, K. (1998). *Teaching with Technology*. Fort Worth, TX: Harcourt Brace and Company.

CHAPTER 2

SINGING UP THE COUNTRY

MULTIPLE READINGS OF A MIDDLE SCHOOL WRITING CLASSROOM AS (CYBER)TEXT

ROB COHEN

"He has almost finished" generate[s] more excitement than "He has almost begun." What if interest were constant?

— Barry McCallion
Art Maxims In A Bronx Fedora (1970)

I'm standing in the teacher's room trying not to appear completely antisocial, asking the few questions I need answers to, taking a rest, when I overhear a conversation about a given student's inability to focus: "she drifts…doesn't stay on task" – this drift, this time on task thing – I wonder about it too; so I listen harder, pretend to be interested in the 27 flyers I just took out of my mailbox. I wonder about the nature of the task this student hasn't been able to focus on, about contexts, models and preparations, scaffolds and the like, but I wonder mostly about wandering; even continents drift and whole galaxies travel through the vastness of space with no particular known destination.

This is nothing new. Teachers have been accusing students of staring out the window meaninglessly wasting time and daydreaming since there have been classrooms for students to daydream in. In third grade, there was a kid named William who sat a few seats in front of me in my row (our desks were bolted to the floor) and who was rudely introduced to the strand of counting beads strung across the front of his desk when he was "caught" fidgeting with them while listening to the teacher (one could not listen without (a) looking at the teacher and (b) taking notes). Yet there are societies whose very essence is based on this idea of wandering. For the aboriginal cultures in Australia, there is a "labyrinth of invisible pathways which meander all over [the continent]…" It is this verb, this meandering which concerns us here. There is no singular path through, rather, "aboriginal creation myths tell of the legendary totemic beings who had wandered over the continent in the Dreamtime, singing out the name of everything that crossed their path – birds, animals, plants, rocks, waterholes – and so singing the world into existence" (Chatwin, 1987, p. 2). Perhaps William was singing numbers into existence; we'll never know. Still, I'd like to think he was on to something that wasn't quite mindless.

Back in the teachers' room, I am struck with a vague realization that the conversation I'm eavesdropping on is focused on endings when it is beginnings, the several attempts students make at inroads – their patterns of mental travel, the patternings allowing that travel – that must be made and remade before a student can do anything.

* * *

Hypertext is "*non-sequential writing* – text that branches and allows choices to the reader" (Nelson 0/2, emphasis in original) and therefore "demands new modes of reading, writing, teaching, and learning" (Delany and Landow, 1994, p.14). Since hypertext is "reading and writing electronically in an order you choose…your choices…constitute the current state of the text. You become the reader as writer" (Joyce 1995, p. 177). This fused position of reader and writer (sometimes referred to in the literature as "wreader") in some ways *limits* the experience of reading, gives *more* control to an author, concurrently giving the reader a kind of free-ranging access to multiple and (it is hoped) related texts (always author chosen), intertexts sometimes unfurling in a grand cascade of fractal geometries, at others collapsing in upon themselves like a black hole left behind by a failed star.

By now we are all familiar with the ubiquitous blue underlined text link on almost every website. Think about what happens, what has happened to any one of us more than once. You're reading an article of one kind or another on the web and inside is a link to another site, so you make the jump. You're a good web reader, so you use the mouse to open the next reading space in another window and start reading anew. You read past the first few links, but now this related material is beginning to catch your interest so you follow a link to another page within the same website, and another. About ten minutes have gone by before you decide to bookmark the current site and close the window to reveal your original text. You find your place and keep reading. You haven't lost focus, or have you?

> | | |
> |---|---|
> | Well, yes. Because, while you remember why you jumped out of the text you started in, you no longer remember the threads you were holding in your head while you were reading the text you began with. It takes a moment to re-orient yourself but you're unable to read as comfortably as before the jump out and back. | Well, no. Because, while you remember what you read when you jumped out of the text you started in, the threads you were holding in your head seemed to keep the newer linked texts at arm's length. Rather than lose your orientation to the original reading, you chose to let the linked text go for the time being. |

Reading hypertext then requires a kind of cohesive wandering. The poet Charles Olson referred to the act of making poetry as requiring a kind of "mindedness." Robert Creeley, writing in the introduction to *Collected Prose: Charles Olson* puts it this way:

> *I miss so much the ranging, particularizing, intensely conjecturing mind he had. Sans mind, no direction – just a rudderless drift. You had to be* minded, *he said. I think of my small town West Acton and his mill town Worcester, and the ocean out there beyond either one of us with its incessant, shifting "place." As he said to Elaine Feinstein, "Orientate me." I loved that word – locate me, put me in the picture, draw me a map (xvi).*

Hypertext requires a kind of positioning of the reader and/or writer that perhaps we haven't encountered in quite the same ways we have in other technologies (like books). Which doesn't mean that hypertext does anything we haven't seen before, just that it does some things in new ways, allows us to make new kinds of connections, some more freeing, and some more limiting. Instead of becoming embroiled in all the arguments about the end of the book, the end of literature, the end of reading, and the end of culture as we now know it, and perhaps the end of the world as well, Espen Aarseth (1997) chooses to call this stance cybertext.

> *Cybertext, then, is not a "new," "revolutionary" form of text, with capabilities only made possible through the invention of the digital computer. Neither is it a radical break with old-fashioned textuality, although it would be easy to make it appear so. Cybertext is a perspective on all forms of textuality, a way to expand the scope of*

literary studies to include phenomena that are today perceived as outside of, or marginalized by, the field of literature – or even in opposition to it…(p. 18).

Let's go back to William and the beads for a moment. His map of the classroom, of his meanderings through learning did not match the teacher's planned terrain. The cybertext he was composing, the connections he was making, meandered along pathways other than those which had been mapped by the teacher. In some ways, William had traveled to a place the teacher had marked with the warning: here there be monsters. Because he chose to follow links that weren't authorized in the original, because he could and would create alternative paths through that lesson, and because the teacher could not or would not read William's map, the two were left stranded on either side of a wide gulf neither knew how to navigate.

* * *

When Bruce Chatwin sits with Arkady Volchok, "a Russian who was mapping the sacred sites of the Aboriginals," and who is explaining the concepts of the songlines, Volchok takes some time to make sure that Chatwin understands just how powerful a force this concept is to the Aboriginals.

> *'Sometimes,' said Arkady, 'I'll be driving my "old men" through the desert, and we'll come to a ridge of sandhills, and suddenly they'll all start singing. "What are you mob singing?" I'll ask, and they'll say, "Singing up the country, boss. Makes the country come up quicker."' (p. 14)*

When teachers maintain that they are the only ones who can "sing up the country," they also distance themselves from students (the gulf between my third grade teacher and William), and negate students' ideas of what a classroom and what learning might otherwise be. I think here of Maxine Greene stating that "imaginative capacity is…the ability to look at things as if they could be otherwise" (p. 19). By insisting that they hold the only true map for learning within the confines of a given classroom despite all the journals and research and reports and movements and what-all, teachers can create environments that feel more like an educational battleground than anything else.

The infusion of technology into a classroom only makes the point more visible, as if all the Aboriginal songlines were now painted on the curriculum being sung into existence. Students live in a world where navigating and/or creating multiple pathways across an electronic terrain is the norm, and a teacher who refuses to acknowledge this remains isolated from both the students and the (un/authorized) learning which is occurring inside the classroom even if the machines aren't physically in the room. (Just about all the students in my school district have at least one computer at home – often they have several). The computers are in the students' lives and that creates change. Students can collect any information they need or want whenever they want it. They can connect discrete bits of data and/or information at lightning speed in previously unimaginable ways. The problem is not that they download their work from an encyclopedia site or homework.com, it's that they can find and arrange unsorted, unfiltered information on arcane topics as fast as teachers can ask for it. It is the very existence of these machines in the lives of our students that creates the need for teachers to recognize the multiple paths that already exist through learning terrains; to help students sing *their* world into existence inside the classroom by extending it. Teachers need to remind themselves that learning is not just about the accumulation of information, that it is also about the creation of meaning in a (social) context along unanticipated (and sometimes uncontrollable) pathways. By not actively embracing and participating in the construction of these paths, teachers run the risk of becoming "rudderless," cast adrift upon the currents of Creeley's ever-shifting ocean, unable to comprehend why things that have worked in the past have ceased to do so. They are faced with the dilemma of one who lives outside the Aboriginal culture and knows nothing of its inner workings.

> *Aboriginals could not believe the country existed until they could see and sing it – just as, in the Dreamtime, the country had not existed until the Ancestors sang it.*
>
> *'So the land,' I said, 'must first exist as a concept in the mind? Then it must be sung? Only then can it be said to exist?'*
>
> *'True.'*
>
> *'In other words, "to exist" is "to be perceived?"'*
>
> *'Yes.' (Chatwin, p. 14)*

In other words, teachers need to read the classroom as cybertext.

* * *

Two years ago I encountered Maria and the homework problem. She never did any. Not just the work assigned in my class, but in any of her other classes as well. As a result, she was considered a borderline student because of the grades she was earning (or not earning). Not that this is unusual or something teachers don't regularly encounter, but Maria was an energetic eighth grade girl who always meant well and just seemed never to get her work done. When asked, she said she didn't like to write and that she only wrote when she had to; and since I was the new writing specialist, she'd have to.

I wanted to know if time was an issue, so I asked Maria to describe her typical day after school. It turned out she wasn't on any teams, didn't participate in band or cheerleading, but simply took the bus home after school and settled in. To do what? Well, she'd unpack her books and organize her homework, then go down to the kitchen and help her mom prepare dinner. After the family ate dinner she would go back up to her room to do her work. So far so good. It's maybe 7:30 and she's starting her homework; time didn't seem to be the problem here.

Then she told me she'd start doing her work and then it's eight o'clock. Here, she paused meaningfully and smiled. I had no idea what she was implying so I asked: what happens at eight o'clock? She'd just giggle, smile, and repeat herself and repeat herself with greater emphasis as if that was explanation enough: *it's eight o'clock*. So I started asking more questions: do you have a favorite tv show you watch? No. Does your family do something together? No. Does your boyfriend call? No. By now a note of frustration was seeping into my voice. *What happens at eight o'clock?* The question felt like it was rattling around with William's beads.

Across the table, Samantha looked up from her work and said concisely, "At eight o'clock we all go online." It seems that the adolescent telephone behavior I grew up with has now found it's way to AOL's instant messenger technology. My students spend inordinate amounts of time instant messaging (IMing) each other; few use the true chats consistently.[1]

I asked Maria how much time she spent on line each night. She told me she'd stay online until she went to bed. And what time was that? Sometimes around midnight, sometimes not until around two in the morning. And you spend all that time online? She nodded sheepishly. I was floored. Here was a girl who readily admits she doesn't get her work done, cannot connect the time online as time away from completing her homework (not just for my class, but for all her classes), and who by her own admission does not like to write, spending 4-6 hours each night writing to her friends, developing as it were, a writerly voice. Clearly, I needed to tap into this energy for words. But how?

* * *

It's 1970 and I'm about half way through my sophomore year of high school. At this point in my life my academic strongpoint is math (it's a long story) and because of one thing and another I am selected with about 10 other students out of a population of over 6000 (well, it *is* Brooklyn, and I *am* a baby boomer) to learn computer programming: Fortran 2. We had one card punch, one card sorter, one card reader, a printer, and a link to the state's mainframe in Albany, New York. Lord only knows what kind of machine our work was being processed on.

Now, my high school, Brooklyn Technical HS, was a science and engineering school with a hands-on philosophy of education that has served me ever since. My point in telling you this is that I want to try to outline here what the experiences in that computer-programming class were like. I remember that the class was my lunch period; as a sophomore I didn't yet have electives; for others in the class who were in the upper grades, it was an elective by invitation. So it was a multi-age, multi-grade classroom. Rather forward thinking for the time.

The class was an apprenticeship workshop. When I joined the fray it seemed that there were others who had been doing this kind of work for a while (I didn't even know the school had a computer link to Albany); truly, I was among a select few or at least it felt that way because the older students were not only able to grasp the concepts of programming more readily than I did, but because the relaxed tenor of the interactions among all the students and with our instructor led me to assume some of them had been at this for a while. I never asked, so I'll never know if my impressions were right or wrong.

What I do know is that we'd been given problems to solve using the computer. And that no one's programs worked first time through (something that seems to be part of the art of writing code...first drafts are, well, first drafts, and are riddled with inaccuracies, inconsistencies and problems). And that the debugging process became a communal effort. We knew instinctively that we couldn't all talk with one teacher at the same time and so chose to talk among ourselves; this talk was not discouraged, it was in fact encouraged.

Thirty-one years later I have some understanding of what was happening: we were entering into a "*Discourse*...a socially accepted association among ways of using language, other symbolic expressions, and 'artifacts'...to identify oneself as a member of a socially meaningful group...or to signal (that one is playing) a socially meaningful 'role' " (Gee p. 131, emphasis in original). Back in 1970, our "socially meaningful roles" were limited to what it meant to become a programmer. We were participants in what Gee terms "*acquisition*...a process of acquiring something (usually, subconsciously) by exposure to models, a process of trial and error, and practice within social groups, without formal teaching" (p. 138). The teaching, and subsequently my learning was dispersed in that what I learned came as much from sitting with another student and trying to figure out the logic behind something called a "do loop," getting confused, and seeking help, as it did from the teacher.

My experience in that class began as an overwhelming set of conflicting and confusing impulses. All my other classes assumed a more or less lecture format, with peer to peer conversation almost non-existent save in the science labs, and even there the talk was monitored. But in the computer class, especially in the beginning, I was never quite sure what I was *supposed* to be doing, only that there were things to be done, and a heightened sense of responsibility to get them done. Gee says "you cannot overtly teach anyone a Discourse in a classroom or anywhere else," that "acquisition must (at least, partially) precede learning; apprenticeship must precede overt teaching" (p. 139). I had been put in a position that forced me to enter a new Discourse or drown in my own uncertainties.

* * *

A few months ago, a pre-service teacher came to observe my classroom. She wanted to see how I was using technology. I have eight desktop computers that range in age from very new to fairly old. They are all connected to a network where students can access their work folders, hand-in folders, etc. And while our school has two state of the art Macintosh G3 labs and numerous other workstations in classrooms throughout the building, we also have a cart of i-books (G3 notebook computers) that comprise a "rolling lab." On this day, the i-books are in my classroom. And all the rules are changed as a result. Rules I never made.

Students who work in the computer center in my classroom are generally social, interacting with each other within the close proximity of the machines as they work, drifting through the inevitable conversations that occur when people work in proximity to one another. Sometimes they are helpful to one another, sometimes they are arguing about boyfriends, girlfriends, makeup, and/or sports. Some will use the web as a diversion after a spell of hard work. There is nothing very unusual about any of this in a middle school classroom.

On most days, work begins with the girls at the tables or in the carpeted reading centre while the boys take over the computer center. The boys soon realize they do not need the computers at that particular moment and so drift back to the tables or the reading centre where a few squabbles occur before things settle. Students are then engaged in drafting, peer editing, revising, the what-all of a typical writing classroom on a workshop day.

But on the days when the i-books are in my room, things are very different. All the gender-specific behaviors delineated above are gone; students are only concerned that there are enough of the notebooks to go around (and there always are). There is a mild buzz of excitement as the students who want a notebook take one and boot up. They sit in mixed groups all around the room. The tenor of the conversations is calmer, and students engage their work more readily and stay focused longer. So what is it about notebook computers?

The pre-service teacher in my room said quite simply: "It just seems normal, like pencil and paper." This is a social milieu these adolescents find comfortable; they can bring the small computers into their private space and use them as they would if they were not in the formal setting of school (no matter how informal a classroom may be). Unlike the labs or the center inside my room where the model for use would likely be perceived as teacher initiated, the notebooks provide a personal space more readily shared with peers.

These are students who are used to interacting with each other as persona. They spend hours on line IMing each other every night and are identified only by their screen names. *In Life on the Screen: Identity in the Age of the Internet* (1995), Sherry Turkle finds that adolescent computer use often involves them in role playing games (RPGs) in multi-user domains (MUDs). Some may be playing more than one game at a time in different domains. Each game requires another character and another identity. Some are also doing homework at the same time. Some are composing interactive fictions which extend the lives of the characters they've created or of those which began their lives as characters in commercial games (talk about dependent authorship). All the while instant messages are being sent and received. On the computer screen, "each of these activities takes place in a window [and] identity on the computer is the sum of [one's] distributed presence" (p. 13). Each window is another place where a composed virtual self resides. None of them are real life (RL). And as one of the college students Turkle interviews says, "RL is just one more window…and it's not usually my best one."

Following Turkle, we could look at school as a kind of virtual environment where each class is a different MUD with different rules for "playing" at the game of learning. Student roles are the ones they assume when they enter a given class. Thus, school becomes a simulation or even a cybertext, where each class occurs in a different window and the links between and among windows are largely ignored. The simulation is fairly "boring" since students can only look at one window at a time: the classroom of the moment.

Think again about the behaviors around the i-books in my classroom. Students are more relaxed because they are working with multiple screens. There is the classroom itself (a lesson and/or conversation supplants IMing), there is the work students are doing on their notebooks including the web pages they are constantly accessing, there are books to read, or an assigned journal to write. Now there are enough windows for them to cycle through, and RL is relegated to its more usual virtual space.

This is *their* world, this fragmented, postmodern, sometimes disconnected sometimes connected, linked, hypertext weave of screens. Turkle tells us "today's children are growing up in the computer culture; all the rest of us are at best its naturalized citizens" (p. 77). These students sing entire universes into and out of existence every day. They are involved with games and simulations and can reset the state of either at any time, thereby offsetting any errors in play. This makes them what Turkle calls "tinkerers." When faced with a problem in the context of a game or simulation, they become "problem-solvers who do not proceed from top-down design but by arranging and rearranging a set of well known materials...bricolage" (p. 51). And they do the same thing with all those windows, whether they are at home in front of their own PC or in a classroom in front of an i-book.

Ruth Vinz (1996) explains this tinkering as occurring along "nomadic lines." There is a kind of contextualized aimlessness here, a wandering in and out of various shifting frameworks, a piling up of meanings accumulated by experiences taking place over time. Years ago when I was an undergraduate I was with my roommate when he had a particularly daunting set of tasks to deal with and didn't know where or how to begin. I responded to his mutterings by saying, "why not just start in the middle and work your way in?"

* * *

In some ways I can thank Maria for helping me to understand all this. When she was my student, she baffled me for a while. What I knew about working with resistance as a teacher didn't include what she was doing. And what she knew how to do wasn't matching up with what she understood as school in general and writing in particular. My systematic and logical approach was getting me nowhere. I privately referred to Maria as "my science project." The only thing I had left going for me was that I was not a technological novice. Nonetheless, Maria was walking along a line I only knew via casual observance; she knew the paths I walked and wasn't interested. To reach her I'd have to learn to use a kind of map I'd never seen.

It occurred to me that IMing was more similar to e-mail than it was different. So I gave Maria my home e-mail address and asked her to write to me one evening when she was on line. One Friday night, to my surprise, she did:

hi mr cohen this is maria! (your favorite student) ok so i'm like riting 2 u so rite bak soon

I felt like the world's best hacker; I had an invitation to come in. I wrote back the next day:

what's on your mind? we said we'd give this a try...so let's try: i got your message late last night when i got in...

I still find it remarkable that you say you don't like to read or write but spend hours doing exactly that on line...what do you find so different about on line? (i'm being curious). ttyl

There were no further exchanges of e-mails, possibly because I pressed too hard for answers too soon, but over the next week of classes, Maria's attitude toward her work shifted; homework assignments started showing up. We were five weeks into a ten-week cycle where she and the rest of her eighth grade classmates had to write a district mandated I-search essay. She had miles to go, but she had begun to work. Ultimately, she finished the project on time. I never got an answer to my question. But I began to learn.

* * *

We can be defeated and disoriented and overwhelmed by the vastness of the learning before us when we start any project. We can try to fit knowledge into neat boxes and discrete fragments – into charts and graphs and tables and units and curriculum. It helps sometimes. (Vinz, p. 6)

Even as the roads we drive are networks of paths, possibilities, apparently limitless, but actually limited, a series of intersecting lines already mapped, a series of (pre)constructed choices – path and destination, a kind of zero-sum multiple choice game, it is always possible to become lost, to need to find new bearings before proceeding. So too with a teacher in a technology enriched classroom. We come up against ourselves, our beliefs and our methods time and time again. Before Maria left my classroom at the end of that marking period, several other students in that section asked for my home e-mail address. They began sending me drafts of their work on a regular basis, more regular than the due dates we had established as a class. We entered into various written conversations about writing and the nature of being a writer that spilled over into the classroom. We began to merge two very different Discourses. And I was learning to read a new map.

Now giving students my home e-mail address is one of the first things I do for each class (I haven't worked up the nerve to try IMing with them; I'm mostly afraid I'll end up with more than I could respond to in a lifetime, or that I won't be contacted at all). Not all of my students send me email, but they all know they can. And very little work comes in late because there's always a way to get it to me. I take an informal survey at the beginning of each marking period when I see new groups of students (as a writing specialist in a middle school I see all 460 students in the building each year; it's a daunting task just to remember who they all are). I ask students to tell me by a show of hands whether or not they have their own computers, many do; the rest have access to one shared by some or all members of the family or to mom's or dad's laptop. Some have T1 lines into their homes, others have cable modems or DSL; very few use dial up connections running at 56k. And then I ask how many have been in chats; about half admit to it. After a few minutes where the students badger each other and I remain silent, the number grows to 80%. Then I ask how many spend time IMing. All hands go up. How many spend an hour on line almost every night? Almost all. Two hours? A little better than half (some start to complain they've lost their privileges for one reason or another). Three hours? Maybe 25% of the class. More? About 10%.

Certainly they are writing. In fact, they like writing to each other electronically so much that some received as Christmas gifts last year a device which is a calculator/dictionary/organizer and which can also send messages across the building to another unit of the same type. For a few weeks students were IMing within the walls of the building; I would suggest there's substantially more to this than simply passing notes or zoning out on a given lesson. This is their Discourse.

Maybe it's my early experience with computers, maybe it's just a function of my stance as teacher, but for me, the new technologies are just there. I don't make a big deal out of them. They're tools. When I taught in a district that had one computer in the classroom capable of going on line, I adapted my teaching to include that use as best I could. I work from the assumption that the machines *can* do what I need them to do even if I don't know how to make that happen; there's got to be someone around who can help me. But the paradigm for technology use seems to mirror what I see generally for instruction regarding that which is deemed to be new material for the learner. That is, we act as though we must have complete mastery of the tool (not just the computer, but the software as well) before we can turnkey its use to students when in fact we need to find a way to gain entry to our students' Discourse.

Some years ago when I was consulting with school districts in New Jersey to help them integrate and infuse technology into their classroom curricula, I found it necessary to give teachers an overview of the various softwares available and what they could do with them in their classrooms. From time to time, I would be called on to show the students in those classrooms how to use software their teachers were struggling with. What stands out most in my memory is the difficulties I went through to get teachers to develop competence in using Hyperstudio (several 1-2 hour workshops across a span of weeks) when juxtaposed with the responses of fourth graders in those same teachers' classrooms. I could give one group of about four students a 30-minute hands-on lesson on the basics of the program and return a week later to find the entire class using the program in ways I'd never conceived. Clearly, mastery does not occur before use.

* * *

About midway through the past school year it occurred to me that there was a space for some of the eighth graders to read novels that were not normally a part of the eighth grade curriculum. So a small group of pioneering and interested eighth graders, along with myself and a seventh grade science teacher, entered into a once-a-week early morning book discussion group. The idea was that students and adults would simply discuss books and the ideas they raise without thought of essays, quizzes, homework, etc. As the year wore on, several more students and occasionally a music teacher joined us.

At the time we began, I started to send notices about meeting times and days via email (we all had email accounts at home), but I also wanted to set up an asynchronous threaded discussion in case our conversations spilled over beyond our weekly hour. I created a "class" at nicenet.org. As soon as I set up the "classroom" and emailed the few initial members of the group of its existence one of them set up a topic for discussion that had us all going for days. We were reading Ken Kesey's *One Flew Over the Cuckoo's Nest* and Langston (a veteran of all kinds of MUD and RPG activities) set up the first forum called "The Combine" and asked us to respond to a question: "Do you think without 'the combine' the world would be better or worse?" I never had to set up a single strand for discussion, someone would always do that as the need arose. There were any number of posts and messages relevant to concepts in the readings until a few of the RPG students got into a kind of flame war. Messages were flying fast and furious. Overnight there were about 15 posts back and forth between two students telling inside jokes at each other's expense.

After I made the point that the forum was not really the place for this kind of behavior, I was struck by the level of insight these students brought to bear on their reading. We arrived at a deep exploration of what comprises the ideal society and I was able to point a few students toward Thoreau and Plato. Later in the year, reading Alan Lightman's *Einstein's Dreams* we delved deeply into the nature of the real and of truth. Dan got things rolling:

> *I find it so hard to believe that two people can look through different pairs of eyes and process the same things in their minds. Truly how do we know that what i think is blue is not what Langston sees as green in his mind but he calls it blue...Now that I think of it maybe we do know with the technology we have...but we only believe what we grow up to live and learn...It just kind of weirds me out when I think about how little we know about what other people are thinking.*

By the end of the week, the conversation had become a meditation on the nature of love. I knew that these students were among the better readers and thinkers across the eighth grade, but I had no idea of their ability to express highly nuanced thinking in writing: little of this had come through in their more formal work for their classes. In fact most of them rarely spoke in class unless called upon directly. The thing that stood out was how fluent they all were in a domain and a Discourse they could call their own. I had some thinking to do.

* * *

None of these moves would have been possible if I hadn't known hypertext. There's a kind of wandering along nomadic lines (Vinz) that occurs in this kind of teacherly composition that doesn't happen in composing other, more traditional teaching and/or classroom texts. Michael Joyce (1997) has a simple exercise he gives his students when he is teaching them about hypertext fiction authorship.

> *What I do is to ask the writers to write four parts of something, keeping the notion of "parts" and "something" intentionally fuzzy but making it clear we are talking narrative...I encourage them to do this very quickly and not to worry about how extensive or finished the writing is.*
>
> *Once this is done, I first have them recreate linearity, that is, link the four parts [sequentially]...to reinforce the concept that in*

> *hypertext even the linear is a choice. Then I ask the question....:*
> *Suppose at this point your reader, before going on, has to reread one*
> *part of what comes before, which would it be? (581)*

In hypertext, "our choices change the nature of what we read. Rereading in any medium is a conscious set of such choices, a sloughing off of one nature for another" (p. 581). And here is the crux of the matter. For teachers to have success in a technology rich classroom environment populated with learners who bring with them each day a terminal ennui begat by their experiences in a Discourse not privileged inside schools – if at all recognized – we need to revisit and reread a part of what has come before, to reconnect, to link with what is clearly present: young minds thinking and connecting and communicating with tools most of us barely understand and can hardly use with the fluidity and fluency of those same learners.

We have long been asked to be reflective practitioners, to notice what we do, the effects, and to make adjustments; now we must also be spectators and speculators, reading our classes for clues, for cues, for entrance points into the Discourse which attends our students and discloses itself in the paths between and among a number of virtual realities, through communication tools which network in some very literal ways. If we are to be something other than rudderless, then we need to choose to encounter our students differently. "Rather than imagining our period of transition to hypertext as a point where something old is replaced by something new, I would be content to see it described as a time when two ways of reading and writing, and two ways of using maps, are plausible at the same time." (Rosello quoted in Joyce, p. 587).

If, like hypertext, the technology rich classroom is a kind of "narrative origami," and can be seen as both folded and folding in and out of itself as well as opening on to new possibilities in the arrangements of learning spaces, then we have a responsibility as teachers to learn to read our old maps against our students' new ones and begin to hold conversations along lines of convergence and divergence; to enter into this notion of classroom as MUD, as a kind of VR which lasts only for a certain number of minutes in the RPG lives of students each day they are in school, to understand school as a medium with multiple screens and open windows, to learn, as it were, to wander the songlines of our own curricula.

Perhaps it is this that most frightens teachers about technology in the classroom. Beyond the unfamiliarity and irrational fears some have around these machines, there is the larger issue of what changes inside the classroom as a result of the kinds of writing that students are capable of doing. Let's forget for the moment the entire issue of kids knowing more about how to use the machines than the teachers. Let's think for a minute what this does to us as educators who used to know how to get something done, but now find that what we know how to do doesn't match what the students know how to do or are willing to do. They know how to connect to all of this technology. They know how to connect it to each other. For them it is a social environment. Its basis is in wandering, in overlapping, in reseeing and rethinking in large patterns. For those who have held on to the notion of controlling the directions and paths of student thought with the teaching we do, the very presence of the machines make obvious the various and variant pathways students take to reach highly individualized learnings. For those who hold the belief that every student leaves a classroom with the same knowledge organized in the same way, the introduction of electronic tools for composition becomes a political threat to the power structures and organization of a linear and cumulative curriculum. All of it breaks down in the presence of the relational structures brought about by the presence of the new media in the classroom.

Think about it. It's remarkable how many sites students know, how many have homepages they post to regularly, how many discuss the real issues of their lives in a code English teachers may or may not know. These learners can create worlds out of words and do so quite readily. The question is whether we want to co-create those worlds and the learnings that take place in them.

NOTES

1. Instant Messenger is available with Netscape even if you don't use AOL's services. It's a technology that lies somewhere between call waiting, email, and television commercials. Both call waiting and television commercials interrupt the flow of whatever narrative is taking place. Instant Messenger allows you to manage a list of correspondents who can "see" when you are online (as you can see them) and who can send brief messages which alert you when they arrive so that you can respond. My small experience with it felt like one of those times I've

set aside to get a particular task done and lots of people kept phoning to talk or stopping by to visit just long enough to break my train of thought.

REFERENCES

Aarseth, E. (1997). *Cybertext: Perspectives on Ergodic Literature.* Baltimore: Johns Hopkins University Press.

Chatwin, B. (1987). *The Songlines.* New York: Penguin.

Creeley, R. (1997). "Introduction." In D. Allen and B. Friedlander (eds.), *Collected Prose: Charles Olson.* Berkeley: University of California Press.

Delany, P. and Landow, G.P. (1994). "Hypertext, Hypermedia and Literary Studies: The State of the Art." In P. Delany and G. Landow (eds.), *Hypermedia and Literary Studies.* Cambridge: MIT Press. 3-50.

Gee, J.P. (1996). *Social Linguistics and Literacies: Ideologies in Discourses.* London: Taylor and Francis.

Greene, M. (1995). *Releasing the Imagination: Essays on Education, the Arts, and Social Change.* San Francisco: Jossey-Bass.

Joyce, M. (1995). *Of Two Minds: Hypertext Pedagogy and Poetics.* Ann Arbor: University of Michigan Press.

Joyce, M. (1997). "Nonce Upon Some Times: Rereading Hypertext Fiction." *Modern Fiction Studies,* 43-3, 579-597.

McCallion, B. (1970). *Art Maxims in a Bronx Fedora.* Somerville: Abyss.

Nelson, T.H. (1987). *Literary Machines: The Report On, and Of, Project Xanadu....* South Bend: The Distributors.

Rosello, M. (1994). "The Screener's Maps: Michel de Certeau's 'Wandersmänner' and Paul Auster's Hypertextual Detective." In G.P. Landow (ed.), *Hyper/Text/Theory.* Baltimore: Johns Hopkins University Press.

Turkle, S. (1995). *Life on the Screen: Identity in the Age of the Internet.* New York: Touchstone.

Vinz, R. (1996). "Dilemmas of Definition: Peripheral Visions on Interdisciplinary Education." Presented at Art, Culture, and Interdisciplinarity. Teachers College Columbia University 4/27.

Chapter 3
Factors Affecting the Adoption and Use of Instructional Devices

George H. Buck

Instructional devices are used in almost all contemporary instructional settings, from formal classes to do-it-yourself presentations in stores. The apparatus used may be as simple as a blackboard or as complex as a computer. The apparatus may simply present information, or it may simulate the actions of either another machine or some aspect of human behavior. In most instances the way instructional devices are used is determined either by an implicit assumption about the ways in which human beings learn, or by following an explicit theory of learning or pedagogy. Devices to assist instruction, or even to undertake some of the duties of a teacher or trainer, have a long and interesting history, and are not recent innovations spawned by the industrial revolution of the nineteenth century.

For our purpose, the term *instructional device* is used. This refers to all devices or apparatus that are used for instruction generally, when it is not necessary to make further distinction (Saettler, 1990). One may distinguish between devices that either provide instruction without a teacher, or which must be used in conjunction with a teacher. Devices falling into the former category are referred to in the literature variously as: *instructional technology*, apparatus that may be used either as adjuncts to instruction, or for providing instruction with or without the presence of a teacher; *teaching machines*, a term describing now-obsolete mechanical devices that purportedly provided instruction to a user by some means, required some form of response, and provided instructive feedback based on the response, but which is now applied in some instances to the use of computers for instruction; *Computer-Based Instruction*, or *Computer-Assisted Instruction*, and related terms, where a computer is programmed to function in the same general manner as a teaching machine, but with a greater degree of sophistication, analyses of response, and speed (Alessi & Trollip, 2001); and *teaching aids*, a general term to describe any material and apparatus that is used by a teacher to enhance his or her instruction. Teaching aids do not provide instruction in and of themselves, but are useful in helping a teacher convey a particular theory or idea. Another category, *necessary tool*, may be identified. Necessary tools comprise those instruments or devices that are essential for a particular activity to be accomplished. A violin, for example, is a necessary tool for violin playing. Similarly, a compass, circle template, or a computer drawing program is a necessary tool for the drawing of true circles in a demonstration of geometry. On the other hand, a violin is not a necessary tool to demonstrate the principles of harmonics to a physics class; it is a teaching aid in this case. While a violin may illustrate harmonics adequately, it is possible to use other instruments and apparatus for this purpose.

The advent of new technologies, or the discovery that they may be applied to education, are usually accompanied by claims that their use will result in *revolutionary change* to the way in which instruction is provided, or that instruction will become more efficient and effective, thus increasing student achievement markedly (Gold, 1999). Such claims are often made before the new devices or technologies are fully deployed or tested in instructional settings. When the first microcomputers began appearing by the late 1970s, for example, some enthusiastic proponents rashly predicted that instruction, as we knew it, was about to be changed dramatically. For example, Alfred Bork (1981) stated,

We are at the brink of a major revolution in ways of learning. Very few people – not even professional educators – understand what is about to happen. The revolution will occur within the next 25 years and will affect our educational system at all levels. (p.1)

Predictions of radical change in education because of an innovation are nothing new. In 1913, Thomas Edison, promoting his motion picture system, stated,

Books will soon be obsolete in schools. Scholars will soon be instructed through the eye. It is possible to teach every branch of human knowledge with the motion picture. Our school system will be completely changed in ten years. (Cited in Saettler, 1968, p. 98)

The inaccuracy of such predictions might seem to suggest that most instructional devices are destined to fail, or that a positivistic attitude about the effect of instructional devices is at best misleading (Postman, 1992); but it is important to consider that some instructional devices have become integral components of many instructional settings. Indeed, many of these, such as the blackboard and its variants, are taken for granted. To gain greater insight into some of the factors that determine whether an instructional device will succeed or fail is beneficial both to educators and to those whom they educate. Earth-shaking predictions of the sort quoted in the previous paragraphs do not account for many key factors that influence the development of instructional devices. For example, was the reason why the motion picture failed to become the primary means of instruction by 1923, as Edison had predicted, the result of poor technology, or was the pedagogical premise of using motion pictures for instruction faulty or misunderstood by educators? Another possibility is that Edison and others considered motion pictures to be a *solution looking for a problem*; an effective entertainment technology, but not essential for improved instruction. Edison and others considered motion pictures in education as a potential market not yet tapped. It may have been hoped that, by using motion pictures, teaching might be improved, and that Edison's company might also increase its profits.

To gain some knowledge of what factors affect the development and deployment of instructional devices, it is necessary to consider their development within the context of a long time frame as well as within the context of the learning theories that they embody (Postman, 2000). Several purposes are served by this approach. First, a more objective view is possible than considering current devices only, since there is now little or no vested interest in devices and methods invented in earlier periods. Second, chronological or linear development patterns of instructional devices and/or learning theories are revealed. Third, a broader perspective is likely to reveal whether recurring claims about instructional devices are either accurate or erroneous. Fourth, any apparent factors or patterns of development discovered may be applied to current devices and situations to enable better forecasting about their usefulness and their possible efficacy in particular educational settings.

Although specifics differ for each instructional device one cares to examine, a common reason why each device was introduced is discernible, *perceived need*. This phenomenon must be explained further, since needs in pedagogy usually arise from some perceived deficiency either in instruction or in resultant student performance. Other factors such as knowledge of available technology, consideration of the economic possibilities and the ramifications of production and use of the device must be considered before an instructional device or an idea for an instructional device can be applied to an existing pedagogical system with any hope of success.

While many authors treat innovations in education as a general subject, in turn the subject of innovations in education is also germane to the introduction and the deployment of instructional devices. Something that is new, or at least unknown to most educators, can be considered an innovation. Although the criteria, models and hierarchies described and discussed in this chapter may be applied to innovations in general, the intent is that they be applied to instructional devices.

Schlebecker (1977) identified four criteria for technological invention, 1) accumulated knowledge, 2) evident need, 3) economic possibility, 4) cultural and social acceptability. The criteria do not explain fully why certain inventions gain widespread use while others do not. From a different perspective, Gaines and Shaw (1986) consider relevant factors as steps in a supposed linear development of an idea or a technology from invention through common use. They liken this development to typical *learning curves* in human beings. With the development of an innovative technology, like a human being learning an idea or concept, there is gradual development following an initial breakthrough. Growth or development then continues at a rapid rate until most of the information is assimilated. A gradual reduction in development follows as the result of *maturity* of the idea or technology. This entire process relies upon previous related developments that have reached maturity. Both Schlebecker's criteria and Gaines' and Shaw's linear steps do little to account for specific factors discernible within educational settings that impinge upon the introduction and the development of instructional devices. More cogent explanations are provided by several educators.

Approaching the implementation of innovation from the perspective of education, Loucks and Zacchei (1983) note that in general, most educational institutions and educators are not implementing innovations. Their analysis of the problem suggests that the reason for this failure is that certain crucial criteria are not considered. Rather than organizing these criteria in linear steps, they are presented as four main *ingredients* that must be present during the process of implementation, if the innovation is to gain widespread use: 1) a well-defined *classroom-friend-*

ly effective innovation; 2) ample and continuous help for teachers from a variety of individuals; 3) a clear direction for administrators; 4) attention to institutionalization. Although the four ingredients help ensure that important factors relevant to the successful implementation of an innovation are considered, the criteria are vague. The meaning of *classroom-friendly*, for example, is not clarified.

In a manner similar to that of Gaines and Shaw (1986), Gold (1999) contends that innovation in education is characterized by short periods of "revolutionary" change that is either followed by failed innovation or by long periods of incremental change based on the initial change.

Employing a different approach, Bishop (1986) proposes a six-step hierarchical process to explain generally how educational innovations may become commonplace. Step one begins with the recognition of a problem, dissatisfaction or need. Consideration of possible solutions comprises step two. In step three, a particular solution (some sort of innovation) is selected as being most appropriate. Trial and evaluation is the fourth step, followed by wider implementation if the trials are deemed successful. The final step is the universal implementation or institutionalization of the innovation.

While Bishop (1986) states that it is necessary to identify the *real* nature of the problem, which in some instances may not lie within education at all, little consideration is given to the possibility of a problem or concern in education being exaggerated or misrepresented by concerns who wish to have a particular innovation or instructional device deployed for reasons other than those of solving an actual pedagogical problem. Many teachers admit, for example, that their teaching methods can be improved. Instructional devices that are promoted as being *time-savers* for the teacher, or devices that are claimed to embody pedagogical methods that will improve student achievement markedly, purport to address the perennial concerns of teaching improvement and efficiency. Many such devices, however, are produced by manufacturers solely for profit, with little or no regard for the improvement of pedagogy (Skinner, 1983; Bennett, 1925). The profit motive solely can induce manufacturers to produce instructional devices. For example, Chalmers (1990) described a local business concern in Edmonton, Alberta, that manufactured varieties of bead frame teaching aids for sale throughout North America. Revenues earned during 1989 exceeded one million dollars.

Concerning the evaluation and selection of innovations, Bishop (1986) states that, "just because something is new or different it need not necessarily be better than the system it is transplanting" (p. 5). Bishop's steps, however, do not contend with many of the intervening factors that can affect the deployment of an instructional device. For example, a *bandwagon* effect, originating either within or without the educational setting, may either spur the deployment of an innovation, or it may hasten its abandonment. In such cases, the actual merit of the device is likely not to be the primary concern.

To better explain the various dynamic factors affecting the development, implementation and ultimate fate of instructional devices, a development and implementation model has been created. Although original, the model incorporates elements from existing models.

While the development and implementation model may resemble some of the linear models discussed previously, movement through this model is not entirely linear as particular points may be bypassed, and abandonment of the innovation can occur at any point if particular criteria and/or circumstances are not met.

INITIAL STAGES

Beginning with a perceived need, either from a pedagogical basis or from some other motive, an individual, group or corporation considers technological possibilities for a device that can satisfy the need. If an apparatus is envisaged that cannot be constructed given the available technology, then the idea is abandoned, or at least shelved until technological advances permit further development of the idea. If the technology exists to transform the idea into reality, then a new device is produced. It is important to note, especially where individual designers are concerned, that the execution of the device may be constrained by limits of the developer's awareness of available technology. In such cases, a new device may be created that is later abandoned when more appropriate technology is applied, rendering the old device obsolete. The replacement of mechanical teaching machines by computers is one such example.

Once a prototype is produced, the developer makes educators aware of the device and the reasons why it should be used. If only a small

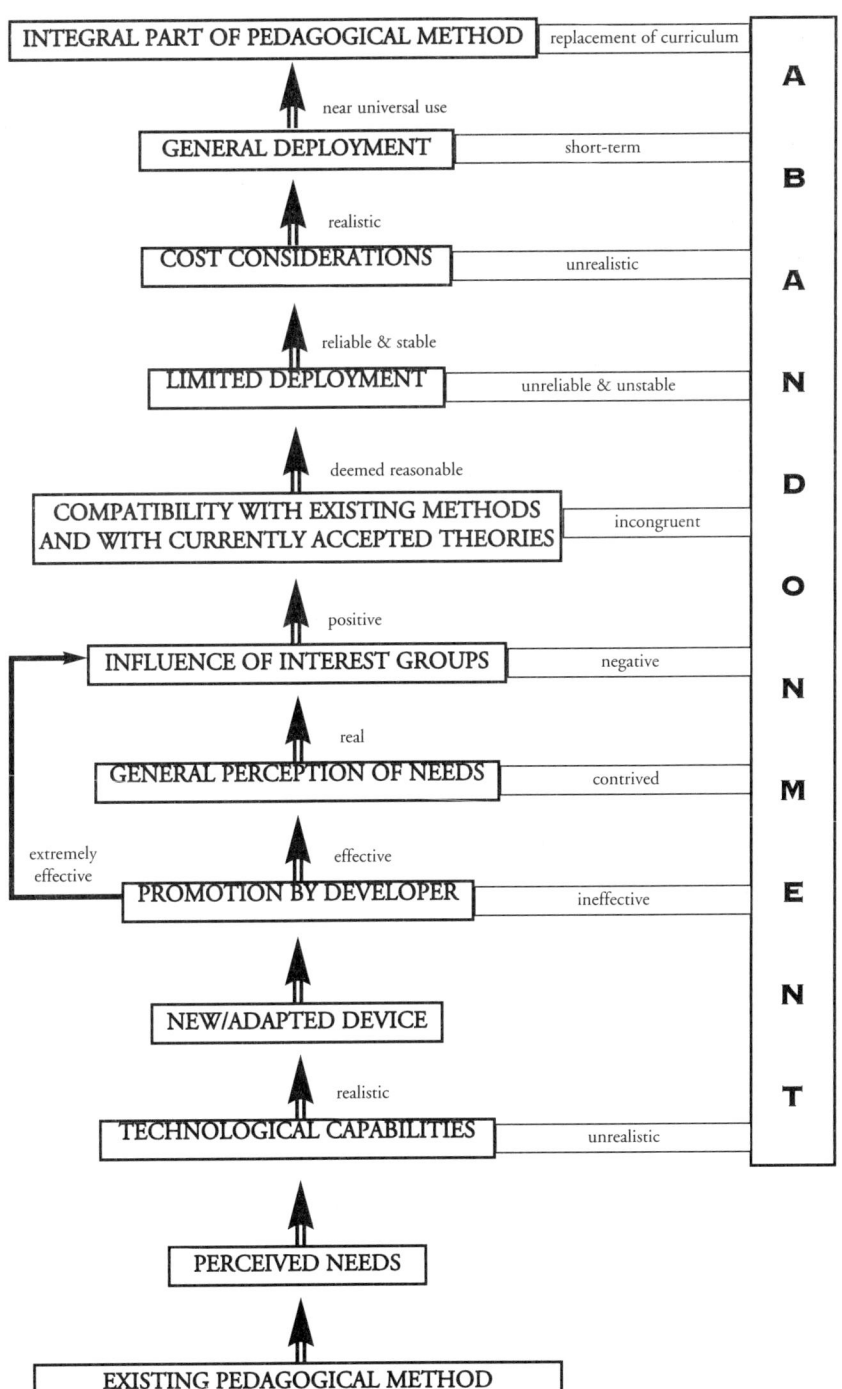

number of people learn of the device, then it is likely to be abandoned through insufficient interest. If the device receives widespread notice, then the rationale and the justification for its use must be recognized by its intended users. Notable exceptions are many of the devices produced for use in the home and in other non-formal educational settings such as day care centres. In such cases, purchasers usually do not consider whether or not the device is effective pedagogically. This step of the model can be circumvented in some instances. If the developers of the device are able to promote it successfully to the interest groups that influence and control the selected pedagogical system, then the device may be introduced without considering the individuals who have to incorporate its use into the curriculum (Stoll, 1995). Havelock and Huberman (1977) also recognized this possibility and caution that innovations forced in this manner, "tend to lurch from crisis to crisis and to end up as large-scale 'pilot projects' with little prospect of being generalized as long as they are propped up by special resources and unusual administrative support" (p. 78). If the general consensus of the interest groups is that the device is inadequate, however, then it is usually abandoned.

BANDWAGON EFFECT

One factor that may lead an interest group to believe that a particular instructional device or a class of instructional devices is appropriate for use, is the so-called *bandwagon* effect. This condition is the result of an assumption that an apparent trend of increasing interest is a reflection of merit and practical usefulness; if a large number of individuals are interested in something, it must be good. This assumption tends to obscure objectivity, so a device or a class of devices may be deployed without considering other factors. A possible result of such action may be that design limitations will affect a large number of people rather than just a few individuals if deployment was limited initially. Another result might be the abandonment of the device because its purpose is not understood by the individuals who are responsible for its deployment or who must supervise its use.

What these statements imply is that the sample which indicates an increasing interest in the device may not represent the level of interest of those individuals who deploy the device or supervise its use. Glaser (1960) provides one example of how the bandwagon effect can lead to erroneous assumptions. He concluded that an apparent high interest in teaching machines was a reflection of their effectiveness. Glaser contended further that teaching machines should be deployed in classrooms as soon as possible so that instruction may be improved. At the same time, there was no indication that the teachers who were expected to use teaching machines shared Glaser's level of enthusiasm for teaching machines. To make predictions based on evidence that does not show a causal relationship clearly, therefore, suggests that the predictions are the result of the bandwagon effect.

Glaser (1965) came to realize the some of the problems that the bandwagon effect can cause,

> *I was greatly concerned that the uncritical rapid acceptance and too-ready use of programed instruction would accomplish two things: that high expectations coupled with awkward usage would result in disappointing outcomes and that the rush toward immediate practicality would pull the field away from its loose ties with the scientific study of behavior.* (p. vii)

Although Glaser qualified his position by noting that actual developments were different from predicted extremes, the bandwagon effect did hinder rather than help the deployment of teaching machines and programmed instruction. It is likely, therefore, that the bandwagon effect is a phenomenon that may affect any instructional device introduced.

COMPATIBILITY

If an instructional device requires a radical change to the existing pedagogical method or system, a drastic change of the teacher's rôle and function for example, then the individuals who have to deploy the device may not approve of it. Abandonment of the device is the usual result of such disapproval. The failure of B. F. Skinner's teaching machines, and others of the same type, to be understood and appreciated by teachers, is an example of how incompatibility of an instructional device with existing methods can contribute to its abandonment (Skinner, 1984).

If the instructional device meets with the approval of those who must make use of it, usually the individual classroom teacher, then the device is likely to be placed in limited use to ascertain its strengths and weaknesses (Schlechty, 2000). Poor performance or poor reliability usually result in the device being abandoned. Evidence showing that the device does what it is intended to do and that its performance is reliable may result in its consideration for general use.

COST CONSIDERATIONS

At this juncture, cost becomes an important consideration, given that large numbers of the device are likely to be required for general use. If the unit cost or the total cost is considered too high either by educational personnel, or by interest groups such as parents or taxpayers in general, then the device will likely be abandoned. If the cost is considered reasonable within the funding available, then the device will be placed in general use. There is a confounding factor that may intervene at this point. The apparent success of the instructional device may encourage other concerns to market similar apparatus. In some cases, the motive of these concerns is only to realize the maximum profit through any means, including misrepresenting the product (Stoll, 1995). A possible result of such unscrupulous marketing techniques is the abandonment of the device because individuals will not buy any model, even though the device is effective, for fear of being cheated.

Other cost-related variables include laws and legislation that permit manufacturers and publishers to gouge buyers of their products. Some concerns employ means provided to them by legislation, to extract money from their customers for protracted periods. An example of this phenomenon is a manufacturer of an instructional device that does not permit the device to be purchased outright, but to be leased on a yearly basis. Not only can the rate charged per year be raised, but the contract may also stipulate that any maintenance and repair work required must be carried out by the lessor. A similar situation can exist with software and courseware for instructional hardware that might already be owned by a school or by some other educational body. Manufacturers may stipulate that a copy of the courseware must be obtained for each machine or, if a site license is requested, an extremely high rate is charged. While it may be argued that the first goal of business is to make a profit, an intemperate desire to gain the maximum profit may result in the general abandonment of an instructional device, since the intended buyers may consider more traditional methods of instruction to be less expensive. A possible outcome of this sort of action, is that any pedagogical merits a device might have will no longer be the first consideration. This is especially true with respect to multi-purpose devices such as microcomputers which can be used for purposes other than instruction.

General Deployment and Integration

When an instructional device is not integrated into the existing pedagogical method because of economic necessity, then its ultimate fate depends upon what happens to it in general deployment. If, after a short-term of use, it is found that the need for the device is no longer present or valid, then the device is usually abandoned. If the device continues to be used for a protracted period, then it is likely to be integrated into the pedagogical method. At this point, the instructional device will continue to be used until a technological improvement makes it obsolete, or until the need for the device ceases.

Examples Applied to the Model

Quintain

There were methods of teaching soldiers how to attack with their swords before the quintain was devised. The paucity of Centurions, combined with high mortality rates on the battlefield as the result of poor sword technique, indicated that a more effective teaching method might improve the efficiency as well as the life-span of the individual soldier. An innovation that would solve the problem without great expense and without increased personnel would be ideal. There was a perceived need for an improvement to the existing pedagogical method, therefore. Although technological possibilities were limited at that time, it was possible to construct a quintain using existing technology and materials (See Buck, 1989, for description and illustrations). The quintain was promoted effectively because of its ultimate widespread use, which also indicates that the need for the quintain was considered real generally. The influence of interest groups was likely positive, since use of the quintain proliferated throughout the Roman Empire. The quintain was compatible with existing methods, since it could replace or supplement the palus. No extensive change to the method of soldier training was required, therefore. Cost considerations do not appear to have been a problem, given that quintains were usually of a simple design and were fabricated from common and inexpensive materials. Limited deployment of the quintain within particular Roman armies resulted in comparisons being made of battle effectiveness between units that trained with the quintain and with units that trained without them. The demonstrated effectiveness of the quintain and its reasonable cost contributed to its general deployment. The near universal use of the quintain resulted in its incorporation into the existing pedagogical method, thus creating a new pedagogical method. The use of the quintain as an instructional device ended with the advent of small firearms, which rendered the older weapons and methods for instructing their use obsolete.

BLACKBOARD

The blackboard is a contemporary example of an innovative instructional device that can be analyzed by the development and implementation model. The blackboard, or its equivalent such as the whiteboard or the electronic *smart board*, is now found in almost every classroom at present. An innovative idea, the blackboard seems to have arisen from a perceived need in an existing method of pedagogy (Smith, 1958). Technological possibilities included both writing on walls and the use of small slates by the late 15th century C.E. (Orme, 1973). The principle of presenting information in such a manner, however, could be realized with blackboards only when technological developments permitted the production of large writing surfaces. Other factors in the development and implementation model were contended with successfully, and the merits of the blackboard as a teaching aid were recognized and accepted generally. Similar devices intended for use in special environments, such as overhead projectors, are no longer considered novel innovations or teaching aids for special subjects or applications.

GERBERT'S TEACHING MACHINE

There are many more examples of instructional devices that have failed to gain widespread use. One example is the teaching machine devised by Gerbert d'Aurillac (ca. 947-1003), who became Pope Sylvester II in 999, for showing the configuration and the location of particular constellations (See Buck, 2000a; 2000b). While the device satisfied a need perceived by Gerbert and by some of his contemporaries as well, it was primarily the influence of interest groups that caused his teaching machine to be abandoned. The individuals who condemned

Gerbert's teaching machines were probably ignorant of their pedagogical merits. This consideration probably did not mollify many educators' fears about possible consequences if they continued to use Gerbert's devices, given the power that the interest group possessed.

TOUCH TUTOR TEACHING MACHINE

A more recent example of instructional devices that failed is one of the many teaching machines that were introduced during the 1950s and the 1960s. The majority of these were based on the behavioristic theories of B. F. Skinner, who also introduced teaching machines of his own. Skinner's endeavors actually represent two discrete innovations introduced at once. A new pedagogical theory, Skinnerian behaviorism, plus an innovative way of providing instruction. Both the theory and the machine were subject to the steps of the development and implementation model. Teaching machines based on Skinnerian theory had greater difficulty of attaining success than instructional devices designed to be compatible with existing pedagogical methods. If Skinner's pedagogical method had happened to gain widespread use first, then each teaching machine would be considered on its own, not in combination with a new theory of instruction. Given that most of these teaching machines were introduced before Skinnerian behaviorism had gained general deployment, it is understandable why few varieties of this type of teaching machine were considered useful by teachers. The Touch Tutor teaching machine was one such example.

Devised by Farrall Instruments of Grand Island, Nebraska, in the early 1960s, the Touch Tutor teaching machine was designed for use in most educational settings. Apart from four prototypes, the machine was never placed in production. The president of the company, W. R. Farrall, explained, "the people in the field [educators] could not understand its value" (personal communication, 1988). Farrall's explanation is partially correct. The apparatus may have been designed carefully and been well-constructed, and it may have been appropriate for its intended purpose as a Skinnerian-type teaching machine. Of greater concern to educators was the value of the underlying pedagogical theory, Skinnerian behaviorism. The failure of most educators to accept Skinner's theories of learning and instruction meant that teaching machines embodying these theories would not be used, regardless of other factors impinging upon the machines.

Devices Adapted for Instruction

Some devices were invented for purposes other than education, and have been adapted for use as instructional devices subsequently. The successes and the failures of these devices may also be explained by means of the implementation and development model. One example is the use of motion picture films in schools.

Although using motion pictures for scholastic instruction was promoted vigorously by many individuals and groups, the actual speed of deployment was extremely slow. This phenomenon frustrated many proponents of this teaching aid, to the extent that some tried to engender a bandwagon effect, thus encouraging others to ignore factors such as cost, compatibility and pedagogical efficacy. For example, Aughinbaugh (1930) complained that most schools continued to resist using motion pictures in their classrooms, in spite of the commercial success of that technology,

> *the world has accepted and welcomed this innovation…With this evolution going on, the schools cannot afford to tarry long. Even now they have lost much of their one-time prestige. When the boy or girl learns something more of geography, history, biology, physics, and so on, from the theater around the corner than he does from his school, the latter is bound to suffer in his estimation. (p. 54)*

Some studies from that period found that learning can occur through watching particular motion pictures (for example Peterson and Thurstone, 1932). Instead of citing such evidence, however, Aughinbaugh (1930) chose to encourage a more rapid deployment of the innovation through the bandwagon effect, "Institutions which fail to keep abreast of the times are swiftly passed. Like China, we cannot worship the past without endangering our position in the present" (p. 54). In spite of Aughinbaugh's spirited promotion of motion pictures for instructional use, he did not address other factors that helped retard the deployment of motion pictures in schools; factors that are encountered in the development and implementation model, such as technological limitations and equipment design.

Computers as Instructional Devices

Some of the problems encountered with using computers as instructional devices bear similarity with some of the factors that have affected the use of motion pictures as instructional devices. The construction of particular machines (hardware architecture) as well as the means by which a user can interact with the machine (user interface) are not standard within the industry. Computer programs (software or courseware) must be configured to conform to the operating characteristics and the constraints of each type of machine, therefore. This attribute forces educational institutions either to select one particular type of machine, or to purchase a variety of machines so that most appropriate software for each can be used. Manufacturer support for particular models of computer can be remarkably short-lived. A school equipped with the latest model in a given year, is likely to discover that it is obsolete within three years. While obsolete machines can continue to be used, they are usually unable to run the most up-to-date software without hardware upgrades, if the machines can be upgraded at all. Older machines, as well, usually cannot take advantage of improvements to the hardware architecture or to the user interface.

Such factors come to bear even when educators themselves design a computer-controlled instructional system. While IBM's 1500 mainframe Computer-Assisted Instruction system was used successfully for instructional purposes by many institutions beginning in the late 1960s, financial and technological considerations resulted in the system disappearing by 1980 (Buck & Hunka, 1995). Similarly, the Canadian-designed ICON microcomputer failed to gain widespread use because of hardware limitations and the inability of the equipment to use software and courseware designed for other microcomputers. Again, factors that now appear within the development and implementation model were not considered by the designers of the ICON, nor by the governmental authorities who perceived the ICON to be the standard for computers in schools.

Appropriate software that is well designed and tested, and which will function in a classroom the way it is intended to, remains in short supply. Much software and courseware relies heavily on the input of the teacher for information. An assumption made is that the individual teacher has both the ability and the inclination to provide the necessary input. Many teachers do not possess this expertise and many expect computers and software to provide comprehensive instruction to students once the hardware is set up and the courseware installed (the so-called *plug-and-play* expectation).

The cost of hardware, software and/or courseware is another major factor determining use. While the cost of an individual computer continues to drop, it remains a great expense for schools to outfit an entire classroom with sufficient computers for each pupil. A one-time expenditure will not suffice, since machines require maintenance, repair, upgrading and eventual replacement (Niederhauser, Bigley, Hale, & Harper, 1999). The cost of software and courseware is significant, even with the provision of site licenses.

NECESSITY FOR INSTRUCTIONAL DEVICES

Most instructional devices fail to become part of a prevalent pedagogical system or method, yet the perceived need for instructional devices appears to be perennial. Why should any new educational device either be developed or considered for use, in view of the dismal success rate of most devices? There have been particular examples, most notably the blackboard and particular flight simulators, which have resulted in notable improvements in the effectiveness of teaching. Where they have succeeded, instructional devices have altered the fundamental pedagogical system, usually to its improvement. It is important to note that the introduction and the use of instructional devices has gradually been increasing since the 17th century C.E. Concurrent with the success of particular instructional devices was the general acceptance of the theory of learning contending that abstract concepts can be learned more effectively if they are related to some concrete representation (Bruner, 1966; 1985). While it has been argued that this idea is not new, many educators, either explicitly or implicitly, accept this theory of learning.

EVALUATION OF THE MODEL AND ITS USES

EVALUATION

From an initial consideration of the development and implementation model, it might seem that it is practically impossible for an instructional device to reach the stage where it becomes an integral part of a pedagogical method. In consequence, one might be inclined to state that this model is biased against the success of instructional devices, considering that there have been a number of them that have become successful. The findings of other educators, however, support the contention that few instructional devices as well as innovations in general, ever gain widespread use. Havelock and Huberman (1977) contend that the main reason for the failure of innovations is that their implementation usually entails changing an existing system, and since most systems tend to resist change, it follows that the innovation will fail to be adopted unless it can be incorporated into the system. Moreover, McLaughlin (1978) as well as Fullan and Stiegelbauer (1991) claim that the reason why most educational innovations fail is because they do not follow any particular model of implementation. Without following a recognizable model of implementation, therefore, it is possible that factors significant to the success of an innovation, such as support from the intended users, can be overlooked with failure of the innovation as a result (Schlechty, 2000). As Elmore (1978) observed,

> *What grates most on the sensibilities of teachers, social workers, employment counselors, and the like is the tacit assumption in most policy directives that they are incapable of making independent judgments and decisions – that their behavior must be programmed by someone else. It is difficult for persons who see themselves as competent, self-sufficient adults to be highly committed to politics that place them in the role of passive executor of someone else's will. (p. 207)*

Kao and Wedman (1995) contend that most innovations in education fail because the complex interaction between organization, people and the innovation itself, is either not considered, or considered only partially. Wirt (1978) noted this problem earlier, and advocates a strategy of *mutual adaptation*, where the needs both of the developer and the user of the innovation are considered and contended with.

USES OF THE MODEL

While examples have been provided to show how the development and implementation model can be used as a diagnostic tool to analyze both successful and unsuccessful instructional devices, the model can also be used for other purposes. Knowledge of the model may help innovators and educators to be aware of some of the major factors that affect both the development and subsequent use of instructional devices. Recognizing and considering these factors may result in developers, innovators, manufacturers and users of instructional devices being able to work more closely together to identify the needs for a particular device, and to ascertain whether or not the device is viable for education in general or only for specific subjects or skills. Similarly, if educators are also aware of the factors in the development and implementation model, then it is possible to minimize the likelihood of such educators becoming victims of the bandwagon effect.

It may appear that the course of most instructional devices follows a cycle, beginning with invention/adaptation, proceeding to implementation and ending with abandonment. While this cycle is borne out when considering older devices, the cycle or pattern is also valid for more recent instructional devices. While some educators and scholars continue to maintain that computers used as instructional devices will change the fundamental methods of education, the failure of this technology to create such change in excess of 25 years, has resulted in some scholars and educators concluding that this goal will never be attained by computers (Cartwright, 1991). Nevertheless, the use of computers in education will likely continue as tools, rather than as instructional devices.

It is more appropriate to consider the cyclical pattern associated with the deployment of instructional devices as an epicycle, especially when considering the context of education as a whole. It appears that in spite of what has happened with instructional devices introduced in the past, many educators, politicians and other educational stakeholders do not learn from what has gone before them, with the result that subsequent instructional devices that arise follow the same epicyclic pattern. This view is shared by Cartwright (1991) who states that in spite of the failure to achieve widespread use of computers as instructional devices, many educators seem anxious to jump on another bandwagon supporting some other new *revolutionary* technology, "Just around the bend on this new electronic highway lies the incredible world of artificial intelligence, virtual reality, and cyberspace. Does anyone feel another revolution coming on?" (p. 155). While enthusiasm for these technologies builds in some quarters in education, it is prudent to recall the cost and difficulty already experienced by military organizations attempting to use elements of virtual reality. Levin (1989) described the difficulties in simulating a dynamic model of a typical protein surrounded by water molecules, "About one hour of Cray XMP computer time is required to simulate 100 picoseconds of behavior" (p. 1456). The cost implications of the previous quote should be compared with a letter written by a teacher in Los Angeles, California. Responding to an article suggesting that educators were slow to take advantage of current technology, since most schools continue to use obsolete microcomputers rather than faster newer models, the teacher wrote,

> *Perhaps he's unaware of how educators struggle to transform outmoded materials into productive experiences for children...The fault...lies not with the educators who always struggle to make do with less but with the legislators who fail to fund education and the public that fails to demand quality instruction. (Penso, 1992, p. 16)*

Forester and Morrison (1990) reiterate a concern discovered with many instructional devices used in the past, they cannot be relied upon as though they do not fail or have limitations. Moreover, the authors state, "this situation is only exacerbated by users [and/or educators] who place blind faith in their technology, developers who abbreviate the design and engineering process, and consultants who are unrealistic in representing the state and accuracy of the knowledge they possess" (p. 86).

Until educators and legislators begin to consider what has occurred in the past and learn to build on both prior successes and mistakes, instructional devices will likely continue to be deployed and abandoned in a cyclical manner. The result will be that constructive progress in education will remain a slow and haphazard process.

REFERENCES

Alessi, S.M. & Trollip, S.R. (2001). *Multimedia for Learning: Methods and Development* (3rd ed.). Toronto, ON: Allyn and Bacon.

Aughinbaugh, B.A. (1930). "The Motion Picture and the School." *School Board Journal*, 81(3) 54, 100.

Bennett, H.E. (1925). *School Efficiency: A Manual of Modern School Management*. Boston, MA: Ginn and Company.

Bishop, G. (1986). *Innovation in Education*. London: Macmillan Publishers.

Bork, A. (1981). *Learning with Computers*. CA: Digital Press.

Bruner, J.S. (1966). *Towards a Theory of Instruction*. Cambridge, MA: Harvard University Press.

Bruner, J.S. (1985). "Models of the Learner." *Educational Researcher, 14*(6) 5-8.

Buck, G.H. (1989). "Teaching Machines and Teaching Aids in the Ancient World." *The McGill Journal of Education, 24*(1) 31-54.

Buck, G.H. (2000a). *The Y1K Situation: Gerbert's Instructional Devices, Their Influence, and Possible Parallels to the Present.* ERIC Document Service: ED443403.

Buck, G.H. (2000b). "Technology Integration in the Mediæval Period: Factors Relevant to the Present." *Journal of Curriculum Theorizing, 16*(4) 79-90.

Buck, G.H. & Hunka, S.M. (1995). "The Development of the IBM 1500 Computer-Assisted Instructional System." *IEEE Annals of the History of Computing, 17*, 19-31.

Chalmers, R. (1990, January 24). "Modest Beginnings Shared by Successful Women." *The Edmonton Journal*, p. D14.

Cartwright, G.F. (1991). "A Decade Up, a Decade Down: Computers in the Faculty of Education." *McGill Journal of Education, 26* (2-Supplement), 149-55.

Elmore, R.F. (1978). "Organizational Models of Social Program Implementation." In D. Mann (Ed.), *Making Change Happen?* New York, NY: Teachers College Press.

Forester, T. & Morrison, P. (1990). *Computer Ethics: Cautionary Tales and Ethical Dilemmas in Computing.* Cambridge, MA: The MIT Press.

Fullan, M.G. & Stiegelbauer, S. (1991). *The New Meaning of Educational Change.* New York, NY: Teachers College Press.

Gaines, B.R. & Shaw, M.L. (1986). "From Time-sharing to the Sixth Generation: The Development of Human-computer Interaction. Part 1." *International Journal of Man-Machine Studies, 24*, 1-27.

Glaser, R. (1960). "Christmas Past, Present and Future: A Review and Preview." In A.A. Lumsdaine & R. Glaser (Eds.), *Teaching Machines and Programmed Learning: A Source Book.* Washington, DC: National Education Association of the United States.

Glaser, R. (1965). "Toward a Behavioral Science Base for Instructional Design." In R. Glaser (Ed.), *Teaching Machines and Programmed Learning, II: Data and Directions.* Washington, DC: National Education Association of the United States.

Gold, B.A. (1999). "Punctuated Legitimacy: A Theory of Educational Change." *Teachers College Record, 101*(2) 192-219.

Havelock, R.G. & Huberman, A.M. (1977). *Solving Educational Problems: The Theory and Reality of Innovation in Developing Countries.* Paris: United Nations Educational, Scientific and Cultural Organization (UNESCO).

Kao, H-F. & Wedman, J. (1995). "Lessons Relearned: Another Faulty Implementation of an Educational Innovation." *International Journal of Instructional Media, 22*(3) 201-16.

Levin, E. (1989). "Grand Challenges to Computational Science." *Communications of the ACM, 32,* 1456-59.

Loucks, S.F. & Zacchei, D.A. (1983). "Applying Our Findings to Today's Innovations." *Educational Leadership, 41*(3) 28-31.

McLaughlin, M.W. (1978). "Implementation as Mutual Adaptation: Change in the Classroom Organization." In D. Mann (Ed.), *Making Change Happen?* New York, NY: Teachers College Press.

Niederhauser, V.P., Bigley, M.B., Hale, J. & Harper, D. (1999). "Cybercases: An Innovation in Internet Education." *Journal of Nursing Education, 38*(9) 415-22.

Orme, N. (1973). *English Schools in the Middle Ages.* London: Methuen & Co. Ltd.

Penso, R.A. (1992, July). "Dvorak's Class Act." *MacUser, 8*(7) 16.

Peterson, R.C. & Thurstone, L.L. (1932). "The Effects of a Motion Picture Film on Children's Attitudes Toward Germans." *The Journal of Educational Psychology, 23*(4) 241-46.

Postman, N. (1992). *Technopoly: The Surrender of Culture to Technology.* New York, NY: Alfred A. Knopf.

Postman, N. (2000). *Building a Bridge to the Eighteenth Century: How the Past Can Improve Our Future.* New York, NY: Alfred A. Knopf.

Saettler, P. (1968). *A History of Instructional Technology.* New York, NY: McGraw-Hill Book Company.

Saettler, P. (1990). *The Evolution of American Educational Technology.* Englewood, CO: Libraries Unlimited.

Schlebecker, J.T. (1977). "Farmers and Bureaucrats: Reflections on Technological Innovation in Agriculture." *Agricultural History, 51I,* 641-55.

Schlechty, P.C. (2000). *Shaking Up the Schoolhouse: How to Support and Sustain Educational Innovation.* San Francisco, CA: Jossey-Bass Publishers.

Skinner, B.F. (1983). *A Matter of Consequences: Part Three of an*

Autobiography. New York, NY: Alfred A. Knopf.

Skinner, B.F. (1984). "The Shame of American Education." *American Psychologist, 39*, 947-54.

Smith, D.E. (1958). *History of Mathematics: Volume II, Special Topics of Elementary Mathematics*. New York, NY: Dover Publications, Inc.

Stoll, C. (1995). *Silicon Snake Oil: Second Thoughts on the Information Highway*. New York, NY: Doubleday.

Wirt, J.G. (1978). "Implementing Diagnostic/Prescriptive Reading Innovations." In D. Mann (Ed.) *Making Change Happen?* New York, NY: Teachers College Press.

CHAPTER 4
THE HAND-MADE'S TAIL

A Novel Approach to Educational Technology

Michele Jacobsen and Ricki Goldman

Introducing the Plot

The intention of this chapter is to challenge the misuse of power and authority when digital technologies are introduced into educational institutions. Using Margaret Atwood's (1985) novel, *The Handmaid's Tale,* as what Goldman-Segall (1998) calls a *subject-to-think-with,* we reflect upon how this Canadian novel can teach us how not to proceed when using new media technologies. Our interpretation of Atwood's novel acts as a critique of contemporary society's eagerness to become part of the technological revolution and yet its unwillingness to assume the ethical responsibilities that accompany this participation. Atwood presents a disturbing account of a future where technology is used to rob individuals and groups of their freedom and dignity. What her tale also reveals is that in oppressive societies, there is resistance to authoritarianism and the interminable search for human kindness.

In our account, we select key scenes and character roles from the novel to explore shifting power relations, not only in the future world of Atwood's Gilead, but in the current world of educational institutions. By comparing the dangers facing learners and mentors with the dangers facing the handmaids in Atwood's depiction of life in Gilead, we address the misuse of educational technology which could rob learners of their rights to an equitable and empowering public education.

The questions we pose are: What are the *multi-visions* of society Canadians want to have and how, given these visions, do we choose what technologies to develop and use to meet those visions? We also ask ourselves: Whose perspectives shape this emerging technologically advanced society? For example, how do stakeholders with diverse interests affect the *product*-ion of knowledge in education? And, how do teachers, parents and learners participate as partners in the development of new learning systems? Most importantly, we ask how equity and social justice can be promoted in the new *knowledge economy* – a term we use gingerly because of its connection to consumption and profit – to ensure the culturally-sound and healthy use of technology?

BEHIND THE SCENES – EXAMINING THE HIDDEN WORKINGS

Selected scenes from the novel provide a staging ground for our analysis of the hidden workings and power plays in educational cultures that are responses to the presence of dominant (i.e., not neutral) information and communications technologies. The roles of the central characters in the novel are explored through the lens of shifting power relations when new technologies are introduced into our learning communities.

In Atwood's Gilead, children are a scarce and highly desired commodity. Those who are able to produce this commodity are sorted from those who cannot. In a remembered incident, a woman goes to a bank and her card disappears in the bank machine. She can no longer access her accounts. We learn that Atwood's main character, Offred, is rendered dependent on and subject to a new societal order for survival. In a botched run for the border, in an attempt to escape the horrific constraints of the new society, Offred's child is stolen from her, and she wakes up from this nightmare as a fertility handmaid, yet another nightmare. A barcode wristband is used to track and control the handmaid's limited movements in society. Fertile women (i.e., only 1 in 100) can become handmaids to the powerful but infertile wives of powerful men. Among the possibilities for an infertile woman are becoming a Martha (i.e., a domestic servant), an Aunt (i.e., the evangelical trainers of handmaids), or an Unwoman (i.e., who is shipped off to slave in the radioactive and toxic colonies).

SCENE ONE – AN INSEMINATION CEREMONY

The wives of the powerful men in the society are infertile. The Reproduction Ceremony, sanctioned by the new social order, sees the handmaid in red veil lying between the legs of the wife in blue veil, being impersonally inseminated by the husband. The handmaid's control over her destiny, her freedom to choose, and her identity are all stripped away. She no longer has the right to say no; she becomes a reproductive vessel, a womb-prosthesis of the infertile wife. She is subject to the will of others.

This scene, selected from the many other disturbing scenes in Atwood's Gilead, causes a particular discomfort. The uneasiness comes from our juxtaposition of the scene with the lives of many educators who feel they are only expected to be vessels carrying required content, ready not to become impregnated, but to impregnate the minds of learners. When grappling with the role that digital technologies will ultimately play in education, teachers can be "veiled" and subject to the will of others in many ways. Teachers are subject to the prevailing power structures, constrained economies and cultural expectations in an educational status quo that often limits how technologies are deployed in schools. The educational formula of a provincially mandated and standardized curriculum, that teachers are expected to divide up and deliver to same grade students, is so ingrained in a collective consciousness that "doing computers" has become normalized in many ways. For too many teachers, their access to a lone computer lab is divided up and metered out in hourly time slots, all in the name of fairness, and educators dutifully march their students down the school halls for keyboarding, word processing and information processing once a week on Tuesday.

Instead of allowing for ubiquitous access to digital technologies throughout the school whenever learners need them, decision-makers often arrange computers in laboratories much like individual desks in classrooms. The computer lab scenario is troubling because of the underlying pedagogical assumptions about content-delivery and control that influence this deployment of technology – a lab set up facilitates a teacher-led class of students doing individual activities at the same time.

One explanation for current lab designs can be found in the early days of computers in schools – computers were expensive, and often unreliable, specialized machines that were usually controlled by the one or two teachers who taught about programming and hardware. Most educators were comfortable leaving computers on the margins – perhaps few imagined that digital technologies would ever have widespread application across the curriculum. Today, even though computers have dropped in price, are easier to network, have multipurpose applications and software packages running on them, the computer lab scenario has survived as an artifact of how digital technology gets marginalized and deployment options get entrenched in education.

Teachers can feel helpless in reaction to the seemingly never-ending supply of institutional barriers to implementing technology. Along with restrictive computer lab deployment scenarios, limited access and scheduling barriers, teachers often run up against problems that result from systematic economic constraints. Although technology acquisitions are still uneven across school districts, many schools have been able to acquire workstations, software and networks for teaching and learning. However, schools often rely on technology-savvy teachers to maintain and support the technology. In corporate environments, the support and maintenance of the technological infrastructure by qualified information systems personnel is taken for granted as a cost of doing business. An accountant is not expected to install, maintain and upgrade the workstation and network needed to do accounting tasks. In schools, however, technology-literate teachers often spend hours installing, upgrading, maintaining and supporting the technology, instead of having release time to support the integration efforts of their colleagues. Unlike their earlier-adopting, tech-savvy colleagues, many teachers are unsure how they might use digital technologies for learning, and school districts have invested unevenly in professional development opportunities to build the necessary capacity for integrating technology among staff. What kind of learning environments enable teachers to confront these uncertainties, and begin to develop digital tools and methods to support learning? Certainly, the new corporate learning monopoly should not be solely responsible for designing and packaging curricular materials according to neatly defined provincial or state standards. Instead, open-ended tools that afford learners opportunities to search databases, design and build artifacts, and communicate openly with each other need to be the essential ingredient in a healthy learning and teaching environment.

Learners are also at risk in the new high tech world. Without mindful consideration of potential misuse, learners could have their privacy and autonomy stripped away in their technology-rich learning environments. What roles should students play in deciding how technologies are used for communicating ideas and representing their thoughts? We know all too well that schools are not always equitable places despite the commitment of educators to treat all students fairly. It is difficult and perhaps impossible to enter into a leadership (i.e., authority) role with students and ensure equity and social justice. Yet, without adults taking leadership, many students might never reflect upon the importance of equity and equality. We ask how educational leaders can partner with learners in ways that evoke personal expression, reflection and construction? And we ask how to examine inequity in education as a philosophical tool for addressing larger political, moral and social questions.

For example, the age-old philosophical debate concerning the nature of humankind, good vs. evil, is being debated in every corner of the world after the tragic events of September 11th, 2001. The destruction of the World Trade Center has become an ephemeral pillar around which we return to earlier theoretical tenets of dualistic thinking. On the one hand, we have witnessed the courage of the commons to act in good faith and with good will to care for others; on the other hand, we are now and maybe forever subject to the malevolence of those who would use terror to gain control. Atwood's tale is more relevant than we think, perhaps not from an internal misuse of power, but from an external and camouflaged entity. That said, we know that, in spite of these horrific events, the world is not demarcated into good and evil, but rather is a complex web of entities – a web of entangled views. In the institutionalized world of education, commerce, and government, complex systems are always at work. One worldview cannot represent or create social justice; instead, social justice is always partial, dynamic, in a state of flux, and can seem frightening because one cannot predict when a flow of events has begun or when it is over. As Goldman- Segall (1998) has stated, for better or worse, people see the world from their various *points of viewing* the world; and within these worlds, learners need to be both in charge of their personal domains while maintaining membership in ever-changing communities of inquiry. And together, learners and teachers need to have the courage to explore issues as complex as equity, humanity, and morality.

SCENE TWO – WHAT'S IN A NAME?

Sacred to those in authority in Gilead is the indoctrination of handmaids in the Red Centres; fertile women were rounded up, against their will, and taught their new role and duty to advance the new society. The handmaids' enculturation begins immediately after their incarceration; their movements are controlled, they are clothed in identical uniforms that proclaim their status, and they are told they are the "lucky ones" because they are fertile. The Aunts teach them how to respond and teach them chants. The handmaids' agency is subjugated to the needs and goals of the ruling class, the new regime. Identity is stripped along with individual agency. We relearn/realize in this scene the importance of "naming" to identity. Disenfranchized because of their fertility, the handmaid's whisper their names to each other in the dark, a covert attempt to hold on to their identity and regain agency. To not only be Off-red but to have a color of her own.

Our reading of the handmaids' enculturation raises uncomfortable images of identity stripping, deprofessionalization and the plug and play approach to teachers, students and curriculum in schools. The handmaids all wear red, the wives wear blue and the marthas wear green. Colors identify role and power, thus reducing the importance of identity. It doesn't matter who you are, and what your unique values, beliefs and relationships are. In education, teachers, students and course subjects are often treated as "plug and play" components. The interdisciplinary connections and relations between subjects are often lost as students get their daily dose of Art, Mathematics, Language Arts and Science as measured out by required seat hours and credits. Into this culture of discretionary units and topics and subjects, digital technologies are introduced that cross boundaries and challenge assumptions about the inter-relatedness of disciplines of study, and the limits of what teachers might teach and students can learn. No longer the exclusive domain of the educational technology folks, digital technologies open up new possibilities for multidisciplinary connections and explorations for students and teachers. In what ways do our current educational systems honor the border crossing and interdisciplinary inquiry opportunities made possible by digital technologies?

Our interpretation of the handmaids "whispering names to each other in the dark" is that even in the most oppressive societies, there is resistance to external control, and an oppositional quest for identity and agency within codes of conduct. Telecommunications technology provides the means by which teachers can connect to each other, and share ideas and resources no matter where they live, or what school they teach in. Later in this chapter we analyze evolving relations of power and control with regard to new possibilities afforded to teachers and students via networks and connections via online environments.

Roles in Atwood's Gilead

Our interpretation of the handmaid's role is to cast her as a USER. Within predefined limits, the USER can access the system designed by others. The USER's movements are monitored and prescribed, and she relies on others who control and design the system.

Role 1 – Handmaid/User

A woman stands at the (Data) Bank ready to receive her Currency dose to move without worry throughout the system, but she is forbidden entry. She cannot contain her need for her fix; yet she has no independent passage in the pipeline. She is forced to become a handmaid to those with access to the DB. As a handmaid, she has her identity and then her dignity confiscated. She is objectified as the wife's womb-prosthesis.

Role 2 – Husband/Commander/CEO

A man is the Commander or CEO of Data Bank Inc., a gatekeeper of the system. The CEO, in his decisions about design specs, enables some citizens better access than others. His concern is for bottom-line decisions ensuring that those who build the Data Bank keep their power, authority and dominion over others.

He too is subject to societal expectations, rules and protocol. However, he is also able to break the rules of conduct and employ others in his duplicity. He wants to get to know the handmaid, to simulate a relationship like in previous times, but still meets her under the cover of night. He complains, plaintively, that he finds the ceremony "impersonal." He plays a word game, Scrabble, both figuratively and literally with the handmaid. He knows she is smart; it serves to amuse him. He is caught in the web as are his wife and the handmaid. The difference is that the web is his design.

Role 3 – Wife/Broker

She trades what she can, never quite subverting the Bank but carv-

ing out a role for herself in a difficult trading market. Her creative juices have dried up; beauty stocks have fallen. She is a defeated woman who used to be a celebrity. Infertility is resolved by controlling the novice USERS, the handmaids, as tools for maintaining compromising positions. Yet, she is a witness, albeit without conscience, of the times yet says nothing. Worse, she is complicit. A pimp supplying the CEO with USERS. She forfeits her creativity in the process. Ironically, her partner, the CEO, needs the USER/Handmaid to understand himself. The handmaid becomes a partner, albeit a coerced one.

Each role has a duty to perform in service of the new society. Duty is defined as obligatory tasks, conduct, service or functions that arise from one's position (as in life or in a group), as well as the work done by a machine under given conditions. An interpretation of duty in the context of three key roles, the handmaid/USER, the husband/CEO and the wife/BROKER, can be understood as the birthing of a new Gileadean order – fertility of a few, and atonement for mistakes. "God is punishing us with barrenness and infertility." The husband, wife and handmaid, willingly or not, can be viewed as simply doing their duty for God and country, fulfilling their obligatory tasks given their position in life. The troublesome kink in the Ceremonial tableau is that the handmaids, like teachers and children in our schools, are often viewed mechanistically given their fertile, but largely powerless, position in the power structure.

The "time before" in Atwood's novel is conceptualized differently depending on whether the forum is public or private. The time before is conceptualized as a period of depravity and sin. History is rewritten; fertile women are considered guilty, and must atone for and carry the burden of past sins that led to societies' downfall (i.e., promiscuity, prostitution, abortion and birth control). In this scenario, handmaids are the ones chosen to restore humanity to its previous state of grace. The time before is also reconceptualized, by those in power who can and do break the rules, as a period of pleasure and freedom. For example, the husband/commander breaks the rules of contact to take the handmaid on a date to Jezebel's, a night club where CEO patrons listen to music from the time before, and participate in historical rituals (i.e., flirting, drinking and smoking). The handmaid's role in the ritual is to uphold the illusion of breaking free within the constraints of the commander's desire for play.

The time before in education, the mythical Golden Age in which homogeneous and respectful children were taught the three R's, teachers spared not the strap to spoil the child and parents knew their place, is often held up as an example of our utopian past. Why corporal punishment is held up as part of a Golden Age is to be considered carefully. The present state of affairs in education is often presented in contrast to this time before, when there were fewer problems, fewer individual differences and less diversity, hierarchies of power, and a black and white definition of truth. Instead of embracing the emancipatory possibilities of widespread, un-regulated access to people and resources on the World Wide Web, this freedom is constrained, and even feared, in schools. Filters and firewalls are constraints that are erected to keep teachers and students in, and dangerous others and ideas out.

When the layers are peeled away, we have to ask, was it really that much simpler in the good old days? Were children any less different from each other? Was brute force necessary in the learning equation? And, did all teachers adhere to a common notion of truth? We authors think not. Education has never been the smooth road that adults, looking back to the past, think it was. The recreation in our minds of what we experienced in schools as children has to be understood as a romantic invention to protect ourselves from what we know to be ill-conceived and hostile to the imagination of childhood.

In our reading of Atwood's tale, the Commander and his Wife represent and protect the status quo, which is regarded as a much better version of society than before. Today's firewalls and filters are instantiations of current attempts to maintain the illusion of freedom but within a strictly defined play area. Contrasting the time before in education with current realities, and the new social order being sought by the characters in Atwood's novel, it would appear that the Gileadeans have achieved a successful return to the good old days of conformity, duty, homogeneity and black and white notions of truth. However, there are also indications throughout the novel that societies' control is an illusion, because in the end, the handmaid finally breaks free. Today's teachers and students also invent ways to circumvent external restrictions on Internet access, and cross boundaries with their inquiries.

Information technology experts who are involved in designing and defining what technologies will be available in schools are often most concerned with what works best with regards to cabling, hardware, network servers and software. To ease their maintenance and support workload, and often with the best intentions with regard to cost-reduction, technology experts seek standardized solutions that can be implemented efficiently across all schools. Information technology curriculum leaders and techno-savvy teachers, on the other hand, are chiefly concerned with designing technological solutions that work best for teaching and learning. Often resisting the techno-centric and problem-reduction agendas of technology experts, these educators seek network and workstation designs that are responsive to the educational goals, local context and expectations of school staff, instead of standardizing on a 'one-size- fits-all' installation. How do technicians and teachers, and even students, participate as partners in the development of technology systems in schools, and whose perspectives [should] count the most in shaping opportunities for learning?

In the "digital commons" (Goldman-Segall, 1998, p. 268), learning environments with online communications and technological devices will not be a better place unless we ensure, from the start, that no one group monopolizes the landscape with their version of 'utopian' software, hardware, or wireless gadgets to be seamlessly woven into the fabric of our consciousness, the public body politic and even into our private bodies. Technological solutions and developments need to arise from the concerted efforts of educators, learners and technology experts who seek designs that provide maximum access and opportunity for students and teachers.

HAND-MADES AND TAILS: REDUCING THE FEAR

Hand-Mades, in this chapter, refer not only to the learners and teachers who make artifacts, but to the digital technologies designed and created by humans. By changing the word from Tale (an account, a story, an imaginative narrative of an event, an intentionally untrue report) to Tail, we question the deterministic stance toward technology and ask whether certain outcomes are inevitable. Are the ways in which we currently use technology for learning determined in advance by the technologies and solutions designed to date? Are the inherent functionalities of technology fixed, or can new uses and purposes be invented?

We critique a deterministic view of educational technology with the postmodern perspective that educators and learners/users themselves create digital environments and *choose* to have more control over how these hand-mades are used for teaching and learning. Teachers and students can choose to shape their futures rather than be subject to them. Instead of the USER/CEO/BROKER model of education that seems endemic to the current corporate knowledge economy, we propose an approach that is open to diverse viewpoints and offers an equitable opportunity for learners and teachers as partners to question their roles. By presenting this alternate interpretation in our novel approach, we aim to ensure that Atwood's vision of the future does not become a prediction: Hand-Made and not Handmaid.

Technology as a human creation is not a neutral or benign force in education. Technologies, as in film or music, reflect their creators. Yet, when we ask about the benefits of using these technologies, we tend to treat them as if they are neutral environments without embedded viewpoints. Thus, when we conduct research on technologies, we fail to consider how technologies are infused with assumptions. Many quantitative researchers have dismissed claims made about the benefits of using technology for learning and the carefully described examples of what works for whom and under what circumstances, with claims that there are *no significant generalizable effects* as measured by standardized exams. Two things are at issue here: the impact of standardized assessments on teaching practices and beliefs, and the belief that there are *no significant effects* of computers on learning.

An explanation for the *no significant effect phenomena* can be found in an analysis of choices about how to use technology with children. Studies that yield no significant effects are often based on comparisons between children using computer-assisted instruction (CAI) versus children taught by a teacher. An integrated approach to curriculum and technology demands and requires that currently held assumptions about curriculum coverage get questioned, and new approaches to investigating enduring questions get explored. Conversely, an add-on approach to curriculum and technology renders digital tools as "one more damn thing to cover." In the add-on approach, technologies are used to do the same things that have always been done (i.e., Math facts, good copy, what did I do on my summer vacation assignments) but at greater speed and convenience. Instead of using flashcards, children press the arrow keys to shoot Math facts out of the sky.

For more than two decades, Gavriel Salomon has discussed the problem of "technology as add-on," and curriculum redesign as "fiddling around the edges" as fearful responses to the threat of digital technologies (Salomon, 1994; Salomon & Almog, 1998). Salomon (2000) describes the use of technology for show in the classroom – the act of "doing computers" in order to have something to mark off on the report card. Far from the transformative effect that appropriate uses of technology in service of learning can have for learners, Salomon's (2000) recent criticism of using technology as an add-on to current ways of teaching and learning, and attempting to preserve the present ways rather than embrace the possibilities offered by digital media, is another instantiation of the futility of rearranging the deck chairs on the Titanic. Our Hand-made Tail is invoked by Salomon (2000) in the following quotation:

> *A most powerful and innovative technology is taken and is domesticated such that it does more or less what its predecessors have done, only it does it a bit faster and a bit nicer. Consequently, nothing really happens, which comes to prove what skeptics have argued all along and what misguided research tends to show: Technology makes no difference in learning. But of course it cannot make a difference since it has been domesticated to be totally subservient to the ongoing practices. Emasculated tools cannot do any harm, but they do not do any good either* (Italics added, p. 16).

Salomon describes the subjugation of the hand-mades, the digital technologies, to the inertia of prevailing views and customs in education. Of course, when an innovative and significant tool is used to prop up conventional approaches, rather than being used for its intended purpose, or even better, for invented purposes that we haven't even thought of yet (but children and teachers often do), then of course it will be rendered sterile, impotent and ineffective.

Core Curriculum: Taking Note

High school teachers in the "core" topics (i.e., English, Math, Science and Social Studies), and indeed university professors, have been heard to claim that there is simply no time to spend on technology integration, digital media and new literacies. Technology is seen as a frill, games, fun stuff, a reward, not hard core learning, because they have to "*cover* the curriculum" for the provincial or end of term exams. It is especially hard to shake the notion of covering the curriculum from teachers who teach high school courses, a time when students are often cramming to pass provincial examinations. In our research and teaching experience, we have independently witnessed digital technologies being used to uncover the curriculum, expose courses of study to scrutiny and ask questions about the fundamental values and beliefs represented by a discipline.

At the same time, meaningful learning goals can be underserved in emerging learning technology environments when technology becomes the course of study. In the new knowledge economy, students are often praised because they can solve technological problems for the class and teacher. Learning is reduced to knowing how to solve a technological problem rather than understanding and producing an original work. When the goal is to learn about spreadsheets instead of manipulating and modeling variables, technology is being used as an add-on. We argue that the goal includes, but should not be limited to, becoming facile with the technology. However, we believe the focus needs to be on learning how to work together to develop knowledge representations within a community of inquiry, and investigating how technology helps us to achieve that end, rather than learning how to run computer applications just in case one might need them for something.

How does technology enable us to share in each other's abilities and achievements? In our research with children in technology-rich learning environments, learners who keep their dignity are not only learning computer skills, they are learning how to participate in a learning and thinking culture, one that encourages them to make things with their hands and heads. As Seymour Papert would say, not only *hands-on* but *heads-in*. In short, learners of all ages need to know how to become their own Hand-mades, maybe even Head-mades, but certainly not Handmaids within what could become an overwhelmingly technocratic society. Imagine the expert game-boy player becoming a fighter pilot. With guidance by a knowledgeable teacher-mentor, this person understands the fundamental difference between a successful click of the wrist that kills his enemy in a simulation versus killing people in real life. This is clearly an example of the ethical use of technology in an environment with knowledgeable guides.

When current high school and university classroom practices are examined, the time spent on teaching and learning is often spent very quietly – rows of students listening to the instructor and copying teacher-prepared notes from an overhead projector. Monday, Tuesday, Wednesday and Thursday, high school and university students take notes from an overhead to prepare for a unit or midterm exam on Friday. Conversely, the learning environment guided by a teacher who is interested in exploring ideas using the full range of technologies available to her is often noisy, active and emergent. Levels of scholarship and notions of quality are predetermined and specific outcomes are negotiated. The ideas, knowledge and questions that students bring are a necessary component of meaningful inquiry and collaborative problem solving. The level of interactive group engagement is often less a matter of the technology being used and more a consequence of the individual classroom teacher's comfort level and the degree to which she requires the class to be silently focused on a given activity – whether that activity is aimed at the group or the individual.

However, the insidious, anti-intellectual notion that teaching practices need not be questioned exists in the current educational culture. *We've always done it this way; it must be right, good for all young people!* Ironically, while taking notes (rather than taking note of what is being studied) from the chalkboard, and now the colorful overhead projector, students sit in darkness with the not-so-hidden curriculum projected on a screen. The real message of schools remains unchallenged. *I, the teacher, tell you what to learn; you, the student, pretend to learn by silently partaking in the ingesting of words, numbers and pictures.* This ritualized activity historically inherited from the blackboard and chalk days has become an unquestioned practice in the high tech school. And once again, we see the handmaids are coerced to accept semen from an infertile system that has already lost its hopes to recreate itself by natural means. The best the ruling system can do is to reproduce itself, creating clones or spending a great deal of time and effort discussing cloning.

Yet, a large number of teachers (and teacher educators) still believe (and tell generations of students) that they learn best by recreating what is already there. They try to convince young adults who are biologically already able to conceive and raise their own children, that this form of interacting with the curriculum – transferring what is on the transparency to their own notebooks, word for word – is essential to learning. This unquestioned and too often buried assumption, which is based on a theory of expert instructing instead of on student construction and an established and static knowledge base, is a major obstacle to effective technology use in our schools. And our teacher education programs bear the brunt of the responsibility for this state of affairs. Instead of enabling education students to break out of the Instructionist box within which they were taught, many teacher education faculties reproduce expert teachers, like themselves, and forget to encourage these new teacher educators to break through the historically limiting barriers raised by former teachers who wanted to contain and shape the minds of young people without expecting any form of serious engagement or interaction, or contribution to the growing body of knowledge. The darkened room with enticing PowerPoint slides is a breeding ground for mindlessness if technology is used only for instruction rather than for visualization and modeling of events that could not otherwise be communicated.

THE RITUALIZATION OF TECHNOLOGIES

The educational community faces an overwhelming task in re-inventing schools and classrooms for a world transformed by digital technologies. Public education, as most have experienced it in the last century, was developed to meet the needs of an industrial, print-based age. Teaching and learning activities in school often share dominant characteristics of that larger culture: they are sequential, hierarchical, linear, externally determined and controlled, and compulsory for all. Perhaps because of societal shifts and changes in response to a major new communication medium, the topic of technology for teaching and learning is fast emerging as one of the forces leveraging educational reform.

Atwood reminds us that both individuals and societies can be caught in the web of technological transformations. What begins as a feminist critique of social discourse becomes a warning about the ritualization of technological integration. In our reading of Atwood, we remind ourselves that schools have always been sites for ritualized grooming. When Leo Tolstoy started his school for the peasants' children who worked on his property in the late 19th century, he dreamed of schools becoming sites of political change. As an anarchist educational theorist (and author), he sought to change the old regime of ritualized servitude using education as the emancipating system. Yet, how does learning a curriculum that is steeped in a culture of containment have anything to do with encouraging learners to experience the world? How do we, and we authors mean *we educators with the will to change things*, promote an equitable educational experience with technologies that will not strangle the adolescent mind, body and spirit? How do we conceive of an education that is not what we do to others but what we, as a community of inquiry, do together – adults and young people as partners in a living culture?

We are witnessing a shift in how teachers regard their roles in the educational "enterprise" (to use [consciously, but not comfortably] business-like terms of definition). Many teacher-scholars are resisting the institutional pressures to conform, to buy in, to accept unquestioningly, the status quo. Teachers, like the wife in Atwood's novel, have little power and often use what little power they have to subjugate those who are even less powerful – students. The cultural expectation in many schools is to not stand out in the crowd, and to please keep noise to a minimum. Intelligent educators are in a position that they must appear to go along with the status quo because of institutional, cultural, economic and positional constraints. However, more and more teachers, like the handmaids whispering in the dark, are questioning the prevailing culture, some only in secret, behind the staff and classroom doors, and some using technologies to connect with one another.

Surely a change in the educational power structure is what Papert, in good conscience, had in mind when he started *Project Headlight* at the Hennigan School, a middle school in one of the poorest communities in Boston. The computer would be the tool, the way to start a cultural revolution in education. It would disrupt current practice by giving power to learners. *Appropriation* and *empowerment* were two words used by Papert to describe his version of a cultural revolution. *Mindstorms*, Papert's book written in 1980, is a treatise to deconstruct the existing educational system by igniting the love of learning that discovery brings. Perhaps this sounds naïve in its pedagogical theorizing at first glance, but it was indeed a headlight for the times.

Papert's theory of Constructionism is more than a learning theory; it is also a spiritual treatise, almost evangelical in its hopefulness and desire for spreading the word. With so much to change in a moribund system that disenfranchises more learners than it frees and empowers, Constructionists (and newer interpretations proposed by Distributed Constructionists and Social Constructionists) may indeed hold a key, a hope. The story is a familiar one: when technologies are first introduced as revolution, innovation and opportunity to change the educational system, creative juices flow. But with time and the call for standardization, integration and using technologies as enhancements to an existing curriculum, the computer simply becomes the better chalkboard where learners sit in the dark mesmerized by flashing slides with digital imagery props. Hand-made becomes reduced to handmaid.

Where are the hand-mades Papert and his team of researchers called for? Has society and teaching become infertile? If technologies hold the promise of ultimate power over our natures, will they also create impotence and infertility, blocking what we know to be humane? Yet, we hold as sacred, with the help of technologies, the advancement of society through the ritualized learning in schools. Should we?

As educators, we need to ask what kind of learning technology we want and what do we not want? How can we use current and emergent technologies to discover new connections with each other? Let's consider the design of networked environments. A school that sets up a network, with a server, some workstations, a network operating system and the mechanisms to link it all together (wires or wireless) can put an incredibly powerful communication system in the hands of children and adults alike. Shared directories can be accessed from anywhere in the school to work on collaborative projects, save and edit media files and print documents. In schools connected to the Internet, the network of networks, students and teachers can also access a vast range of experts and resources, participate in tele-collaborative projects with children and adults from many other cultures and countries, and download helper applications, resources, tools and files as they need them for the work they want to do. Or not.

Unfortunately, many schools and school districts enforce strict security and control when designing networked environments. Desktop choices are made before the user logs in and configurations cannot be altered. Net-savvy elementary students might try to get around disabled disk drives by uploading their homework to their personal web sites for access from school, but downloads are prevented just-in-case someone harvests a virus from the World Wide Web. Protecting the technology from the teachers and students becomes the overarching goal.

The Internet connects people to each other and provides a space in which the human voice can be rapidly rediscovered (Levine, Locke, Searls & Weinberger, 2000). Remember the handmaids whispering names to each other in the dark? Unlike top-down broadcast media controlled by the privileged few (television execs, radio announcers, newspaper editors), the Internet is an interactive and emancipatory communication medium in which users can and do resist artificial constraints. In the online world, participants have endless information and play choices, as well as new publishing opportunities. When the choices are not overwhelming, as they can be, young people can produce and publish their own video, audio and animated creations. An elementary student can publish her perspectives that uniquely reflect her concerns and worldviews. Or not.

When the World Wide Web was first born, there were thousands of teachers who figured out how to download and set up free web servers, construct web documents using HTML and share their work with the world. These upstarts published ideas and plans, got projects going with kids and teachers in other schools and created online environments that were exciting, creative and unique. But then, someone at the school board caught on to what was happening and brought the excitement and unchecked communication to a screaming halt. In many school boards across North America, web pages have to be formally approved and are required to publish prefabricated logos and messages that are standardized and sanitized. Although many of the same upstarts have figured out ways to get around these requirements (by using free web space or their own home Internet accounts), there are many teachers who cannot.

Technologies can lose their luster, however bright and shiny they appear now, as opportunities to rethink the meaning of our learning institutions, and can merely become used as props to support more oppression, more of the same in schools. As educational researchers and creators of these new technologies, we can become like the commander and his wife – seduced into a belief that the current technology vision is the only vision of the future. The potential seduction of the computer is more problematic once it has been sanitized and ritualized into the school system. Ironically, in the end of *The Handmaid's Tale*, the handmaid escapes from Gilead to a new world, rather than confront the existing system. Is the hope for the next generation of technological devices and their accompanying theories another escape to the edges of a wilderness, the edges of the known, a place not yet envisioned by Tolstoy or Papert? A place and time where creativity is not an inspirational phase but rather a continuum of invention? Or should one stay put and change the system from within the existing structures that exist to perpetuate themselves?

LEARNERS AS INSTRUMENTS OF CHANGE

At first glance, young people seem to have a better understanding of digital technologies than most of the adults charged to teach them. The shifting power relations associated with who is expert, who is in control and why this matters, often leads to tension and conflict in the technology-enhanced learning environment. The same scenario is acted out in university settings between graduate students and faculty. Or in companies between programmers and CEOs.

As in every generation, young people have grown up with the emerging technology of their times as a natural part of their daily landscape. It becomes part of their culture more easily and so, even though young people don't often create the culture, they more easily adopt and perpetuate it. Adults, on the other hand, are more skeptical and cautious, having been through their own revolutions and realizing that revolutions tend to fade. Children of the 1980s and 1990s grew up expecting that digital tools work a certain way, and often interact with physical and digital interfaces using their whole bodies (i.e., watch how a child uses both thumbs to dial a cell phone, held like a game controller, compared to an adult who pokes with one index finger). Digital technologies, like the cell phone, are used by children for both intended and unintended purposes, and also for invented purposes. Intended use – to maintain contact between two or more parties. Invented purposes – to arrange for a meeting with a friend in another class during math period.

Today's children play with digital devices and highly complex toys. And yes, there is a serious problem in that playing outdoors may be reduced because of their fascination with digital and multimedia tools and devices. Yet, in the course of our research in diverse settings, we have spoken with learners who are articulate about their learning needs, reflect deeply on their learning and how they learn best, and are currently caught in a system that often doesn't recognize their diverse skills and strengths. As one student from Goldman-Segall's research with children from Project Headlight told her: "Only teachers who don't know what they're talking about have to use curriculum; they don't have anything else to teach without it." Josh's ideal school would ensure that for half the year, children should be able to do whatever they wanted. As he says, "if you want the teacher to help you with ideas and everything, then you can ask her." According to Josh's theory, teachers should not coerce children into doing things that they don't want to do; they should help children when asked; and, most important, they should let children follow through on their ideas. When Goldman-Segall asked Josh what happens to children who don't have any ideas for self-directed projects, he said: "Ricki, all kids have ideas...You get imagination just from facts that you see, things that you see." When she asked Josh whether there should be a "curriculum" for teaching the program language, Logo, Josh said it would be "punishment" if there were a curriculum in Logo, because it is important for children to follow the ideas they have – especially in Logo. "'Cause, you see, no one thinks it's fun, if you're drawing something and you want to do something else, and they're making you draw something that you don't want to do. And if you have another idea, it would be like punishment for the kids who really don't like it." (To view the video and add comments, go to http://www.pointsofviewing.com and then click on p. 173.) Josh, like many motivated learners, feels punished when someone takes away his freedom to express himself in self-directed work activities.

In ways that are similar to Atwood's handmaids, learners want to be recognized and valued as individuals, and have ready access to technology in schools like they do at home, instead of being subject to the one-size-fits-all roles that society has for them or could have for them if technologies are used in a standardized manner.

We need to turn students' quests for freedom and dignity into strength, rather than conceiving of it as a problem to be solved. A space needs to be opened in which diversity can be honored and guided, rather than be conceived of as something to fix. Today's students need not conform to traditional notions of literacy, competency and relevancy. We cannot afford to lose or discredit even one voice. The argument we are proposing is not for a rampant state of relevancy in which every idea or thought is deemed valid, but instead for a collaborative learning community in which learners [teachers and students] are regarded as travelers in search of deeper understanding. We argue for epistemological integrity and rigor to guide the development of digitally enhanced and enabled learning environments for scholarly communities that promote creative and innovative thought and reasoning. We propose a multi-vision community, not a mosaic of different parts neatly fitting together, an image so entrenched in the Canadian consciousness, but rather a conversation with each voice affecting the other, continually evolving as characters in a novel make up a story at any given moment in the plot.

How do we change the story so that all teachers will recognize when students themselves are onto something big, are creating a digital representation that is profound, or inventing something important to them in their understanding? How do teacher education programs encourage teacher-mentors to hear children make those fundamental connections to the world, instead of saying, "Oh, that's interesting" and then move on with their own agenda? DiSessa (2000) describes how teachers and researchers need to challenge current assumptions about curriculum and what is possible for children to learn, and then revise our community affiliations as telecommunications become an integral part of computational media. As advisors and mentors, educators and parents need to question how to guide newly birthed ideas and computational literacies to fruition, leverage the power of technology to facilitate new learner interactions and develop methods that guide epistemological explorations to the next level of complexity. Better still, we need to question how we can cultivate the child's budding questioning and inquiry into the human family. Because of the widespread influence of computers, science and business are not remotely the same practices they were 20 years ago (DiSessa, 2000). How can we open up spaces in which digital technology can have similar influences on the cultural practices of schooling?

THE PLOT THICKENS: *THE LEARNER IS US*

To answer the questions we posed in the beginning of this chapter about how to create a multi-vision culture, we now thicken the plot to recommend that teachers and learners reflect upon, critique and expand the theory of multiple *points of viewing*. How do we accomplish this?

First we need to collectively design (virtual and real) safe spaces in which teachers and learners can be lifelong explorers. Teachers need not have to pretend to know everything about our complex world. Second, those responsible for the learning environment need support and protection to collaboratively construct new learning cultures not based on competition, but on co-operation. Third, teachers and students need to be able to select and to design the technologies they will use in their classrooms and schools. This does not mean that every teacher needs to be able to program (diSessa, 2000). It means that teachers and students need to have open-ended tools to be able to re-invent curricular goals and turn their classroom into an ecological community rich in diversity and experience levels.

In the research we have conducted in schools over the last 15 years, teachers become energized and renewed as professionals when they are provided with mentoring, support and on-site professional development with the new technologies. Teachers who are provided opportunities to question, to inquire into and to experiment with knowledge, and are supported in their efforts to design this type of technology-enhanced learning environment for students, undergo a transformation that prevents them from going back to the daily compromise of prepackaged and predetermined units of delivered content. When teachers are provided with opportunities to interact with each other and with their students in intellectually demanding ways, and within enabled environments in which they can plan, implement and evaluate meaningful projects that leverage the power of digital technologies, they feel invigorated as learners again. When honoring teachers, we need to remember that most are people who choose teaching, not necessarily because they love to teach, but because they love to learn. The majority of teachers are passionate about learning, are curious about the world and have years of wisdom in how to explore and question knowledge in the world. And they entered the teaching profession because they love and want to share their enthusiasm for learning.

Indeed, the future role for teachers is to become learners again, to see themselves in novel environments where they are empowered and empowering. When we ask to locate the learner in the new digital media culture of learning and teacher, our focus must be reflective and reflexive. We must look within for changing the world we live in. Only then we can help the others we share our worlds with to change and become the persons they are meant to be. Only by changing ourselves can we mentor others. If schools are to become rich learning environments in which we prepare students for today and their future, and not our past, then it stands to reason that teachers need to be provided with opportunities to develop and negotiate their own relationship with digital technologies. Teachers have a right to experience the type of learning environments that they are called upon to provide for children. And they need faculty mentors in teacher education colleges who are passionate about the exploration process. They need to know that learning is the natural response to living in a creative environment. They need to not see themselves as gatekeepers and guards, managing and disciplining those who have not yet found joy in learning, but rather see themselves as people who open the doors for others to go further than they have. They need to see themselves as learners.

It was Oliver H. Perry who, on September 10, 1813, wrote to General Harrison: "We have met the enemy, and they are ours." More than a hundred years later, Walt Kelly, in his cartoon section, "Pogo Looks at the Abominable Snowman," wrote:

There is no need to sally forth, for it remains true that those things which make us human are, curiously enough, always close at hand. Resolve then, that on this very ground, with small flags waving and tinny blasts on tiny trumpets, we shall meet the enemy, and not only may be ours, he may be us *(*The Funnies, *p. 292, italics added).*

"We have met the enemy and he is us" is probably the most famous line that remains of Kelly's work and it was subsequently picked up in the 1960s by revolutionaries as a call to change oneself. More recently, in a keynote address at a symposium called *Locating the Learner* at the University of Washington, Goldman-Segall (May, 2001) built upon this history of word play by stating: "We have seen the learners, and they are us."

Conclusion: From Instructionism to Social Constructionism

A number of researchers argue that there is a qualitative difference in how adults and children learn when using technologies (Howard, 1994; Jonassen, Peck & Wilson, 1999; Norton & Wiburg, 1999; Papert, 1996). The widespread access to electronically published information has created a change in the roles of both teachers and learners. Clifford, Friesen & Jacobsen (1998) describe the shifting nature of power and learning in classroom contexts when teachers put the power of adult tools in the hands of children. For example, teachers, who were trained to deliver instruction based upon an industrial age model, knowledge packaging and transfer, are under tremendous pressure to use communications technology that can essentially shift the balance of power in the classroom, and change teacher and student roles. Teachers become mentors and guides; students teach their peers and share their knowledge with others, teachers included. Leaping into the knowledge age is less about technology integration *per se*, and more about the fundamental changes to teaching and learning that are enabled and required by the new medium.

Many teachers feel caught between Instructionist approaches with prescribed curriculum objectives and standardized exams, and the technology-enhanced Constructionist environments, where learners become builders and designers and work on projects as a community of inquiry. Faculty in Teacher Education Programs often do not know how to create these learning environments in spite of the fact that they might teach about Constructivism and Constructionism as viable and alternative methods to classroom life. Constructionism does not lend itself well to the contemporary discourse riddled with words like *accountability* and *national initiatives* aimed at higher scores. And, when students enter into the constructionist learning environment, they too are often resistant to the freedom they are offered. After all, how can they feel they are learning if the standard signs of achievement are changed? If their ability to solve problems counts more than getting the right answer, how do they measure up? And how do parents respond to Constructionist innovations when most parents want their children to do better than other people's children?

The new knowledge environment of the information and communication age calls many of the Instructionist assumptions of the print-based transfer models of schooling and teaching into question. The emerging technologies require thoughtful (and intellectual) teachers to face fundamental issues and ask critical questions about the intent, value and fundamental goals of schooling. For example, what is the changed nature of literacy in a hypermedia environment? Composing and representing with text and graphics in a digital environment calls for fundamentally different skills, dispositions and critical abilities, many of which are undervalued, and some of which are actively discouraged, by traditional text-based orientations in school. How do teachers, parents and students negotiate these new expectations?

In *Points of Viewing Children's Thinking*, Goldman-Segall (1998) describes the fundamental cultural, pedagogical and epistemological shifts that occur when children use digital technologies to become knowledge producers rather than knowledge consumers. Goldman-Segall builds upon the shift in technology from broadcast to interactive media to promote the idea of the learner constructing artifacts that represent their cultural consciousness. The paradigm shift from Instructionism to Social Constructionism, where communities of inquiry design environments using digital video media, is discussed most poignantly in her understanding of gender. When young people use new media, Goldman-Segall (1998) maintains, they have the opportunity to flex their epistemological *attitudes*. She departs from her Piagetian (1969, 1952, 1930) and Papertian (1992, 1991, 1987, 1980) roots of stages and styles to examine gender as both a social construction as well as a biological tendency. With new media technologies as tools for playing out new roles, young people explore their sexuality and, more importantly, their thinking about role in the social and biological world.

At issue, then, is not simply whether technology offers a better way to learn or not. In a very serious and troubling way, the educational worldview is being challenged. What happens to those who are on the edges of the prevailing view of education relates back to the changed worldview in *The Handmaid's Tale*. Those who fight against it get hung on hooks with bags over their heads as grim public examples. Innovative teachers, who often occupy the borders and margins in schools, those who teach in generative ways in response to children's questions and ideas, embracing the power of digital technologies, are too often poorly defended by administration and teaching colleagues.

In a study of primary school teachers who use digital technologies in their teaching, Julie Wood (2000) describes how innovative teachers can be hindered by their jealous peers. Wood found that pioneer teachers often downplay their expertise or novel teaching strategies to avoid evoking jealousy from their peers. In the typical elementary school culture of "all-for-one, one-for-all," drawing attention to oneself is regarded as showing off and invites a hostile response from peers. Being open about one's innovative teaching strategies, and worse, the advances in student learning, can result in other teachers using intimidation tactics and flatly rejecting what the teacher is trying to achieve with technology (Wood, 2000). Unfortunately, this state of affairs promotes mediocrity, and often drives innovation underground. It is a common expectation that every school must be treated the same, and must essentially look the same. School principals and teachers must not be seen to be openly innovative. Wood (2000) summarizes this growing uneasiness, experienced by traditional teachers who resent those who are innovative, as a feeling that their hard-won teaching style is rapidly becoming obsolete – and so are they.

Digital technologies are a major information and communications revolution. Digital technologies can change forever how people manage, exchange and share information. The integration of technology into classroom teaching and learning requires new questions, shifts power relations and roles, and demands that educators evaluate the needed changes that will enable students to take advantage of unregulated on-line resources, and to contribute to and extend those resources as they share their knowledge with the world. Unlike students in the industrial-model, information-consumer generation, today's students can be constructors and producers of information and share their perspectives with a worldwide audience.

The integration of technologies requires that assessment and evaluation structures be reconceptualized. Educators need to evaluate the quality of the new knowledge and representations that students produce, and communicate new expectations with parents. Teachers and students need to learn to live and work in an environment in which time, distance, cultural differences and relations of power no longer divide us in traditional ways. As exciting as are the opportunities, it will not be an easy road to travel.

In Atwood's *Historical Notes* at the end of her novel, a group of university professors have gathered for a symposium on Gileadean Studies in Northern Canada. Atwood pokes fun at those who study culture and interpret history (and not make it?). She roasts academics for their subjectivity to multiple, and often incorrect, interpretations. Is Atwood's goal in closing with this provocative tail of her novel to poke fun at how her work is often misinterpreted? Her academics are analyzing audio tapes recorded by the main character about her experience as a handmaid, and their inferences about what happened are usually wrong, sometimes amusingly so. The academics only have part of the data – the tape recordings, whereas the reader has Atwood's entire story (presumably the whole story) based on Atwood's account. And, of course, even Atwood is not privy to understanding what she has written.

The authors of this chapter offer diverse perspectives and different parts of the story about educational technology. In this, the tail of our chapter, we wonder what our peers will question when they deconstruct the Social Constructionist novel approach to examining collaborative and computer-supported teaching and learning environments. We are curious about future critical discourse in which academics and other analysts deconstruct and interpret current approaches to teaching and learning with technology early in the 21st century. In this chapter, we analyzed how multiple educational perspectives and shifting power relations currently shape learning and teaching opportunities in digitally enhanced learning environments. The approach taken in this chapter contributes not only to an ongoing critical discourse about curriculum, technology and learning, but also calls for reflecting upon the literary genre to make sense of how technology-rich learning environments can achieve the multi-visions of society. It is the time to open the doors to interpretation and critique and invite communities of practice to consider alternative methods of analyses of the complex technological learning systems. We may find, in this journey, that in our enthusiasm to infuse the educational world with technologies, we have lost something of humanity along the way. Something that connects us to each other, face to face. Real-time. We may find that time and place cannot be replicated on a computer monitor. That caring for each other and the life of all species who inhabit this world cannot be reduced to the integration of technologies or to quantitative analysis of how many schools use computers and how school grades improve with the use of computer technologies. Accountability should be understood as the willingness of citizens to work together to create humane places for children and adults to learn and to share their learning with each other. To become accountable to each other and to themselves. This journey will never be easy but it will be the challenge of our lifetime. And, as Atwood has shown, it will take place far away from Gilead.

REFERENCES

Atwood, M. (1985). *The Handmaid's Tale*. McClelland and Stewart.

Clifford, P., Friesen, S. & Jacobsen, D.M. (1998). *An Expanded View of Literacy: Hypermedia in the Middle School.* Proceedings of the ED-MEDIA AND ED-TELECOM 98: World Conference on Educational Multimedia and Hypermedia & World Conference on Educational Telecommunications, Freiburg, Germany, June 20-25.

diSessa, A.A. (2000). *Changing Minds: Computers, Learning, and Literacy.* Cambridge: MIT Press.

Goldman-Segall, R. (1998). *Points of Viewing Children's Thinking: A Digital Ethnographer's Journey.* Mahwah, NJ: Lawrence Erlbaum Associates. For viewing video and adding comments, go to http://www.pointsofviewing.com.

Howard, D. (1994). "Human-computer Interactions: A Phenomenological Examination of the Adult First-time Computer Experience." *Qualitative Studies in Education, 7*(1), 33-49.

Jonassen, D., Peck, K. & Wilson, B. (1999). *Learning With Technology: A Constructivist Perspective.* Upper Saddle River, NJ: Prentice Hall.

Levine, R., Locke, C., Searls, D. & Weinberger, D. (2000). *The Cluetrain Manifesto: The End of Business as Usual.* Cambridge, MA: Perseus Publishing.

Norton, P. & Wiburg, K. (1998). *Teaching with Technology.* Orlando, FL: Harcourt Brace College Publishers.

Papert, S. (1996). *The Connected Family: Bridging the Digital Generation Gap.* Atlanta, GA: Longstreet Press.

Papert, S. (1992). *The Children's Machine.* New York: BasicBooks.

Papert, S. (1991). "Situating Constructionism." In I. Harel & S. Papert (Eds.), *Constructionism.* Norwood, NJ: Ablex Publishing.

Papert, S. (1987 [1985]). "Information Technology and Education: Computer Criticism vs. Technocentric Thinking." *Educational Researcher, 16*(1), 22-30

Papert, S. (1980). *Mindstorms: Children, Computers, and Powerful Ideas.* New York: Basic Books.

Piaget, J. (1969). *The Child's Conception of Time.* London: Routledge & Kegan Paul.

Piaget, J. (1952). *The Child's Conception of Number.* London: Routledge & Kegan Paul.

Piaget, J. (1930). *The Child's Conception of the World.* London: New York: Harcourt, Brace and World.

Salomon, G. (2000). "It's Not Just the Tool But the Educational Rationale That Counts." Keynote address presented at *Ed-Media 2000*, Montreal, Quebec. Canada. http://construct.haifa.ac.il/~gsalomon/edMedia2000.html

Salomon, G. & Almog, T. (1998). "Educational Psychology and Technology: A Matter of Reciprocal Relations." *Teachers College Record,* 100 (1), 222-241.

Salomon, G. (1994). *Interaction of Media, Cognition, and Learning.* Hillsdale, NJ: Lawrence Erlbaum.

Wood, J.M. (2000) "Innovative teachers hindered by the 'green-eyed monster.'" *Harvard Education Letter,* 16(4), 7-8.

CHAPTER 5

OBJECT LESSONS

CRITICAL VISIONS OF EDUCATIONAL TECHNOLOGY

SUZANNE DE CASTELL, MARY BRYSON AND JENNIFER JENSON

The rapidly evolving landscape of higher education has changed the way institutions of higher learning must think using computing technology....As creators of the course management system used by the largest, most advanced, and most diverse base of institutions and students today, WebCT is uniquely positioned to develop and deliver technology that helps institutions achieve these goals...WebCT Cobalt, our next generation e-learning platform, will be the first educational solution to combine course management with state-of-the art application architecture and customer relationship management technology, and the first such system, to deliver significant benefits to students, instructors, administrators, and CIO's. WebCT: Leveraging Technology to Transform the Educational Experience. *(June, 2001)*

Universities are not simply undergoing a technological transformation. Beneath that change and camouflaged by it, lies another: the commercialization of higher education. For here as elsewhere technology is but a vehicle and a disarming disguise. David Noble: Digital Diploma Mills: The Automation of Higher Education.

The stage upon which are enacted contemporary debates concerning the significance and proper deployment of educational technologies is populated with a familiar set of characters – the concerned parent, the enthusiastic child, the harried teacher, the bewildered administrator and the miracle worker. Within the high-stakes context of the current imperative to "Get Connected, and Share in the Dream," the implementation of new information technologies, miracle workers occupy an *apparently* facilitative and enabling role as expert cultural interpreters of what Mark Poster has dubbed the "Second Media Age."

In the early days of educational computing, the miracle workers' yellow brick road was paved by techno-gurus like Seymour Papert (the classic text is *Mindstorms,* Papert, 1980). He created a digital artifact –

LOGO – around which, like a campfire, members of a fervent group of users sang the praises of that particular solution for today's .com challenge to education – the integration of digital tools into the resiliently analogue environment of the typical public school. In the current climate, miracle workers, conversant in a digital Newspeak (Orwell, 1987), peddle a discourse peppered with buzzwords, such as: "E-solutions," "information societies," "personalization," "pipelines," "connectivity," and "learning content management." The miracle worker appears like a mirage – just-in-time assistance to get out of the mire that typically follows in the frenzy that is produced by the imposition of technological change on a massive scale. Miracle workers are often located in universities, and take the form of "high-flyer" academics with branded and quasi entrepreneurial mega-projects and high-profile revenue-generating products (e.g., Canada's TeleLearning Network of Centres of Excellence, http://www.telelearn.ca/g_access/news.html), whose impressive resources open doors to schools and/or communities caught up in the frenzy to "Leverage technology to transform the educational experience" (WebCT, 2001).

Alarmist rhetoric, reminiscent of earlier debates about the so-called "literacy crisis" (see Graff, 1988), survives today in a wide range of educational policy documents (see, for example, WebCT, 2001) and promotional materials that urge educators to grapple with the implications of an "explosion in knowledge, coupled with powerful new communication and information processing technologies" and, thereby, to promote widespread "technological literacy." Arguments that enthusiastically promote the widespread implementation of educational computing typically predict that these technologies will (a) facilitate and transform teaching processes, and (b) promote significant positive gains, both academic and vocational, for students. The obstacles standing in the way of integration efforts are immense. And so, there is a frenzy of activity at present dedicated to creating Success Stories with digital technologies.

Consider the following headline (May 21, 2001) from *Wired News*:

Bringing the Information Super Highway to the Dirt Road

Surfing the Net is second nature to most American schoolchildren these days. But not on the Pala Indian reservation in Southern California. That's about to change, thanks to a partnership between Native Americans Indians and researchers at the University of

California at San Diego.

The High Performance Wireless Research and Education Network (HPWREN) team is creating, demonstrating, and evaluating a high-performance, wide-area, wireless network in a number of "hard to reach" areas in San Diego county...Located at the foot of Palomar Mountain in east San Diego county, the Pala Indian reservation is home to 600 tribal members including more than 150 children who attend elementary school on the reservation. Until last month, the tribe could only dream of access to high-speed Internet connectivity...

Success stories like the one above equate integration with materiality, that is with the acquisition of hardware and software (i.e., "connectivity"). Integration in each of the following contexts, however, is accomplished very differently discursively despite like-minded exhortations and proclamations. Consider these two rather divergent views (cited in Bryson and de Castell, 1998, pp. 542-543) of what bringing digital technologies into a school means:

The most significant impact of technology on education will come from an extensive transformation of the curriculum and instructional practices... Technology-based education makes learning more active and interactive for each student. Technology brings resources to the classroom that motivate, stimulate, and encourage students. Computers are an integral part of many of today's jobs, and computer literacy will be even more essential in the future. Our job is to help learners today to prepare for the challenges of tomorrow. School District, District Technology Policy

It's just simple things that drive me crazy. Like, we have this lab of new computers and this great paint program, and no mice. Can you believe it? It's been three months since they delivered those machines, and no one knows who is responsible for getting the mice. So they sit there. New Technologies and the Primary Program Project Teacher

We know, from our own small-scale educational technology research, as well as from large-scale studies carried out in public schools of the actual uses made by teachers of new information technologies, that the level of implementation of these new tools has not come close to matching their apparent promise.

In the U.S., Henry Becker and colleagues recently completed an important national study of teachers and computer use (Teaching, Learning, and Computing, http://www.crito.uci.edu/tlc/html/tlc_home.html). The authors report that whereas until recently, teachers' computer use has been limited by the computer/student ratio, by 1998 the typical school had one computer for every six students enrolled, or about four computers per classroom if they were actually divided equally among all instructional rooms.

Becker's analysis of the survey data suggests that at the high school level, the majority of intensive experiences with computers that students have are in courses outside of the academic core, and often in computer studies and business education classes. Becker's results indicate that a majority of teachers across grades 4 to 12 either do not use computers at all with their students or do so only occasionally. The "typical" teacher provides students with fewer than ten opportunities to use computers during a school year.

This apparent and longstanding lack of success in reaching implementation goals with respect to uses of digital tools in schools has created a specific niche for the working of miracles: the provision of digitally-mediated environments within which to re-mediate the production of knowledge in educational contexts. Today's education workers are accorded a special role in the "knowledge society" – the catch phrase that is driving a significant segment of activity in the implementation field – the educator as broker of information.

Within such a context, the miracle workers' effectiveness is measured by their capacity to spin narratives of success against all odds by providing tools that appear to transform students' engagements with information – or, worse, info-tainment. Moving from a banal reproduction and passive consumption of existing forms, to a productive and dynamic apprenticeship in a constructivist community of practice, these romantic narratives about the significant changes that invariably ensue when a school adopts the miracle worker's platform are the stock in trade.

It could be argued at this point that we lack an educational theory of technology (which is not the same thing as a theory of educational technology, of which we have of course a number.) The difference between these is that theories of educational technology take for granted, whether as good or as harmful, the integration of education and technology. An educational theory of technology, by contrast, would investigate technology from the standpoint of educational values and purposes, and with reference to what can be discerned from a study of the technology as a socially-situated artifact. Such a theory of technology would offer material grounding to a rethinking of educational epistemology. Accordingly, an educational theory of technology would seek to articulate particular machine capabilities with specific epistemic purposes. In order to learn from our tools, we have also to study them, as well as the context of their intended use.

We take seriously Ursula Franklin's (1990) insistence that technology is not only an artifact but also a system of social practices, but this is not to say that technology has no relevant artifactual status at all. So while an educational theory of technology need not be technologically determinist, reading off what can and should be done in education from purported structural and material features of the machine, neither can it sensibly be technologically indeterminist, as if artifactual capacities and limitations were not any kind of consideration at all.

A potent irony is that, confronting a range of enormously powerful, radically transformative digital tools, educators have sought to render their and their students' encounters with and uses of these transformative tools (a) familiar and (b) comfortable. Take a look, for example, at an online educational environment, "HomeRoom," which encourages teachers to: "Create customized, skill-specific tests for your students, aligned to state standards or a specific state test." (http://www.home room.com/educators/scr_assign.asp). Like an endlessly rehearsed mantra, we hear that what is essential for the implementation and integration of technology in the classroom is that teachers should become 'comfortable' using it.

We might well stop a moment and consider the absurdity of such a demand: we have developed a powerful means for reshaping human knowledge, communications, educational structures and relations, epistemic concepts and practices, and have incalculably increased the amount and kind of information available to ordinary people worldwide, we have a master code capable of utilizing in one platform what have for the entire history of our species thus far been irreducibly different kinds of things – writing and speech, images and sound – every conceivable form of information can now be combined with every other kind to create a different form of communication, and what we seek is comfort and familiarity?

What about novelty, unprecedented innovation, intellectual challenge, ideological dissent? Why are these sidelined by familiarity and comfort? How is it even conceivable that the latter can stand in for the former? Nevertheless this has been education's' typical response to digital tools. And to that end, lesson plans are devised and promoted through education 'portals' or templates or programs and environments are designed by educational technology experts that as nearly as possible replicate the traditional school-like questions, tasks and activities that this new technology threatens to replace. Beyond being the means of its OWN production, how is this use of technology better than a textbook? How, indeed, is it any different? What has an on-line lesson got to do with digital tools at all?

Typically, therefore, it is remarkably traditional content that we deliver by computer, on CD-ROM or via the web, using few of the tools of the computer or the web beyond their capacities for display and distribution. This is equivalent to using a high end, multicapacity, powerful server for typing practice – another not unfamiliar school-based practice we would never find in any other context. We have to begin to see this as no less ridiculous than using a jackhammer to insert a picture hanger into drywall. From this standpoint we might reconceive teachers who resist technology less as uninformed Luddites and more as the only folks capable of seeing the nakedness of the emperor, and honest enough to say so (an argument that is fully developed in Bryson and de Castell, 1998.)

In trying to develop an understanding of what technology can do for education, it is important to look at particularly well-regarded instructional uses of technology in education, the innovations spotlighted in media celebrations of "technology in the classroom". Consider here just two genres of prominent and "successful" computer-supported learning environments: the programmed instruction package or "integrated learning system" (e.g., SuccessMaker, http://www.suc cessmaker.com/) and the networked E-Learning environment (e.g., WebCT, http://www.webct.com), where a range of online tools are provided to support both teachers and learners in a form of activity typically characterized as "collaborative knowledge-building."

There are a number of "integrated learning system" software packages available for sale in schools today. Each utilizes an extensive and sophisticated database to deliver multi-level use drill and practice software to individual students. The software also provides individualized error analysis profiles, specifying areas for remediation and providing instructional tasks that promise to bring the learner up to the prescribed standards for their grade level in each subject area. Here is the all-purpose individualized curriculum delivery tool.

These curriculum delivery tools, however, provide no room for invention and no room for production. They are systems built for compliance and as such embody no educational theory: education is reduced to instruction, and the extent of its theorization consists in these imperatives:

* Deliver set curriculum
* Meet set standards
* Evaluate outcomes based on these pre-established criteria
* Administer remedial practice where students' work fails to meet these criteria, and above all
* Track, record, document.

Online E-learning environments like WebCT (see www.webct.com) emphasize networked communication and integrated course delivery and management tools, and are represented as a very different kind of technology: a toolkit for collaborative knowledge-building that explicitly encourages active involvement in its production on the part both of instructors and students. This technology, its proponents would argue, DOES embody an educational theory, and it goes something like this: the systematic development of cognitive and communicative skills which are constitutive of learner-effectiveness and engagement and, therefore, directly facilitative of students' educational success. However, a closer look at WebCT, which is now in wide use at universities and colleges, reveals that its WYSIWYG interface is intended to make it easy for instructors to put course content online, which then makes it possible for educational administrators to reduce face-to-face instructional time and replace expensive faculty teaching time with "plug-and-play" content modules, sessional instructors, and a heavy reliance on machine-scoreable multiple-choice assessment protocols. One of the more recent additions to the WebCT toolkit – the E-Pack – signals the trajectory that this form of educational technology is traversing through the rough ground of implementation. WebCT has partnered with major textbook publishers to create online versions of high-use texts, eliminating in one easy and seductive step the need for any faculty involvement in designing university-based courses.

E-Packs make it easy for instructors to start teaching online without having to create a course from scratch. E-Packs provide instructors with fully customizable course materials around which to build their courses, including video animations, sample syllabi, lecture notes, quiz and test banks, and glossaries, combined with the functionality of WebCT's course management software. (http://www.webct.com/content/)

Looking more closely, we see a difference more of degree than of kind between an integrated learning system's use of large, elaborate data-bases to provide step-by-step programmed instruction and up-to-date, "on-demand" individual assessment, and an online E-learning environment that provides instructors with powerful and integrated "learning and content management" tools designed in order to engender mindful collaborative learners with explicit "higher-order" cognitive dispositions and abilities. While the former is more obviously a totally routinized, content-corrupt, pedagogy-corrupt system to promote and enforce learner compliance to a fully pre-programmed curricular delivery system, the latter's fundamental structures are themselves built entirely from traditional school-knowledge resources and their activity-systems are no less categorically pre-scripted.

Another respect in which these celebrated educational technologies are similar is their high cost and re-location from the sphere of educational research and development to the high-stakes corporate environment of E-Business.

A question arises for us at this juncture – can a different kind of work be done that involves immersion in a culture of digital technologies, and yet that takes into serious account the threat of cultural colonization inherent in this brave new world, even as it produces engagements with these tools. And is it possible to do this work in a guise distinct from that of the newly hybridized miracle-worker-entrepreneur?

The advent of post-structural epistemologies and research traditions has provided a new field for research endeavors where the aim is no longer to reduce complexity by the disciplined reinvention of the familiar in a play of simulations, but rather, to cultivate novelty, to nurture difference, and to inject complexity into its question in ways that prohibit easy readings or unproblematic interpretation.

Like many who work with new information technologies and educational settings, our program of research has been inspired by Donna Haraway's (1991) imperative, best elucidated in the "Cyborg Manifesto." We believe that as minorities, like ourselves, get involved with digital tools and delve deeply into the possibilities for creating new and potent forms of subjectivity in our engagements with the cyber-mediated world of zeros and ones.

Most educational technology design and development, we argue, has been predicated on the uncritical simulation of culturally valued knowledge, roles and practices. These traditionally imitative practices – thinly veiled "be-like-me" injunctions to mimic the cognitive styles and work practices of recognized 'experts', whether in science or research or programming or literary production, insofar as their modus operandi is simulation, do not allow for the kinds of parody, irony, or other intentionally transgressive disruptions, that the evil twin sister of simulation, dis/simulation, or *parodic* imitation does.

And so we have found it interesting to think about the scope of a technology-intensive, educationally oriented invitation to play, to produce, and to dis-simulate expertise. In short, a program for the deployment of digital tools used not for replication and reproduction, but for creation. An initiative for *authentic, that is, agentive* production, for hacking into the codes of conventional schooling, and introducing viruses into its well-ordered set of assumptions and structures. As some would put it, to deploy digital tools in order to engage in "culture-jamming."

Culture Jamming (see Lasn, 1999) provides an interesting example of a politically articulate intervention and strategy of representation where agency is evident in the active contestation of oppressive regimes of truth – and that could as easily be a description of the research mandate of the first of three projects we will briefly describe next – to interfere with the construction of and silences about "the normal" in and out of school.

For the past eight years, we have been working collaboratively with a group of women in a research collective called GenTech (http://www.shecan.com). Our focus has been a phenomenon that has received much media attention of late – it has become commonplace in social science communities in North America to represent as "problematic" that many girls and women are neither full, nor even interested, participants in the digital world of the 21st century (find a description of this project at Bryson and de Castell, 1996). Whereas female students have made impressive gains in some areas like math and science, *girls and women are staying away in droves from computer-intensive areas of the curriculum* – and of the culture. "Culture Jamming" seemed to us to point to one way out of the paralysis that postmodern theories engender in their ambivalence toward intervention or agency in research where marginality is the dominant narrative. Hence, in the GenTech project, we deliberately interfered with the gender order of the masculinist culture of computing, looking critically at how to overturn the established order governing relations among girls, tools and schools.

Axiomatic to GenTech's school-based intervention work (http://www.educ.ubc.ca/faculty/bryson/gentech/sshrcreport2.html) were the presumptions that:

- Kinds of tool-use, a particular stance in the face of power tools, and restrictions on access to new tools are easily identifiable as vital cultural locations where the performances of gender take specific shapes
- Heteronormative gender performances are overwhelmingly hegemonic for many women
- Therefore, to queer gender it is essential to interfere with the representation of, as well as actual access to and uses of technology by girls and women.

In this project, we worked with small groups of girls, who then taught peers and younger girls, who then trained boys. This was to try to invert the usual power structure of the culture of school-based computing, in which girls are absent and silent, and their absence and silence are typically invisible to their teachers. We made efforts to expand and enrich the community of female experts by inviting mothers to the school to see, and hopefully to encourage and be encouraged by, what their daughters were learning. The teachers responded to learning new technologies predictably: they were apprehensive, already had labeled themselves as incompetent – "dumb people click here"– and at the same time were visibly excited by and absorbed in the learning, even as they remained highly skeptical about computers in general, (and for good reasons that we won't go into here, but we describe in detail in a paper on the GenTech web site called "Teachers as Luddites").

The instruction we provided to teachers and students was both extremely simple and extremely time and labor-intensive. We worked intensively with a group of five female teachers, once a week for a full school year to help them learn basic skills to facilitate the integration of technology into their curriculum – something that none of them had done before. There are thousands upon thousands of schools, classrooms and teachers who are presently expected and increasingly required to use new technologies, but if teaching a single teacher requires at least a half-time person one day a week for a full year, then clearly that requirement will simply not be fulfilled, and indeed this is the case today: there are NO resources available to teachers to do the kind of work we were doing in the Einstein's Sisters Project. In the hopes of providing some means of filling the "training gap" we were beginning to understand, we decided to create a digitally-mediated learning environment titled "Computers for Lunch" (see http://www.computersfor lunch.com).

At the end of the school-based project, we didn't want to just pick up our tools and leave. We felt an obligation to the people who had worked so hard to make the project successful. And we well knew that we ourselves were at risk of playing miracle workers with this project (indeed, and ironically enough, we *were* positioned in 2000 as 'miracle workers' with a "pioneer in new media" award for the GenTech project from a national women in technology organization!).

We were very much aware that our intervention, which looked so good on the surface, was completely non-scalable and non-sustainable. So our challenge now was to devise a way to provide instruction and support, not just for five, but for an unlimited numbers of teachers at once, after the grant funding had run out and it was no longer possible for us to be physically present. We wanted Computers for Lunch to be free, accessible to anyone at anytime, directly relevant to teachers' work with students, and very well scaffolded so as to preclude "failure" – an important requirement for novice users. We wanted to use what we had learned from our years of school-based fieldwork to design a learning tool that would be scalable and sustainable for this *particular* – but nevertheless highly *generalizeable* community of elementary school teachers and learners.

This meant that we were adamantly committed to the use of appropriate technology. We wanted only to use software teachers would already find on their school computers, and the program had to be usable in low-tech, poor connectivity contexts, because that is the state of internet access in most public schools. We wanted streamlined content that would strip away all the info-bloat instructional sites usually have, and, very important for a mostly female user-group, which would keep technical language to a minimum, and would be activity based.

This next stage of our work involved creating a free, fully accessible, practical resource on-line for learning essential computer skills in a way that would engage elementary teachers and their students, and paid particular attention to ways of more equitably supporting learning by women and girls.

Computers for Lunch consists of over 600 inter-linked web pages covering seven different kinds of activities. It is written in html, using Dreamweaver and Flash animation, and it also comes in a CD-ROM format for schools with no or low connectivity.

The next step has been to put the tool to use in a range of other kinds of contexts and try to see how it works, to see, in particular, what kinds of supports novice learners need to utilize on-line resources, and from that basis, to begin to build a new and more sophisticated learning tool.

Since the educational problems of technology (and not, it must be stressed, the problems of educational technology) are global and mass-scale educational problems, we would argue strongly that any innovation represented as a solution to these educational problems must be scalable and accessible.

The consequences of educators' and particularly educational theorists' failures seriously to engage with educational questions about technology have had a devastating impact on both research and practice in this domain. It is neither correct nor right to distance oneself from the fray, and to assert that one doesn't use technology: we all use a range of technologies in our instructional practices. There is of course no obligation to use particular digital tools, but here is surely an obligation to have a thoughtful and informed understanding of how one's educational purposes are best served, and by means of what cultural tools. Why would educators who work, as we here do, under conditions where computers are ubiquitous, where they represent the fastest growing career opportunities for graduates, where they are the primary site of curriculum revision, pedagogical changes, policy formation and professional development, where computers are used in almost every cultural context, just say no to technology in our classrooms? Two reasons: time and resources. Ministries and departments of education everywhere are urging teachers to "integrate technology into the curriculum" but are providing neither the time, nor the tools, to do so. What public educational funds as are being made available, are being disbursed either on hardware, like computers and scanners and high speed Internet access, or they are being disbursed for the purchase of rights to use educational software designed less for public education than for monetary gain, and then marketed to the educational system as 'educational technologies'.

We argue it is irresponsible for educational administrators in ministries of education, school districts and schools to utilize resources provided for integrating technologies into the curriculum to support what is now a burgeoning corporate involvement in educational software design. Rather, they need to provide the time and resources needed to enable teachers and learners to harness the new forms of intelligence and the new functional capabilities of digital tools to participate in the world of technology as purposeful and capable producers and not merely consumers of the products of others. We argue the public school today has become the charitable arm of technology industries, scaffolding and supporting their growth and development rather than supporting the technological growth and development of teachers and learners.

Speaking not of educational but, more broadly, of cultural technologies, Constance Penley and Andrew Ross (1991) observed in their introduction to *Technoculture,*

> *...we fully recognize that cultural technologies are far from neutral and that they are the result of social processes and power relations. Like all technologies, they are ultimately developed in the interests of industrial and corporate profits, and seldom in the name of greater community participation or creative autonomy. (p. xii)*

In educational terms, we know that the odds are firmly stacked against educationally productive uses of technology, and that so-called educational technologies will seldom be developed which actually serve the aims of developing and supporting a critical, informed and responsible global citizenry. We know that, "in many cases" as Penley and Ross go on to note, "…the inbuilt principles of these technologies [both educational and cultural] are precisely aimed at de-skilling, information gathering, surveillance and the social management of large populations." However there *are* possibilities within this environment for knowledge creation and communication that explicitly seek to promote public educational goals. Because there are also in these unregulated spaces quite remarkable and historically unprecedented opportunities for educators and for educational institutions, to re-consider 'business as usual" and to make of public education a better place, to better ends than its traditional form has nowadays become. For probably a very short time, digital tools have given the public (a global public) the possibility of unregulated knowledge-transfer and infinite interpersonal relationship capabilities. Because of the interpenetration of the market with these technologies – technology as the proverbial Trojan horse – there exists tremendous pressure on public education to reorganize itself along business lines. This has wrought, for the integration of technology into education, a frenzy of simulation, of which this is only one example:

> *As photo opportunities go, this one was perfect. Except it was mostly a sham. While their husbands talked affairs of state in the Oval Office, Hillary Rodham Clinton and Aline Chretien ventured into a poor, black neighborhood [Burrville] where, through the wonders of technology, they watched the students of twinned schools in Washington and Ottawa share their hopes on a live, audio-visual Internet hookup. But soon the screens would go blank and be carted away, leaving Burrville's students taking turns on their single slow computer before the Chretiens finish[ed] their state visit today.*
> (The Globe and Mail, *1997*)

Educational research thus far may not have told us much of use, but it has surely made apparent to anyone with eyes to see, the partial success of the project of building an educated public. It is of importance to us in thinking through these ideas to look at how new technologies – the first in human history capable of addressing a geographically unlimited public sphere – might yet be deployed in the service of creating a different and better incarnation of public education.

To see what these might be, we need to look to our tools.

REFERENCES

Becker, H. (1998). *Teaching, Learning, and Computing.* Available: http://www.crito.uci.edu/tlc/html/tlc_home.html).

Bryson, M. & de Castell, S. (1996). "Learning to Make a Difference: Gender, New Technologies, and In/Equity." *Mind, Culture and Activity, 2*(1), 3-21. Available: http://www.educ.ubc.ca/faculty/bryson/gentech/learning.html

Bryson, M. & de Castell, S. (1998). "New Technologies and the Cultural Ecology of Public Schooling: Imagining Teachers as Luddites In/Deed." *Educational Policy, 12*(5). 542-567. Available: http://www.educ.ubc.ca/faculty/bryson/gentech/Luddites.html

Franklin, U. (1990). *The Real World of Technology.* Montreal: CBC Enterprises. Available: http://www.masseylectures.cbc.ca/M_Audio.html#franklin

Graff, H.J. (1988). Whither the History of Literacy? The Future of the Past. *Communication, 11,* 5-22.

Haraway, D. (1991). "A Cyborg Manifesto: Science, Technology, and Socialist Feminism in the 1980's." In D. Haraway (Ed.), *Simians, Cyborgs, and Women: The Reinvention of Nature.* New York: Routledge.

Lasn, K. (1999). *Culture Jam.* New York: HarperCollins Publishers Inc.

Noble, D. (1998). *Digital Diploma Mills: The Automation of Higher Education.* First Monday, 3(1). Available: http://www.firstmonday.dk/issues/issue3_1/noble/

Orwell, G. (1987). *1984.* New York: Chelsea House.

Papert, S. (1980). *Mindstorms.* New York: Basic Books.

Penley, C. & Ross, A. (1991). "Introduction." In C. Penley & A. Ross (Eds.), *Technoculture.* Minneapolis: University of Minnesota Press.

Poster, M. (1995). *The Second Media Age.* Cambridge, MA: Basil Blackwell Inc.

WebCT. (2001). *Leveraging Technology to Transform the Educational Experience.* Unpublished manuscript. Available: http://www.webct.com

Wired News. (2001, May, 21) Available: http://www.wired.com/news/school/0,1383,43718,00.html

PART II

CASE STUDIES AND CLASSROOM USES OF ICT

Chapter 6

TEARING DOWN THE WALLS

New Literacies and New Horizons in the Elementary School

Heather Lotherington, Mary Leigh Morbey, Colette Granger and Lara Doan

Before I built a wall I'd ask to know
What I was walling in or walling out,
And to whom I was like to give offense.
Something there is that doesn't love a wall,
That wants it down.
– excerpted from Robert Frost, Mending Wall *(1914)*

INTRODUCTION

In this chapter, we discover how two elementary schools in metropolitan Toronto found creative ways to implement information and communications technologies (ICT) while meeting the requirements of provincially defined curricula. In the process, each school imaginatively reconfigured the educational script by dismantling many of the walls that segment traditional schools. The pedagogical choices made in each school, and the resulting achievements are distinct; the successes of both schools illuminate new horizons for 21st century educators.

Our research group came together as co-researchers in a Canadian study within a large-scale multinational and multisite research project that examined factors contributing to innovative ICT pedagogy under the auspices of the Centre for the Study of Computers in Education at York University.[1] We come from diverse age, cultural, social, and disciplinary backgrounds, yet we share an interest in the critical implementation of ICT in education. This chapter presents our triangulated observations of these two innovative schools.

Our work brings together case studies of two public elementary schools located in different pockets of the city of Toronto. Ravine School and Main Street School are each located in what one school authority described as "inner-city" neighborhoods, now labelled "special needs" by the Toronto District School Board based on low socio-economic status relative to the city as a whole. (The names of the schools, teachers, and students have all been changed in accordance with research assurances of anonymity.) In addition, in each case the local constituency includes a high proportion of recent immigrants to Canada. Both schools have been designated pedagogically innovative in their uses of ICT by Canadian federal and Ontario educational agencies.

We visited each school for a week to learn about their programs. Having piloted our protocols at Ravine School in June, 2000, we conducted our case studies at Ravine School in November of 2000, and at Main Street School in December of 2000. The case studies examined teacher in-service programs, other professional development activities, and school philosophies and strategies, with the aim of locating those circumstances most likely to produce meaningful ICT pedagogical practices. Interviews were held at each location with the school principal, a school administrator, the computer specialist, the librarian, several groups of teachers involved in innovative ICT collaborations, a student focus group, and a parent focus group. Along with collecting interview data, we made observations of classes in progress, and documented uses of learning spaces.

Working with Nvivo and ATLASti software for qualitative research, data analysis and interpretation employed both manual and electronic coding of patterns and themes. Moving beyond a positivist approach, rather than surface manifestations we sought deeper and more subtle understandings of our observations and our conversations with the school-based personnel (Glaser & Strauss, 1967; Strauss & Corbin, 1990).

A Pedagogical Understanding

In thinking through the data that emerged from our interviews, a framework we found helpful for our understandings of what had transpired in both the Ravine and Main Street School settings was a text originally published in 1970: Paulo Freire's *Pedagogy of the Oppressed*. In this influential text, Freire, a Brazilian adult educator, attended to various oppressive practices of schooling, explored the possibilities of dialogue, and articulated visions of a new emancipatory literacy. We revisited what Freire called the "banking concept of education" (1998: 53):

> *Education thus becomes an act of depositing, in which the students are the depositories and the teacher is the depositor. Instead of communicating, the teacher issues communiqués and makes deposits which students patiently receive, memorize, and repeat. This is the "banking" concept of education, in which the scope of action allowed to the students extends only as far as receiving, filing, and storing the deposits. They do, it is true, have the opportunity to become collectors or cataloguers of the things they store. But in the last analysis it is the people themselves who are filed away through the lack of creativity, transformation, and knowledge in this (at best) misguided system.*

In this model, Freire argued, the teacher is the subject of the learning process, while the students are objects or containers that are filled by deposits of sanctioned information. Pedagogy is thus conceived as a fixed unidirectional process: teachers' teach, students passively 'receive' the teaching and the possibilities of dialogue are minimal. The teacher talks, the students listen, and knowledge is framed as a commodity "owned" by the teacher to be deposited into the learners. Though globally many educators have taken up Freire's critique, the banking model of education still prevails in many sites of formal schooling in North America. Freire proposes an alternative to these prevailing and anaesthetizing educational practices. This latter model, he explains (1998: 61):

> *...breaks with the vertical patterns characteristic of banking education... Through dialogue, the teacher-of-the students and students-of-the-teacher cease to exist and a new term emerges: teacher-student with students-teachers. The teacher is no longer merely the-one-who-teaches, but one who is himself (sic) taught in dialogue with the students, who in turn while being taught also teach. They become jointly responsible for a process in which all grow.*

Stated differently, in this latter model – what Freire calls "problem-posing education" (1998:60) – students and teachers participate through dialogue, as subjects, in the re-envisioning, critical intervening, and reconstituting of their social realities.

Freire's work is directly relevant to our discussion about how information technologies are conceptualized and employed within school practices. The increasing presence of ICT in home and school domains has subtly altered the traditional balance of power between knower and learner, for example. For some educators the introduction of information technologies has effected in essence a "reversal" in the transfer of information, in that students may know more about many of the nuances of ICT than their educators. In the words of one teacher:

> *I think that what I find with the computer, I never feel adequate. I always feel that I'm lagging behind. You know, I brought pictures in and I scan them. Lorraine taught me to – and then I sent them over to Britain and I was so excited. But then I see primary classes, young classes, doing that and I think, Oh.*

Borrowing from Freire, educators' might ask: why are practices of education conceived as merely processes of information transfer? But bounded by rigid formulations of who teaches and who is taught, there is a marked reluctance on the part of educators to pose such questions. Spaces for dialogue and innovative ICT use can be stifled by the preoccupations of those who are lodged in concerns about who is entitled to transfer bytes of information.

Although the depositing of information still conceptually grounds many schooling practices at Ravine and Main Street Schools, we also noted a different conceptualization of knowledge: more specifically, a view of knowledge that closely resembles the praxis for which Freire advocated. Further, we observed how the uses of information technologies in the formal educational practices of both schools were inseparable from the guiding methodological philosophies at work. The educators with whom we spoke thought carefully and collaborated with each other, the students and the principal about the socio-political implications and educational uses of software, hardware, and the Internet at Ravine and Main Street Schools and beyond. This pedagogical understanding situates our chapter, opening doorways to new possibilities for the interconnection of ICT, literacy, and pedagogy in the elementary school.

RAVINE SCHOOL

A mid-sized school of about 400 students, Ravine School includes Junior Kindergarten through Grade 6. All students come from the surrounding neighbourhood, which is characterized by high-density, often subsidized, housing. The students attending Ravine School represent the bottom 10% socio-economic grouping in the Toronto District School Board. The student population is culturally diverse, representing households in which 24 languages other than English are spoken. The school provides students with high quality programs that emphasize numeracy, literacy, and social responsibility. A central focus at Ravine School is the development of a wide range of computer skills, and the integration of computer and library programs with regular classroom instruction.

Our visits to Ravine School, the aim of which was to query manifestations of ICT innovation, were illuminated by non-traditional notions about learning, internally organized professional development, and the facilitation of computer mediated instruction through efficient teaching co-operatives. Students, teachers, and principal, through an innovative triad[2] partnering arrangement – focused on grades 4, 5, and 6 – embrace new ways of constructing and interpreting knowledge as well as of developing new literacies.

THE TRIAD INNOVATION

The triad formulation, an innovation originating in Ravine School discussions, is a collaboration of the teaching school librarian, teaching computer specialist, and classroom teacher, who work as an integral unit interconnecting a particular curricular focus through a combination of classroom, computer lab, and library instruction. A three-pronged teaching construct brings together teachers of varying subject backgrounds and computing knowledge and experience to work collaboratively across curricular aims in ways that entrust them to contribute their strengths to the learning context. The triad innovation at work embodies an alternative to traditional modernist approaches to teaching and learning, making relevant and interconnecting the curriculum, dialogic discourse, professional development, and collaborative learning through ICT. Whereas in traditional practices of schooling, knowledge is often treated as a commodity, innovative practitioners at Ravine School work with the relationship between discovering and creating.

The collaborative nature of these processes reveals itself through the imaginative re-invention, reconstruction, and risk-taking in relation to the pedagogy we observed at the school.

The Ravine School principal's articulation of her guiding approach to innovation illuminates a dialogic and collaborative process – a process that contributed to the birth of the "triad" construct.

> *What we try to do here is for people. What is it they want to know? [Our computer specialist] also thinks about what it is she thinks [her fellow teachers] need to know, what is new, what is different, what is exciting. And it is always that blend of what your experts know, what have they learned, what your visionaries [offer], what …your other people want, and somehow or the other you have to combine these.*

Echoing the principal's viewpoint, the Ravine School teaching computer specialist reflectively articulates the creative, experimental, risk-taking, collaborative, and integrative approach that underlies the triad concept:

> *I am in total involvement with the teachers…And the teachers will come to me. [I] was thinking about web pages and one teacher came to me and said, 'Okay, we are doing projects on space, black holes in particular and I am trying to think what we could do with this information? Well, I guess'…since I just learned how to do Web pages six months ago,… 'maybe they [the students] could do web pages.' And so they [the students] are all doing… Web pages. And he said, 'I can sort of see that we could have this model of a black hole turning around in 3-D.' And I am going, 'Oh, yes, I think that is possible. But…I don't know, I have never done this before.' We put our heads together and I found a program that actually creates a model and then would create it into a movie. Then I got someone to show me how [to] put the little video on to the Web page. And now all these kids have these great movies of a black hole, and it is from a graphing program. It is this colorful object moving, it is how a black hole moves in space.*

INNOVATIVE LEARNING SPACES

Ravine School literally knocked down the physical walls existing between the computer lab and the library to carve out a space supportive of multiple literacies. The material space was transformed with the goal of facilitating a fertile gathering place for knowledge constructing using both electronic and paper artifacts mediated by dialogue.

The opened up computer lab-library space flows from a circle of outward-facing networked computers surrounding a smaller inward-facing networked computer grouping, both supervised by the teaching technology specialist. This lab space moves through an open doorway and a wall of picture windows into a small working group area on the fringe of the library, providing an interchange between screen and page references. The library space, supervised by the teaching librarian, opens into a small group working area analogous to the computer-lab small computer grouping. This library working space leads on into the stacks culminating, at the other end of the room, in a couple of quiet reading areas replete with comfortable sofas and chairs. One recreational reading space is centered around a fireplace, another around a central reader in story-telling space.

The Ravine School teacher librarian muses about how the removal of the library/computer lab wall and the opening up and integrating of physical spaces is reflected in the cognitive activities of the students.

> *All along we kept saying the problem is…we really need a connection between the two rooms [the computer lab separated from the library by a solid wall] so that there can be an easier flow, so that maybe [the technology specialist] can come over [to the library] sometimes or I can go over [to the computer lab]. At least the kids don't have to walk around. It's to facilitate that going back and forth of ideas and movement of the children themselves. [The architects and engineers designed the space for back and forth flow]. We were simply chosen by the [Board] to be the first school, the or the second school. That had walls removed.*

The transformed physical area of the computer lab/library pushes and at once supports pedagogical possibilities. Working with contemporary and traditional literacies, electronic and paper texts, students and educators alike enter this space where mutually confirming dialogic relationships are mapped out between and among people and all kinds of texts. The principle of breaking down the physical walls effectively creates a climate for inclusive learning, encompassing both modernist notions of 20th century hierarchically organized print literacies, based on historically sanctioned writers, and evolving postmodern 21st century screen literacies. Within this space of mutual respect and mutual accessibility, teachers and students effectively develop and share knowledge about using computers for learning, employing truly multimedia resources and blending knowledge that crests the wave of technology with more classical ways of knowing. At Ravine School, the theoretical underpinnings work with, not against, the interminability of knowledge itself. As such, this formal space for learning is open to both the transformative and disruptive moments that shape the very nature of learning experiences.

TEACHING AND LEARNING AT RAVINE SCHOOL

Veidi, a Grade six student, comments about how the triad program with computers has changed his life as a student and has helped him to do things he would otherwise be unable to do. In his triad schoolwork, he fluidly moves back and forth between the library and computer lab, between print and screen literacies;

> *I think computers have helped us a lot throughout because...if you want to research in a book, the book might be a 1996 [text about] the Olympics, and...you need [information] on the 2000 Olympics. [Those] books are still not out, [not yet] published. So you could go [onto] the Internet, [and] you could get updated facts about the [2000] Olympics.*

At Ravine School a grounding premise might be stated as *we all learn and teach together.* Simply put, teachers at Ravine School support specialists who share a vision of facilitating collaborative and innovative approaches to knowledge construction and of promoting students' active involvement with processes of learning. Teachers with little confidence in their computer literacy are involved in triads because they have valuable knowledge and experience in other fields. In this way, a fluid sharing of knowledges, literacies, pedagogies, abilities, and resources is facilitated. One of the triad teachers, Belinda, echoes these understandings.

> *But where my teaching comes through is working with the computer teacher, I'm part of a triad. And [when] I meet with my other two partners, we plan cooperatively what I'm going to do. I can't do it all on my own yet. I have ideas and [our computer technology specialist] will then take the ideas, [and see] that they're carried through. [B]ut in all fairness, the computer work is done in the computer lab with [the] computer teacher teaching. I attended the*

classes and I sit with the kids and as [our computer teacher] is telling kids what to do, I'm teaching it at the very same time. I need a lot of support, though. The classroom information comes from me but not the technology.

The teaching and learning experiences of teachers and students alike illustrate how the triad conception situated in an open, fluid library-computer lab space facilitates teacher-student, teacher-teacher, and student-teacher collaborations through dialogue and exchange.

MAIN STREET SCHOOL

Main Street School is located on the outskirts of an industrial area within the city of Toronto. Main Street School, like Ravine School, is a mid-sized school of about 400 students. The school teaches Junior Kindergarten through Grade 5 students. Main Street School is situated in a mixed-income neighborhood in which high-density, partly subsidized rental housing is interspersed with middle class single dwellings. The principal informs us that Main Street School students live, overwhelmingly, in the low cost high-rise accommodation. Children living in better circumstances in this traditionally Roman Catholic neighborhood, into which the newly arrived families of Main Street School students have moved, attend the neighborhood Catholic school.

The Main Street School student body is highly multicultural; students speak a wide variety of languages other than English at home come from the low socio-economic status typical of newly arrived working class immigrants. Boxes of mittens sit on a shelf, destined for children whose families cannot afford what are not luxuries in Toronto's climate. In order to help introduce families to ways of life in Toronto, the school provides an extensive outreach program, which includes, among other things, the provision of information on social services translated into numerous languages. During our visits to Main Street School over the course of a week in December, during which a massive snowstorm all but paralyzed the city, we had the opportunity to see the school putting into action its philosophy of community outreach – a philosophy which equally underpins the incorporation of ICT in education at Main Street School.

ICT AS AN INNOVATION AT MAIN STREET SCHOOL

In contrast to Ravine School, ICT is approached at Main Street School less as a particular curricular innovation and more as a mobilizing force in equalizing opportunity for the children who attend the school. The school sees itself as a social resource for the community.

[This is a community where the income levels are not very high, and access to technology is very limited; a lot of them are new immigrants. So they are still getting used to coming in and living in Canada....[We] had to provide them with technology in the schools because they are not the kind of community that would even go to a library. The kids tend not to have access to the kinds of technology or other life experiences that [other] kids would. (Principal, Main Street School)

The staff's – and the leadership's – shared vision of ICT is a logical outcome of its overall commitment to meeting the needs of the community the school serves, particularly in relation to concerns of equity. Issues relating to their students' perceived disadvantages include teacher perceptions of inequities between the students at Main Street School and those at other schools as well as their concerns about the students' access to technology, home backgrounds, academic skills, and opportunities. The principal states emphatically that ICT implementation

is very clearly aligned to our school plan; it is very clearly aligned to the initiatives that we have determined and we have to address in this school. Some of them are equity issues and one of them that comes readily to mind is the whole issue around females and access to technology.

INNOVATIVE LEARNING SPACES

At Main Street School, like Ravine Street School, the library is an open, integrated space intertwining digital and paper text literacies. Part of this fluidly designed, circular space is an open amphitheater where readings and performances can take place. In such a space, more traditional understandings of textuality are opened up to include post-modern screen literacies and performative texts. Conceptions of literacy introduced to school children are thus significantly broadened and made more contemporary.

Whereas at Ravine School the librarian works hand-in-hand with the teaching computer specialist, at Main Street School the librarian *is* the teaching computer specialist. Computers are interspersed with bookshelves in the library such that there is no discernable architectural division between library and lab. In addition, classrooms are equipped with a small number of networked computers. Students are supplied with intranet email facilities as well as various software packages.

EQUITY CONCERNS

The school community is perceived by the principal as one in which, for cultural reasons, parents "tend to spend more time with their boys than with the girls in terms of getting homework done" – whether this is directly related to ICT or not. Although the principal acknowledges that there are no simple solutions, efforts are made to "find appropriate software that would hook [girls] into using technology and not shying away from it." Given that girls' "confidence level is much lower especially vis-à-vis technology…we certainly want to track whether looking at particular software applications is going to engage the [girls] much more."

One concern about equal access voiced by the principal is grounded in issues of the special needs of some students, while others are founded on the issue of unequal access to all educational resources, including but not limited to computer technologies. For example, music is cited as a program that has benefited from the cost-effective implementation of ICT:

> *[The computer allows a greater equity towards achieving [access to music education for all students]…[M]usic is an expensive pursuit and it's usually mostly upper class that's able to afford it. (Teacher, Main Street School)*

This example falls under the umbrella of socio-economic issues, with respect to which the former Main Street School vice-principal also has a point to make. She believes that for students from

> *a school that does not have a strong ICT program and students who do not have computers at home…[there will be] a big gap between those, and schools that do have a strong program, and students who go home to computers. This is one of the negatives in terms of our own greater society. Schools in lower socio-economic areas are disadvantaged.*

But students' exposure to technology is not the only issue. Another important equity-related concern, arising from the fact that many families are relatively new to Canada, is that students may be at a linguistic and academic disadvantage because it is believed that the language and educational backgrounds of their parents may provide limited exposure to the kinds of communication and literacy practices expected and valued by the school. A teacher at Main Street School observes:

> *Most of our kids are Canadian born but a large percentage of their parents are rural Vietnamese families where they didn't have schooling. So the problems that we've experienced because of that are more of the communication problems. Clearly they don't know how to write a sentence, they don't know any of that because their parents can't provide them with that kind of support. Their oral language is Vietnamese but they can't even read to them in Vietnamese because they are illiterate in their own language. So that's more of an issue, more than money.*

It is important to consider the ways in which issues of equity are addressed at Main Street School, especially as they relate to and inform choices that are made about ICT. It is a widespread phenomenon within education that much ICT implementation does not go a great distance beyond what de Castell, Bryson, and Jenson (2000) identify as the "remarkably traditional content that we deliver by computer, on CD-ROM or via the web, using few of the tools of the computer or the web beyond their capacities for display and distribution." While it may be the case that competent use of technology requires substantial literacy skills, many of which are those skills traditionally understood to contribute to school success, it is important to note that too much emphasis on the skills alone, without consistent efforts to use both skills and technology in new ways, can actually result in fewer demands and the resulting creation of deskilled individuals (Aronowitz & DiFazio, 1994). One reason for this emphasis on "the basics," however that term is defined in an ICT implementation context, might simply be that educators themselves have not yet discovered ways in which to implement technology less traditionally. Another reason might be, as discussed above, that hegemonic views prevail: education functions primarily as a conservative institution that tends to reproduce the social conditions in which it operates.

Teaching and Learning at Main Street School

The principal has decorated the school halls with works of art and philosophical quotes from international sources alongside student-generated art. Also prominent in the halls is evidence of the awards teachers at this school have won. The principal at Main Street School believes in her teaching staff and supports them through trial and error in new ways of teaching and learning, as does the principal at Ravine School. The school is committed to providing each teacher with a laptop computer in order to make education more portable, and to encourage teachers to be more exploratory with software outside school hours. Given its reliance on portable classrooms, the school is also looking to acquire more wireless technology. The goal of going wireless is an additional response to the school's commitment to extend flexibility in the use of computers in the school, with the aim of encompassing a broader community focus, although insurance and other difficulties have yet to be resolved.

In addition to the more traditional uses of ICT at Main Street School there have been several initiatives that have engaged technology with student learning beyond the walls of the school, including a newspaper production project. This kind of initiative, which extends both curriculum and technology and gives students the opportunity to do "real" work, constitutes more than an effort on the part of the school to make curriculum "fun" for students. Such projects also make connections between classroom practices and the kinds of life experiences that result in authentic learning for students.

Educators at Main Street School are also engaged in mutually supportive learning networks which, while not tied directly to curriculum, as is the triad program at Ravine School, function to guide and support new teachers. "Supervision for Growth" is a mentorship program at Main Street School that links beginning teachers with more experienced staff members and with the principal, and supports their personal and pedagogical development in the use of ICT. The principal describes how new teachers have created "growth plans," which

> *because of the heavy emphasis on technology had to do with how they see technology. Some of them wanted to look at literacy, some of them wanted to look at social studies. They identified basically the areas that they [were] going to focus on for the year. Myself, the*

> *vice principal, the senior [teacher], and the beginning teacher would work closely as a unit.*

The Main Street School community has adopted teaching and learning practices that are new, surprising and potentially beneficial for the entire community, particularly for the students. Simply put, while the educators at Main Street School articulate concerns about their students with respect to questions of equity, including gender equity, socio-economic disadvantage, and what are generally known as lesser "life chances," they also acknowledge that unlike in most areas of curriculum, where teachers are expected to be "knowers" – Freire's depositors – who pass on their knowledge to students, in the case of new information technologies, this is not always so: indeed often it is emphatically *not* the case. Still, it can be exceedingly difficult for teachers to give up what they might perceive as their position of power within the classroom. Despite the inevitable growing pains which result when popular and yet restrictive models of schooling are challenged by more equitable approaches, students at Main Street School have been encouraged to take up the role of "teacher" – both with students and even with teachers – actually helping both teacher and students to acquire new skills and to work in different ways.

ICT thus extends present models for pedagogical change, and reinforces new meanings for *collaboration* and *collegiality* within the school. The idea of students-teaching-teachers can be seen as threatening in educational circles still grounded, even if unknowingly, in a banking model of education. However, such practices can empower students with the knowledge that they have useful and significant contributions to make to teaching and learning within the school community as a whole. Students teaching teachers can re-orient power relationships within classrooms, giving students a more equitable voice in relation to the authority figure of the teacher; and can suggest to other students, who perhaps might not have the confidence or the skills to take on such a role themselves, that it is possible for learners to contribute to the life of the classroom in active positions of leadership rather than as mere respondents to the teacher's input. It can free the teacher as well as the students, for example, by allowing teachers to provide more individual attention to students who need it. Main Street School staff members, commenting about ICT, tell us:

> *Right now we have some students that are well ahead of many*

adults in the building and are actually demonstrating for the teachers and helping teachers out. I see that happening frequently. (Principal, Main Street School)

A couple of my kids brought in CDs they had at home and showed them....I have learnt a lot from the kids....I love that. Once they've shown it to me, I would tell the class that Jerry has brought in a CD and he is going to show how to use it. So I have the kid show the whole class rather than just me....It gives them confidence and ownership. (Teacher, Main Street School)

[What has to be done is to] do PD for the teachers to build the skill level of the teachers and wait for that to trickle down to students. Or you build the skill level of the students and have them adopt the skills and then sort of influence teachers. (Librarian, Main Street School)

Of course, such change is not only possible in the realm of information technology. In all areas of curriculum there may often be activities at which some children excel that could be shared with, or taught to, their peers and their teachers. But in the normalized discourse of education, it is rare for such possibilities to be considered. One speculation is that the very characteristic of technology – as new, challenging, and less familiar to educators than to some of their students – may help both teachers and learners to negotiate practices of pedagogy that gesture toward Freire's suggestion of a potential model of "teacher-student and students-teachers" that "breaks with the vertical patterns characteristic of banking education..." (1998: 61). That is, the novelty of ICT itself might open up the possibility for such a change to pedagogy, giving new meaning to *collaboration* and *collegiality* within the school.

The changes in pedagogical practices at Main Street School – specifically both the mentoring programs and the development of a student-as-teacher/teacher-as-student model – mark the beginnings of a new pedagogical project, one which might involve educators learning to think in new ways about the possibilities for learners to direct their own learning, and to interact in mutually beneficial ways with other learners and other teachers in a community. And this returns us to the original idea of Main Street School as a community of individuals working together to accomplish the common goal of learning.

IDENTIFYING WALLS

In the context of education there are many walls that cannot be seen. Tearing down the material wall between the library and the computer lab at Ravine School led to other intangible walls being dismantled. An obvious first step, in asking how challenges are met, obstacles are confronted, and such metaphorical/theoretical walls are torn down, is identifying those challenges and obstacles. For those implementing ICT it is important to know what the wall is, what it is made of, in order to work at climbing over, working around, or pushing through it.

EXTERNAL WALLS BETWEEN SCHOOL AND COMMUNITY

At Ravine School, the principal, teachers, and students focus collaboratively on challenges of pedagogical, ICT, and social concerns in the working of the triad formulation: hence, the removal of traditional pedagogical and physical walls within the school building. One of the challenges now facing Ravine School is the question of how to begin to meaningfully break down walls between the school and the community. Ravine School is actively seeking ways in which to foster the kinds of rich approaches to moving beyond and jumping over the walls separating school and community that have been undertaken at Main Street School.

At Main Street School, the teachers perceive social and pedagogical challenges within the school itself, and obstacles in the relations between the school and the community it serves, as at least partially surmountable by ICT. Yet they also perceive distinct – though ultimately related – difficulties concerning both ICT as such and its implementation.

GIRLS' AND BOYS' SPACES

Other less visible, and more educationally insidious walls also exist. de Castell (2001) points out that in schools, computer labs are typically seen as boys' spaces, whereas libraries are seen as girls' spaces. The architectures of both Ravine School and Main Street School carefully merge these gendered territories so that there is a flow not only of interconnecting literary resources, but also of social comfort zones in accessing those literacies.

In *Object Lessons: Critical Visions of Educational Technology* (2000), de Castell, Bryson, and Jenson state that in "the usual power structure of the culture [of] school-based computing...girls are absent and silent, and their absence and silence are typically invisible to their teachers". In another paper (1996), de Castell and Bryson point out that this "invisibility" must be understood within the context of schools generally. "School contexts," they argue, "are locales where scripts for the enactment of appropriate gender identities are always already entrenched ...". In other words, within and outside the context of formal schooling, performance of gender has predefined roles: the partriarchal culture that scripts these roles also enforces the scripts. With respect to relations with computers, for example, it is expected that girls are to be timid and apprehensive. Given the ways in which gender performances are cemented into the landscape of formal schooling, perhaps not surprisingly gender inequities were not perceived by the teachers interviewed to be a barrier in the use of computers at Ravine School. Echoing conclusions reached by other participants in the study, one teacher asserted: "I haven't seen any differentiation in gender." (Teacher, Ravine School)

At Main Street School, in contrast, while some participants, such as the former vice-principal, found "no differences between boys and girls," others did note qualitative distinctions between girls' and boys' interactions with technology. The principal, for example, wondered: "Why do [girls] tend not to be attracted by technology? Is it just the hardware or is it the...kinds of software...out there that [are] much more attractive for young boys than for young girls?" Observing that girls' "confidence level is much lower especially vis-à-vis technology," she asserted that her goal was "to track whether looking at particular software applications is going to engage the women much more."

The librarian recounted similar observations in relation to boys' and girls' attitudes toward ICT:

I have library helpers and I try to sort of keep a diverse group. What might happen occasionally is that you would have student helpers that may be a little bit more male-dominated [though] I am sensitive to that, I don't see it much.

He went on to recall showing a class a software application related to website creation:

> *Two days after I showed them, there was a little group of boys there and all they wanted to do was create their own [website]...You [could] see that they [had] just sort of taken the ball and were going to work on it that night to build a Web site. I didn't notice that in the girls, it wasn't that kind of excitement.*

Like the principal, the distinctions the librarian noted between girls and boys were differences in interest, confidence and motivation.

> *I don't see any differences in terms of skill, in terms of capability, and in terms of whom I would depend on. I think the key variable here is if students have had time on tasks and time on the computers, there is no difference.*

TECHNOLOGICAL PROBLEMS

The Ravine and Main Street School communities benefit from a widely shared vision of the importance and usefulness of ICT in education. Inevitably, however, technical difficulties do arise, and in addition, lack of government funding and support have a major impact on the acquisition and maintenance of hardware and software, as well as on opportunities for professional development. It is worth examining how the staff at Main Street and Ravine Schools manage to persevere with the implementation of information technology.

On the most material level, ICT can only be implemented if it is available, if it works, and if teachers know how to use it. The computer teacher-librarian at Main Street School concisely summarized this issue, saying that a successful implementation requires that "things work and [the teachers] have support and time to learn." Teachers at Ravine School also stated that there simply weren't enough computers. Other teachers spoke frequently of feeling frustration when computer hardware was not available or not functioning properly. Among them is one teacher for whom this issue is closely tied to teacher resistance to ICT implementation:

> *I think resistance to technology has occurred because of frustration of the effectiveness of the machines....[P]eople go in and they want the kids to all do this database and make this chart or something and half the computers don't work or the printers don't work. After that occurs numerous times, people stop using [the computer equipment]. They can only tolerate so much of that.*

Relatedly, the librarian at Main Street School commented on the need for sufficient hardware and software to justify planning time for the use of technology in a busy classroom:

So if a teacher is doing a reading group and she has seven students in it, for her to program, you'll only have one disk – it's not efficient. But [if] she s/he has four machines and you can put two earphones in each,...[there are] eight potential spots here, that's a reading group, that's worth my time....

One very computer-savvy teacher maintained that without support (including informal technical support and professional development), and without sufficient hardware (laptop computers), "resistance was a genuine fear, not an attitudinal thing." She continued,

Why wouldn't you have resistance? ...[You] plan this great activity, for half a day you've got the lab booked and the WIN is down and you can't do anything. So it's very frustrating.

Technological obsolescence was cited as another frustration: "Some of the programs haven't been adapted to the faster machines, which is sad, because the old machines aren't being repaired."

At Ravine School, where staff also alluded to increased workloads, less preparation time and fewer professional development opportunities, a creative budgeting solution was developed for these problems, viewed as emanating from the continuing serious erosion of funding and time that teachers in Ontario have been struggling with under the present government. Whereas in both schools it was noted that school volunteers, largely comprising parents of children attending the school, played an essential and highly valued role assisting teachers and administrators where required throughout the school, these were generally roles requiring human warmth and understanding as opposed to particular pedagogical skills. Through creative budgeting at Ravine School, a source of funding was located for the hiring of a technically competent paid teaching assistant, whose role included trouble-shooting technical breakdowns. At both schools, the combination of a shared pedagogical vision, and an orientation toward collaboration with respect to ICT, encouraged and maintained by strong leadership on the part of the principal and several other key individuals, enables the staff collaboratively to deal with problems that inevitably arise with the more technical aspects of ICT implementation.

DOING IT ALL

Theoretically oriented concerns about curricular requirements on one hand, and student learning on the other, result in tensions. In the view of one teacher:

The only resistance is that there's probably a worry that with the focus on technology that area perhaps may need some really important aspect of literacy and the needs of the students might be ignored.

Concerns about meeting the requirements of the curriculum and time constraints are echoed by teachers at Ravine School:

It's just that we're loaded with everything else, it's trying to find time to allow the children onto the computers. My kids don't get on often enough in the classroom, because I'm afraid that if they're on that, then they're missing the other lesson and if they're doing their research or they're doing some reading on the computer, then they're missing their spelling or their missing their math or they're missing their science. It's just really difficult with all the other stuff that we have to present to find time in the classroom to do computers. (Teacher, Ravine School)

One of the main constraints, of course you'll probably hear a lot about, is time. There isn't enough time to teach these kids so much of what they could be learning right now. And the thing is that when they're at this age, it's just like learning languages, they're learning all these skills on the computers, and I'm sure everything else. And they sort of retain them for a long time, for the rest of their life; these are life-long skills. And so the more they can learn right now, I think the better off they are. And first of all they don't get enough time using the computers. Even in a school like this, they don't have enough time for computers, which they could be using for all different subject areas and stuff. And then there is equipment, so there are more computers and then more teachers who know how to use it in the classroom and they could be doing this. And I'm just happy to help and guide the teachers and the children as to what software to use for different areas. So I can see it totally integrated and it's not as much as I would like to see it because of those factors. (Computer teacher, Ravine School)

Some teachers, particularly older members of the staff, expressed candidly their fears of using computer equipment:

I'm always afraid that I'd do something to the computer or the program that is going to fry it. And my son keeps telling me, You can't do that, mom. There is nothing you can do that's going to bother the machine, just shut it off and start over again. And it's just that comfort level, it's improving but...

Another, more digitally literate teacher also found that a lack of ICT expertise, and a corresponding lack of time for sufficient professional development, hampered the implementation and increased resistance. She related:

I think that some teachers are really genuinely scared of technology. ... There is a belief that teachers don't believe in technology, and I don't feel that anyone has said that. I think that they are just afraid because there hasn't been the PD. Professional Development days have been taken away so there is no time for it.

The computer teacher-librarian at Main Street School explains further that

[We have teachers who just have not had an opportunity to see how to integrate [ICT]... They've sort of been overwhelmed with perhaps software or hardware glitches that have shown up. That happens all the time. If there weren't people to persevere, I don't know what would have happened to a lot of technologies, but they just don't have the time and inclination.

A corresponding problem is the load on those who have technological expertise:

One of the other barriers, if you want to look at it that way, is if you have a limited number of people who have the expertise like Lorraine, you burn her out. And I think this is quite a major problem that the government needs to look at and the Board and everybody else, because they are going to whoever your expert is. So you need to spread the expertise base, and we've tried to do that. In fact, we talked about it at the staff meeting...[S]o you tell yourself, 'We've got to do something about this. So we're going to change Lorraine's timetable a little bit and we're going to identify people here in the primary wing and if you have a problem, would you please ask Andrew or ask Denise. If you're in the junior wing, you know, there are several people, try ask somebody else before you go to Lorraine.' (Principal, Ravine School)

TEARING DOWN THE WALLS

Technology is socially applied knowledge, and it is social conditions which make the crucial difference in how it is applied. (Kress, 1997: 53-54)

PEDAGOGICAL WALLS: REDEFINING THE TEACHER, THE LEARNER, AND THE LEARNING

Computers have been shown to be catalysts for social interaction if student work groups are carefully constructed (Rickards, 1996). In addition to interaction between groups of students, the process of ICT implementation has the potential to open up surprising possibilities for new and useful kinds of relationships between students and teachers.

The blossoming practice, at both Main Street and Ravine Schools, of students becoming involved in *teaching their teachers* as the latter move through the process of ICT skills acquisition, is one way in which the very newness of technology can contribute to a shift in the framing of education – from traditional transmission paradigms to innovative models of student-teacher collaboration. This kind of reframing of practice demands a concomitant theoretical gesture toward recognition of the value of the knowledge students bring with them to their encounters with education, as well as a relinquishing of traditional understandings of power relationships with the teacher-learner relationship.

LANGUAGE WALLS: WORKING TOWARDS MULTILITERACIES

Paulo Freire enjoins us not to dissociate "reading the word" from "reading the world." Becoming literate means thinking differently than one did previously, seeing the world differently, and this suggests that there are many different literacies (Papert, 1992: 10).

Balancing traditional and evolving literacies is important. Critics of technology in education, such as Stoll (1999), question where the balance point lies with children and computers, pointing out that too often ICT bulldozes prior literacies. The open library-lab spaces at Ravine School and Main Street School find a balance point between paper and screen literacies and learning how to access them separately and in tandem as purpose demands.

The majority of students at both these schools come from minority language backgrounds, a common characteristic of many schools within the Toronto District School Board. However, school literacies tend to privilege English, according little or no recognition to literacies in other languages and cultures (Lotherington, in press). Use of English is implicit in ICT.

Ravine school used a dyad model to support English language acquisition. Explained one teacher:

We have students here from whatever the country the kids are coming from and we mentor, partner off. And so they can teach each other, they can speak each others' language and the more experienced students will be working with the student who's new, so that they mentor each other beautifully.

This dyad model, we were told, extends to working with and on computers. Explaining how this is done, one teacher said:

They are buddied up with someone who knows about the computers, so it's a lot less frightening and a lot less intimidating when they have a peer showing them what to do.

At Ravine School, the types of software programs selected for students, who were in the beginning stages of learning English as a second language, were primarily icon based.

They don't even have to do anything; they just click on the different pictures and the words will come up and a song will play, or whatever. (Teacher, Ravine Street School)

The software applications used were geared toward English language acquisition, with an emphasis on explicit step-by-step mastery of phonics and whole-word skills. The selection of these particular software programs privileges one model of language acquisition to the exclusion of other models. However, while students in their beginning stages of English language acquisition were receiving instruction of a compensatory nature supported by educational software, these students were not cast off into the domain of isolated learner of basics. These students, like all students at Ravine School, simultaneously engaged in activities that required them to construct new knowledge within and amongst the larger community of learners. The combination of dyad mentoring, with and without computers, and the integration of computers at all levels is consistent with Ravine School's guiding framework of learning and teaching together.

The Main Street School librarian asserts that at the school there is a prevalent "mind-set in and around inclusivity...in terms of equity." Coupled with this mind-set is the strong belief among the staff that can arguably be generalized as a wish to serve the students well in terms of the dominant culture in which they live. Although mention is made of ways in which the school attempts to respect its community's social backgrounds, cultures and languages, the discourse that informs the teachers' and the principal's statements is one of success, comprising notions of *skill building, opportunity, getting ahead*, in terms of the dominant culture. The aim of such a vision seems to be to prepare the students for a life in the English-speaking, Canadian middle class. That this goal is of primary importance may be controversial, but it is not surprising. While of course not the only objective possible, it is one on which much of current education is based: schools function to reproduce the structures and norms of the dominant groups in society (Hodas 1993). In sum, the teachers' general view is that the acquisition of computer skills as economic and cultural capital (Bourdieu, 1973) is a necessary prerequisite to later life success for all students. In the words of the principal,

> *the whole society has sped up so much in terms of information technology...[so that] if you even hope to keep up and position yourself to be successful in life, you need to have access to the computer age. So for these kids to be successful in life, whether we like it or not, that is how the world is working.*

This assertion indicates the uncritical pervasiveness of English as the carrier of technoculture; a melding of the notion of literacy and English, which is characteristic of literacy assessment mechanisms in Ontario as well as further afield in other English-dominant cultures (Lotherington, in press). Hawisher & Selfe, however, critique the modernist notion of the global village – a virtual space operating in the main in a sort of cyberEnglish – which they suggest is a colonial notion of highly technologized western nations (2000:28). They suggest a far more fractured future in terms of identities constructed through digital media that increasingly forge collectivities through particularized global communities that include languages amongst other social threads.

SOCIAL WALLS: REDEFINING COMMUNITY

The concept of *community* has been redefined in the context of Main Street School, which is open to the families of its students in technologically as well as socially inviting ways. A more seamless notion of education is created within the school community by dissolving the walls that traditionally isolate teachers within grade or subject-specific classrooms, as well as those separating the school from the community. This sense of the school expanding its reach into the community is in sharp contrast with dystopian visions forecasting the demise of the school as a social institution (Papert, 1980: 177), although in both scenarios, ICT is seen as a facilitating influence.

Additionally, working towards a vision of more socially equitable experiences of schooling, traditionally gendered library-lab territories have been merged in both Ravine and Main Street Schools.

LEADERSHIP: BREAKING DOWN SCHOOL HIERARCHIES

Collaboration is a hallmark of both Ravine and Main Street Schools; it is part of an overarching school culture that permeates all areas of school life. It comes about in large part as a result of the leadership that the principals provide. From hiring practices that focus on engaging staff who "believe in the kinds of things that we believe in here" (Principal, Main Street School) to the mentorship program known as *Supervision for Growth* at Main Street School, to the working of the triad at Ravine School collaboratively interlinking classroom teachers with the librarian and the computer specialist, the vision of both Ravine and Main Street Schools' principals is clearly the construction and maintenance of a school environment that fosters co-operative learning for everyone.

> *My sense is that [the teachers] want to learn and they come to the ICT workshops, I don't make them mandatory, they are all invitational. It is rare that [the staff] don't show up. As long as you don't make it very threatening for them. Some of us will proceed slowly, some will take giant leaps but we are all here to learn the best way we know how. (Principal, Main Street School)*

In discussion about a commitment to people and her vision for Ravine School, the principal's growing articulation of an alternative sense of professional development emerges. Her view of professional development comes from years of experience and critical reflection about how to meaningfully "design" professional development possibilities for her staff within their particular context.

> *The more you know about people, the more willing you are to disagree, and the more open you are to doing something creative. It all fits together. If people are afraid to approach the computer lab person, if they think their ideas are going to get shot down, you are not going to get any of the innovation or any other creativity. That is why…that if I go into another school and it would take a few years …I could do the same thing that has been done here [at Ravine School]. It might not be in computers, it might be in music, again, something I have no expertise in, but you build on what you have and where you have it.*

This understanding that individual teachers not only join the staff with different levels of expertise, but also that they learn in different ways and at different rates, exemplifies a philosophy that helps make it possible for teachers to confront and work through problems with information technology as such, and to work toward furthering their own technological skills as well as increasing and improving the ways they teach students both *about* and *with* ICT.

MAINTAINING TECHNOLOGICAL AND PEDAGOGICAL MOMENTUM

The guiding vision of the Ravine School principal facilitates teacher innovation, professional development, and learning through dialogic, communal notions. An inventively designed computer lab/library space optimizing multiple literacies was created. Specialized computer and library teachers were selectively and democratically hired to give shape and life to the triad concept; the school staff voted on the hiring of both teaching computing and library specialists. Collaborative teacher triad networks were facilitated across professional interests, experiential and administrative levels, and expertise, in areas both directly connected and seemingly unrelated to ICT. The Ravine School teachers we observed implementing the triad formulation are active teacher-learners. Observed also was the emergence of professional development internally within a school through dialogue, collaboration, risk taking, re-invention, and reconstruction in light of what "local" experts know, what "local" visionaries offer, and what "local" teachers and students want.

The staff at Main Street School also share a strong commitment to collaboration in the implementation of ICT, and the usefulness of such a collaborative approach is demonstrated time and again; in fact, formal professional development has proven less important than informal support from the Main Street School community itself. For example, one teacher speaks about Dorothy, a helpful computer-literate teacher, as a strong resource for her colleagues who need technical assistance, saying that

> *a lot of people don't want to go out of this school for professional development because it tends to be people who talk 'techy' talk and it goes right over your head. That's why we love having [Dorothy] here because she tells you exactly a way that you know how to use the computer and it makes sense. I know people are reluctant because they've gone to one or two [formal workshops] and they said that they didn't understand anything that they said anyway.*

It is not hard to understand why Dorothy is so appreciated. Seeing herself as a kind of "technology leader at the school," she herself demonstrates an understanding of the need to provide both technical and moral support, contending that

> *you sort of have to be a psychologist as well and support these teachers that don't have the experience and have fear about it. There's a couple of teachers who are scared but are willing to learn and you need to be really gentle with them.*

In sum, both Ravine and Main Street are schools that are working together; schools in which the lines between teacher and learner are blurred, and the educational goals are clear.

NEW LITERACIES AND NEW HORIZONS IN ELEMENTARY SCHOOLING

In a culture like ours, long accustomed to splitting and dividing all things as a means of control, it is sometimes a bit of a shock to be reminded that, in operational and practical fact, the medium is the message. This is merely to say that the personal and social consequences of any medium – that is, of any extension of ourselves – result from the new scale that is introduced into our affairs by each extension of ourselves, or by new technology...Many people would be disposed to say that it was not the machine, but what one did with the machine, that was its meaning or message (McLuhan, 1965: 7).

How has the implementation of information technology changed, and how is it changing, teaching and learning?

In these two elementary schools, teaching and learning roles have been rethought to include dialogic supports across and between school literacies, technological literacies, and communities of learners. Although the walls "torn down" in these two elementary schools are predominantly figurative, they do include material walls. At Ravine School, these were opened up to provide spaces in which new ways of teaching and learning could be facilitated. In so doing, the divide between traditional and computer literacies was also bridged; transforming the library and the computer lab into a continuous space allowing modern and postmodern literacies to be accessed in complementary ways using both paper and screen texts.

At Main Street School, the library-lab-theatre is in the round and does not have any walls. However, the curricular incorporation of ICT dismantled real, albeit theoretical, walls in pedagogy: those separating teacher from learner and those defining "the learner."

At both Main Street School and Ravine School, learners have been empowered in different ways to take on leadership roles in the classroom, where they have facilitated digital literacies. The social walls isolating teachers within classrooms have also been dismantled at Ravine School through the triad innovation, and they are being continually chipped away at through Main Street School's mentorship program and informal computer literacy support networks. Also at Main Street School, walls separating the school from the community have begun to crumble, eroding the boundaries of learning.

We leave you with questions emerging from the two schools studied. How might the innovative understandings and applications of pedagogy and ICT in both Ravine and Main Street Schools be sustained in light of changing Ontario provincial philosophies and practices of education, changing school administrative personnel, and changing teaching staff personnel? How might the understandings of these individual case studies be thought about and employed by other elementary schools?

In summary, both elementary schools have created new literacies and horizons through:

1. visionary leadership dedicated to the meaningful pedagogical inclusion of information and communication technologies;
2. an enactment of Freire's "problem posing education";
3. redefined, innovative, open library-lab spaces that collaboratively integrate ICT, pedagogy, knowledge bases, expertise, and literacies;
4. provision of opportunities for teachers to learn about ICT, resources, and related pedagogy with ongoing support given for its incorporation;
5. a dedicated teaching staff employing collaborative self-help networks; and
6. a positive school climate in which teachers are consulted, valued and supported.

As students of the digital era are forging their own new literacies and identities, teachers at Ravine and Main Street Schools are working closely with them. Everyone is learning.

NOTES

1. Ravine School and Main Street School studies are components of two larger research studies examining factors that contribute to innovative teaching with ICT: 1) the Second International Technology in Education Study (SITES) Module 2 linked to an Organisation for Economic Co-operation and Development study, and 2) the Canadian Telelearning Network of Centres of Excellence Theme 7 Educating the Educators study. The concluding discussion in the *Canada (Ontario) Pre-Pilot Report* (1999) for SITES-M2 notes that "[a]ccording to the criteria established by the SITES-M2 study, a pedagogical practice using [computer-based] technology is considered to be 'innovative' if it (1) shows evidence of significant changes in the roles of teachers, and students, the goals of the curriculum, and/or the educational materials or infrastructure, (2) shows evidence of measurable positive student outcomes, and (3) is sustainable and transferable."
2. The triad collaborative team consists of the grade level teacher, school librarian and computer specialist working in tandem to plan and teach the curriculum. In cases, more than one class teacher is involved in the grade level, so the triad consists of a three-part union, but it may

include more than three people.

REFERENCES

Aronowitz, S. and DiFazio, W. (1994). *The Jobless Future: Sci-tech and the Dogma of Work.* Minneapolis: University of Minnesota Press.

Bourdieu, P. (1973). "Cultural Reproduction and Social Reproduction." In Brown, R. (Ed.), *Knowledge, Education, and Cultural Change: Papers in the Sociology of Education* (p. 71-112). London: Tavistock.

Bryson, M. & de Castell, S. (1996). *Learning to Make a Difference: Gender, New Technologies, and In/equity.* http://www.educ.ubc.ca/faculty/bryson/gentech/learning.html

de Castell, S. (2001, March). Girls, Tools and Schools: Gender, Equity and New Information Technologies in Education. Presentation at the faculty of Education, York University, Toronto.

de Castell, S., M. Bryson, J. Jenson. (2000) *Object Lessons: Critical Visions of Educational Technology.* http://www.educ.ubc.ca/faculty/bryson/ObjectLessons.html

deCastell, S, A. Luke and C. Luke. (1989) *Language, Authority and Criticism: Readings on the School Textbook.* London: Falmer Press.

Freire, P. (1998). *Pedagogy of the Oppressed* (M.B. Ramos, Trans.). New York: Continuum. (original work published 1970)

Gee, J.P. (1994). *Social Linguistics and Literacies: Ideology in Discourses.* London: Taylor & Francis.7

Glaser, B. & Strauss, A. (1967). *The Discovery of Grounded Theory.* Chicago: Aldine.

Hawisher, G.E. & Selfe, C.L. (2000). "Conclusion: Inventing Postmodern Identities: Hybrid and Transgressive Literacy Practices on the Web." In G.E. Hawisher & C.L. Selfe (Eds.), *Global Literacies and the World-wide Web* (pp. 277-289). Longon: Routledge.

Hodas, S.S. (1993). "Technology Refusal and the Organizational Culture of Schools." In *Educational Policy Analysis Archives, 1*(10):1-19.

Kress, G. (1997). "Visual and Verbal Modes of Representation in Electronically Mediated Communication: The Potential for New Forms of Text." In I. Snyder (Ed.), *Page to Screen: Taking Literacy into the Electronic Era* (pp. 53-79). St. Leonards, NSW: Allen & Unwin.

Lankshear, C. J., Gee, M., Knobel, and C. Searle (1997). *Changing Literacies.* Buckingham, UK: Open University Press.

Lotherington, H. (2000, November). ESL Literacy and New Media:

Reshaping Literacies in the Age of Information. Invited plenary address presented at TESL Ontario 2000, Toronto.

Lotherington, H. (in press). "Multiliteracies in Springvale: Negotiating Language, Culture and Identity in Suburban Melbourne." In R. Bayley & S. Schechter (Eds.), *Language Socialization and Bilingualism*. Clevedon: Multilingual Matters.

McLuhan, M. (1965). *Understanding Media: The Extensions of Man*. New York: McGraw-Hill.

Morbey, M.L., Lotherington, H. & Doan, L. (2001, April). Lessons From an Elementary School: Thinking, Space, Computers, Innovation. Paper presented at the 2001 Annual Meeting of the American Educational Research Association, Seattle, Washington.

Nardi, B. & O'Day, V. (1999). *Information Ecologies: Using Information with Heart*. Cambridge, MA: MIT Press.

Papert, S. (1980). *Mindstorms: Children, Computers and Powerful Ideas* (2nd edition). New York: Basic Books.

Papert, S. (1992). *The Children's Machine: Rethinking School in the Age of the Computer*. New York: Basic Books.

Rickards, H. (1996). "Getting the Best Out of Computer Technology in Primary Schools." In T. Gill (Ed.), *Electronic Children: How Children are Responding to the Information Revolution*. London: National Children's Bureau.

Stoll, C. (1999). *High-tech Heretic: Why Computers Don't Belong in the Classroom and Other Reflections By a Computer Contrarian*. New York: Doubleday.

Strauss, A. & Corbin, J. (1990). *Basics of Qualitative Research: Grounded Theory, Procedures and Techniques*. Newbury Park, CA: Sage.

Chapter 7
Lessons Learned

Three Case Studies of ICT in Teaching and Their Implications for Practice

Herbert H. Wideman and Ronald D. Owston

Teachers and other educators are continuing to envision and develop ever more varied ways of applying ICT to teaching and learning. Already, only a decade after the first widespread distribution of computers in schools, a practicing educator faces a bewildering sea of choices when deciding how best to make use of this new tool. The relative ease with which ICT can be configured and adapted to varying pedagogical styles and learning needs, the possibilities for interactivity and communication it offers, and the broad range of curriculum to which it can be applied have fostered this explosive growth, and as the technology becomes ever more powerful, the trend will accelerate. Teachers need to know how to separate the wheat from the chaff by understanding the factors that contribute to the educational effectiveness of different forms of ICT use, and here is where educational research can make a significant contribution. In this chapter, we explore the findings from our studies of several very different applications of ICT in education, and review the factors that contributed to their success or failure. These cases provide a vision of the possibilities and problems that ICT use can bring to the classroom. We also consider the lessons to be learned from these cases that can assist practicing teachers in making the most of ICT's educational potential while avoiding mistakes that might lead to wasted time and effort.

A. A Comparative Study of Two Online Learning Projects

In our first study, we investigated the inter-relationship of implementation processes, pedagogical perspectives and practices, and perceived outcomes in two Canadian national telelearning projects based on different pedagogical models and delivery systems, one of which was judged by participating teachers to be more successfully implemented than the other. By means of a comparative analysis of the two programs, we sought to determine what teacher and practice factors contributed to their relative success or failure, and to describe how these factors interacted with implementation concerns.

The two projects we studied were Writers in Electronic Residence (WIER) and the Satellite Networked Schools (SNS) project. WIER uses a Web-based conferencing system to link English and language arts students to Canadian authors, teachers, and each other for the exchange and discussion of students' original compositions. WIER is a relatively large telelearning network by Canadian standards, involving the participation of up to 120 classes in any given year from all areas of the country and including students ranging from the junior elementary to the senior high school levels. It is also one of the few Canadian projects at a mature stage of development, having been in operation for over 13 years. The SNS project linked three Canadian schools via digital satellite to a commercial curriculum content provider headquartered in the United States. Although the SNS service was well established in many schools in the US at the time of the research, only three Canadian schools had been connected. We studied all three of these sites during their first and second years of implementing the service.

WIER has three primary learning objectives: 1) making use of computer and network media to enhance students' creative autonomy and to broaden the scope and shape of classroom experience; 2) helping students to (re) consider the value of revision in the writing process and the students' role in using language to interpret and understand as well as be understood; and 3) prompting these novice writers to revisit their creative efforts in the light of the ideas that they receive and generate in their conferencing interactions with both author-mentors and their peers. Students "post" drafts of creative works into forums which the assigned author reads and then responds to, posting back comments and suggestions for revision to the student (which others accessing the conference are free to read). Students also read and respond to work posted by other schools. WIER strongly encourages participating teachers to require every student who submits a composition to provide a written response to two other student works.

SNS is a curriculum resource delivery service that was purchased by the schools primarily with the goal of enhancing mathematics and science teaching and learning. The service provided teachers in these schools unlimited access to their collection of over 12 000 videos indexed to the K-12 curriculum. Teachers interacted with company personnel via a two-way television channel to search out and select relevant videos. In addition, the company would develop "custom curriculum" upon a teacher's request, incorporating new or existing videos and live interaction with a subject specialist if desired. As part of its service, the company also provided a Web site, printed curriculum resources delivered via a faxback service, and a selection of interactive software in CDI (Compact Disk Interactive) format. To ensure that all elements of the service interoperated, the company sold a complete turnkey installation to schools, including a file server, networked computers with Internet connections, fax machines, digital satellite receivers and an antenna, TV monitors, and VCRs.

In order to investigate teachers' experiences in the WIER and SNS programs and to collect their reflections on program implementation and its effects, interviews were conducted with staff directly participating in the programs. For WIER, we interviewed teachers using the program in 11 participating schools across Canada. These teachers had recently completed or were completing 12 weeks of WIER activities with at least one class in either creative writing or language arts. (The normal duration of a WIER project is 12 weeks, however, schools may elect to participate in many projects.) In the case of the SNS program, we conducted preliminary interviews with teachers and principals at each of the three schools at the beginning of the project and returned a year later to interview the same staff on their experiences during the intervening period. A total of 38 interviews were conducted.

Our analysis of the interviews suggested that at the end of two years, the SNS project was perceived by most teachers to have had very limited success. This was especially true at the two high school sites. On the other hand, WIER was roundly praised by teachers as being a very successful online experience. The apparent success or failure of a program is obviously a function of many factors; this study focused on the teacher-related dimensions that determine the success of an online program.

One of the major factors found to be of significance to the teachers' experiences of the two programs was the nature and extent of professional training and support they received in the use of the innovation. Teacher development and support for WIER was largely limited to online activities and some written materials: no in-person training or support was provided. In an initial two-week online orientation period, teachers learned from written materials how to get connected and join the WIER forums, and how and when to post students' work. WIER also involved students in the orientation by asking them to submit brief compositions about the communities and to read and respond to others' work. WIER does not dictate the way in which their service is integrated into the classroom curriculum or what pedagogy the teachers employ in using it, but it does have tightly scheduled periods for posting new works and for reading and responding to the efforts of others that participating teachers are not free to alter. A separate forum is available throughout the program for teachers seeking answers to technical or programmatic questions; certain experienced teachers act as mentors and moderators in this forum, providing answers and pedagogical guidance.

The SNS program provided a much more intensive, face-to-face set of training and support activities for participating teachers. At the beginning of the project, teachers at all sites were trained on how to access the SNS network in a workshop led by a company project consultant. This initial training was largely devoted to understanding the technical and operational aspects of the system. After the initial training the burden was on the teachers to decide what resources they wanted to use, how they would incorporate them into their curriculum, and when and how often they used the company's services. If teachers had any difficulty with the system, they had several choices: (1) they could call the company's toll-free number and set up a video conference with support staff to answer any technical or curricular questions, (2) they could call the company's project consultant – a former assistant superintendent of a large Canadian board of education, (3) they could wait for the consultant's next scheduled visit to their school for further training and assistance, or (4) they could seek help from the head project teacher at the school who was specially trained to provide on-site support. Based on feedback and expressions of interest from participants, periodic on-site follow-up training sessions were also offered by the consultant.

Despite the greater variety and depth of the training and support offered to teachers in the SNS program, they expressed much more dissatisfaction with these facets of their program than did the WIER teachers. While SNS support staff were described as "friendly" and "helpful," there was often a lack of promised follow-up to teachers' queries about operational or curricular aspects of the program. Given the great technical complexity of the system's operation, this could be crippling. Promised video segments were frequently not delivered on time, video requests were lost, and custom-developed curriculum segments were too slow in production. Timeliness of response was a critical issue for these teachers, since they would schedule video from the program into specific time slots in their curriculum – delays in delivery or in operational support made the late materials virtually useless. Moreover, even though the company claimed that their staff were "master teachers," nearly all the high school teachers using the system found the staff's subject matter expertise wanting. Commented one teacher when asked about this issue:

The competency there is poor…there's one person who understands something about physics and I talked to him at some length and he seems to be okay. But in general, I would say, no; they're trying to stretch very, very hard to cover things. In one lesson for elementary teachers [that this teacher saw], the staff were trying to explain Newton's three laws of motion…Newton was probably turning in his grave!

Overall, the combination of insufficient training and the service provider's staff not being able to support the teachers in meaningful ways was discouraging. As one middle school teacher said:

There are no real exemplary models to show [the service's] full potential. It's kind of like stabbing at the dark, you're just reaching out and grabbing things and hoping that when you pull them through the darkness that they're going to be effective. And I think for a lot of people the time it takes and that hit and miss [approach] has really had a negative impact on people's desire to use the services.

The experience of the teachers in the WIER program was considerably more positive, despite the lack of on-site or face-to-face training or support. The initial printed training materials provided to participants, along with the two weeks of orientation and training activities offered through the WIER conferencing system, made it possible for teachers to access and use the conferencing system with little difficulty, although in schools with networked computers some onsite technical support to establish an initial connection was sometimes provided by a computer teacher or technician. Teachers found the opportunity to raise questions and issues with more experienced peers and WIER staff in the online staff forum met nearly all of their support needs beyond localized technical issues. A few teachers did remark that they found the initial exposure to the WIER FirstClass desktop with its numerous "writing salon" folders for different grades a little overwhelming, and thought it should have a simpler user interface for the orientation period.

The most interesting question here is why, despite its much greater commitment of resources to training and support, the SNS program was considered far weaker on these dimensions by program participants. One important element was the relative degree of technical and operational complexity of the two programs. While WIER did make considerable logistical demands on teachers, obligating them to upload and download numerous compositions and comments to appropriate forums on a regular basis, it only required teachers to master one fairly straightforward conferencing system. SNS, on the other hand, forced users to learn a range of more complex services – selecting and using different software programs, working with SNS staff to search its 12 000 title video library for appropriate resources, previewing and scheduling video delivery, and placing orders for the creation of custom video segments. The technical and operational demands of this far more complex program were sometimes overwhelming despite the available support. Equally important, while the scale and range of training and support options for WIER were far more limited, they were more carefully targeted to the immediate practical needs of programme participants. Orientation materials walked new users through introductory activities that allowed them to become comfortable with WIER operations prior to involving students in the program. Students were given orientation before beginning the process of sending drafts to authors.

The timeliness of the responses provided to enquiries was a third element in WIER's favor. When a teacher wanted to discuss a pedagogical issue or an operational concern, experienced teacher-mentors would respond promptly to questions posted in the teacher forum. SNS users, on the other hand, could experience delays of days or weeks in getting needed information – if they got it at all.

In addition to the nature of the training and support provided, two other factors did much explain teacher experiences of these two programs. These were (1) the teachers' perceptions of the value of the program for students, and (2) the congruence between the pedagogy implicit in the program and the teachers' own practices. The SNS project fared poorly on both criteria. While a few teachers did find some elements of the program, such as specific video segments or live teleconferences, educationally valuable and relevant for their students, the overall perception of the low levels of quality and curriculum "fit" of the materials being delivered was such that teachers found the service to be of marginal value. Canadian content was lacking, and materials provided as appropriate for a given grade level were usually found to be too simple.

At the SNS sites, the decision to acquire the service was made by senior board personnel; teachers were not involved in the process (with the exception of one teacher who recommended against acquisition). The expectation was that teachers would make routine use of the service: at the middle school, SNS was to be used by all classroom teachers; at the high schools the focus was chiefly on use by mathematics and science teachers. This expectation put pressure on teachers to change their practice in ways that were not necessarily congruent with their pedagogical beliefs, practices, or goals. Even when teachers were able to obtain resources that were both timely and on topic, most were not particularly happy with the pedagogical approach employed by the SNS producers. Said one middle school teacher:

> *I personally don't like the approach that they tend to take with a lot of the Social Studies things. They seem to have a lot of B movie actors, dressing up in strange costumes and acting silly and pretending to be Einstein or whatever. I guess the disappointment for us is that as a middle school, it's the sort of thing where we would have the kids dress up in silly costumes and do the research, find out enough about it and put their own skit on. Instead, this is adults doing it for kids.*

On the surface, ordering custom curriculum appeared to be the solution to inappropriate stock resources. However, as another teacher explained, even the custom material was found to be wanting because of its design:

> *Each teacher has a reality of what he's trying to get across and in most cases, when this material is being presented from a different way of life or bias, it doesn't come across the way you want it.*

A few teachers did see the SNS materials as providing a different, non-teacher directed vehicle for learning, some of which could be self-paced. By employing a number of different media for information delivery, the SNS resources brought variety to the learning process, which would sometimes heighten students' motivation to learn:

The main thing is that the kids like being there. That's a huge asset. Some of the things on the disks are kind of fun. There'd be a little game the kids can play, like answering against a certain time and they're given a score. And there are things that we're doing in class, so its kind of fun for them and it practices certain skills.

But even then the role of SNS resources in the classroom was largely subsidiary. As one teacher put it,

I would strictly use this entire package as support for what I am already doing. I can't see it replacing me. Perhaps for small lessons I could completely rely on the computers to do that. Probably very rarely…

The experience of teachers using the WIER program offers a dramatic contrast to the disappointments experienced with SNS. Both in terms of perceived value and congruence with pedagogical beliefs, WIER received a strong thumbs-up from participants. With only one exception, the 30 or so teachers interviewed considered the educational value of the WIER experience to be very significant, with its benefits outweighing all the challenges and demands it imposed. Even the one teacher who was "somewhat disappointed" with the outcomes from her classes' involvement with WIER considered this to be an artifact of the rushed implementation and her lack of experience – it was her first exposure to WIER – and she still hoped to use it the following year, as she thought it had great potential.

The most frequently cited desirable outcome was a significant jump in students' motivation to write. For the great majority of students, having access to professional authors as an audience for their creative efforts generated considerable enthusiasm for writing and posting stories and poems. "You could see the enthusiasm" was a typical teacher comment.

The contributions made by the professional authors were found to be valuable for several reasons. Teachers saw them as bringing an element of expertise and authenticity to the student writing process they could not provide on their own:

> *I think it's a fantastic opportunity for students to have feedback from published authors. People who are working daily at writing. That's a kind of experience that I, although I'm a teacher, can't bring...to bear on their work.*

The quality of the commentary that these authors provided was praised by most of the teachers. In the words of one teacher:

> *I loved how positive the comments were – how constructive they were...every little thing, a spelling error was well looked at and deeply and thoroughly just considered and I think the kids really appreciated that. It made me realize, well, the kids really do like to have a lot of time spent on their stuff...but also that maybe you can achieve it verbally.*

WIER was seen by many of the teachers as helping students develop the ability to take constructive criticism in the way it was intended rather than as a personal affront. As one teacher put it, "They are more comfortable with me looking at the criticism and asking me for suggestions or direction as a result of the criticism." Another teacher, reflecting on students' growth as writers over the course of the WIER program, cited the value of learning from critiques:

> *[They're better writers] because they have gone through that experience of having people respond to their work. And that's a huge hurdle to get over, to be willing to expose your writing to other people. So I would say all of these kids who come through it, partly as a result of WIER, will be more ready to have their writing looked at by other people.*

Several participating teachers cited a growth in self-confidence in writing on the part of many of their students. For some, this seemed to lead to a general increase in the student's self-esteem.

In addition to valuing the outcomes of the WIER program, teachers found the philosophy and pedagogy embedded in its practices to fit comfortably with their own methods and goals. Its process-writing orientation was in accord with the pedagogical approaches to writing taken by the more expert teachers in the program, who were for the most part employing a manner of instruction modeled on the Writers' Workshop. In the words of one teacher,

> *It's sort of like a chicken and egg situation, you know. You get involved in WIER because you have a certain philosophy of how*

> *students should write, and you stay with it because it supports what you believe.*

Most of the teachers when asked indicated that making use of WIER had not changed their basic approach to the teaching of writing; rather they saw it as providing a very valuable adjunct that increased the efficacy of their pedagogy:

> *I think it was parallel to what I believe for the Writers Workshop. So it seemed like in Writers Workshop the more people you can have interacting around the students' writing, the more valuable it is. So it's something that I would keep in my program, because just me responding to the students' writing or just other students responding I think is not enough.*

Another teacher commented, "What delighted me most was that all the comments were spot on. It reinforced the very kinds of things that I was trying to do."

For those teachers less expert in writing process pedagogy, WIER offered opportunities for professional development which they came to value: "I have to say that I've learned a lot about teaching writing, and the kinds of things that you can tell students to do, ways you can tell them to improve their writing." These teachers found that engagement with WIER led to changes ranging from minor to major in their method of teaching writing. The most commonly cited change was a role shift away from functioning as an evaluator of the finished work or draft to working as a facilitator helping students prepare compositions for posting or interpreting feedback from other WIER participants. One teacher commented on how her relationship lwith her students had changed:

> *We became probably friends and we were side by side looking at the computer screen and experiencing together...They were just kind of coming to me as a buddy, as someone who could help them through it and I didn't feel as pressured to look over their work and say, okay, change this. A lot of pressure of doing that was put onto the authors...*

Other teachers noted that reviewing the authors' comments on their students' efforts gave them considerable insight into how to more deeply and effectively respond to young writers. This is exemplified in the comments of one participant:

The only difference is…having somebody who is a professional author. I find I've learned from this in terms of his responses to the kids. I found that very insightful as a teacher. I'm not a published author, well I've written a thesis. But I wouldn't consider that in terms of what he's written. Especially Kevin Major, he stands out. When I look at some of the things he has said to the kids I don't know if I ever would have thought of having said those…

Training and support, perceived value, and pedagogical congruence – our comparative study of SNS and WIER suggests that these three factors are critical to the success or failure of any major application of ICT in the classroom.

B. Streamed Video on Demand: A Pilot Study

As broadband Internet access becomes more ubiquitous and affordable, new possibilities will open up for the creation and delivery of high-quality learning materials incorporating many modes of teaching and utilizing different media. Two of our studies have examined projects that have developed exemplars of these new forms. The first assessed a pilot study of a new technology and interface for the selection and delivery of educational video segments taken from the large video library of a major public educational television channel to teachers in the classroom. Digital streamed video-on-demand seems to offer significant potential to enhance and enrich classroom learning. In theory at least, the medium can deliver to the computer desktop high quality educational resources keyed to curricular outcomes. Students can view the content on its own or build multimedia presentations and reports incorporating segments of the streamed video. Teachers can construct Web-based learning activities and instructional units that contain video components which explain, illustrate, model, or simulate concepts or events in ways that would be extremely difficult or impractical using traditional teaching methods or media. The reality today is that this technology is still in its infancy and not sufficiently robust for widespread use in schools. Nor do the networks and servers in educational institutions yet have the capacity for large-scale simultaneous delivery of content to teaching desktop, although that day is coming soon.

The pilot examined the feasibility of video delivery to a school lab equipped with very high-speed Internet access and a 100 Kbyte/second Ethernet network. A Canadian educational television broadcasting agency entered into an agreement with a large Ontario school board to conduct a test-of-concept of streamed video delivery to one of its high schools. The agency views the delivery of streamed video to schools as part of a strategic direction it wishes to pursue. For the pilot project, a small group of teachers selected from the agency's vast archives of educational programming videos that they believed would be valuable supplements to the high school mathematics and science curriculum. The agency digitized these programs and made them available to the school from a video server via high-speed cable using a proprietary database and interface. In preparation for classroom use, the teachers developed Web-based lessons which incorporated links to selected video clips. Several of these were used with students in a grade nine Science and Technology class during field trials in December 1999.

Data were collected through a series of interviews with the teachers over the course of the project, through observation of the classroom trials, and through analysis of the capabilities and limitations of the specific software tools and lessons used. We assessed both the educational value and practical viability of streamed video delivery into the classroom.

The commercial software application used for creating video clips, linking these to documents via URLs, and streaming the video proved to be underdeveloped and plagued with bugs that initially prevented it from operating in a stable manner. The teachers assisted the software developers for several months in the process of debugging the software and by December it was considered stable enough for classroom trials to proceed. The Web-based lessons developed used TVO video segments to illustrate complex physical processes related to the topic (electricity). The segments held students' interest, and video was clearly a more appropriate medium for teaching about and demonstrating dynamic systems of this type than text or static images. However due to recurring software problems, video playback was often problematic when more than a few students attempted simultaneous access, and the result was a rise in student frustration and an increase in their off-task talk. Teacher time largely had to be devoted to resolving operational issues rather than providing pedagogical support to students.

Despite these difficulties, the trials did provide a positive proof of concept. Streamed video can offer teachers an efficient and effective way of teaching about dynamic and/or multivariate systems not possible using other media by allowing them to easily select short segments of video precisely targeted at the desired learning outcomes. The viewing of video can have real value in helping students understand the dynamic processes that are part of the complex systems studied in science and mathematics. Its use can address some of the pedagogic weaknesses inherent in teaching approaches that rely solely on verbal or static graphical representations of dynamic events involving many variables. Streamed video also has potential applications in the arts and humanities, where it could bring new insight and color to learning activities. And by giving students the ability to play, pause, and replay segments to meet their individual learning requirements, streaming has the potential to be more interactive, engaging, and educationally effective than whole-class video viewing.

While critical of the technical problems and limitations imposed by the video delivery system used in the trial and the time these consumed, the participating teachers were of the opinion that the goal of using streamed video was worth pursuing. They saw it as having considerable educational potential, and thought that with a simplified, stable editing and delivery system a typical teacher could be making effective use of it after a one-day professional development session.

C. A HIGH-BANDWIDTH, WEB-BASED MULTIMEDIA TUTORIAL

The second development project we looked at that focused on extending the range of the possible in Internet-based learning was directed at creating a series of tutorials for undergraduate university courses, tutorials which incorporated a number of different media elements and programmed interactive elements (applets) and required a broadband, high-speed network for delivery. At the invitation of the developers (the CulTech research group at York University), we conducted a formative evaluation of one of these tutorials, created to augment a face-to-face "Introduction to Computer Technology" course.

The tutorial development process had been lengthy and expensive; the creative team involved included Web designers, graphic artists, video technicians, and programmers. The tutorial was intended to eventually serve as a stand-alone course that could be accessed remotely via a broadband Internet connection such as cable modem or ADSL. For the trial, students accessed the tutorials through a campus computer lab running on a very high speed network, which allowed real-time 30 frames per second delivery of high quality video when necessary.

The Web-based tutorial covered all aspects of the course, most in greater detail than was possible in the lectures and labs that were part of the traditional course structure. Video clips of the professor or outside experts were embedded in Web pages to introduce new themes and explain key concepts. The use of custom programming was extensive; many interactive Java applets allowed students to run small trials and experiments to explore key areas, such as the conversion of base ten numbers to binary numbers and the use of logic gating in computer design. Incorporating many background readings and links to other information sources, the tutorial in its final form ran to several hundred web pages.

During the trial, students were not given any class or lab time to access the tutorial, but it was available for use as an optional study aid and was available whenever students could get to the lab. At the end of the course, data on student use of the tutorial was collected through a brief questionnaire completed in class, as well as by undertaking an analysis of the log files generated over the term by the tutorial Web server. The latter allowed us to determine the frequency with which different sections and elements of the tutorial were accessed on a page-by-page basis and to review the patterns of use over time. In addition, focus groups were conducted with 16 students in order to illuminate their perceptions, attitudes, and reflections about the tutorial.

About one quarter of the students used the tutorial over the term. Access was generally distributed evenly across the term, except for a brief period of heavy usage for the two days before the focus groups were conducted. The log file analysis revealed that most students' use of the tutorial was far from comprehensive. Typically, it was limited to particular sections and subtopics, with certain areas that received less attention in class being rarely visited. Two usage patterns predominated. In the first, which might be termed *exploratory browsing*, students first worked their way through some of the introductory section and then looked at pages in one or two of the other sections (usually Hardware or Software – the History section content was very rarely accessed). In the second, *focussed work*, students did not spend time in the introductory section; they proceeded directly to work with resources in one (or infrequently two) focused domain areas – accessing, for example, several related pages on data representation in the Hardware section. These students would go more deeply into the tutorial sections than others, exploring pages three or even four levels "down." Students were roughly equally divided between these two use patterns. Many of the resources that were the most expensive to build into the tutorial, such as the interactive Java applets and some of the multimedia clips, were virtually ignored – pages containing them were rarely accessed.

In commenting on their experience with the tutorial, most students indicated that they found it "easy" or "very easy" to use; however further inquiry revealed specific problematics with the design that might have inhibited deeper exploration. The use of highlighting on the contents page was inconsistent, leading users to think that clicking on any subtopic below a given topic would just take them to that chapter rather than the specific subtopic. The use of hidden menu trees that only popped up when a mouse was over the superordinate label also led to students missing certain content areas. Navigating back to the top-level contents page was difficult for some. Several thought the hyperlinks should use the same color scheme as Netscape Navigator to avoid confusion about which links had been explored.

All of the students interviewed felt that the tutorial flowed well and was organized in a logical manner. There was a strong consensus that the text of the tutorial system "read" better than the course textbook, and was easier to understand. About 85% of the participants thought the general balance between text and other multimedia elements was appropriate. Still, many students felt that some portions of online text were too long and could be more efficiently read if the text was broken up by more graphics, animation or videos. Some students felt that examples would help them understand the material more effectively. One student commented, "I don't know if it gives any examples of the codes, the binary stuff. I didn't see any examples; I need examples to show continuity and the context of what happens."

The interactive applets were generally thought to be effective learning aids, although a few students thought they should be accompanied by voice-overs to explain processes more thoroughly. The use of the interactive elements was considered important; they were seen as a major advantage over reading text on-screen, which could be more easily accomplished using a textbook.

Three quarters of the students said that the online tutorial enhanced their learning in certain topic areas. A typical comment: "It's educational. It gave you a lot of insight into theory." A substantial minority of participants saw their tutorial experience as heightening their interest in the course content. One student had this to say: "I think it enhanced my interest, in terms of future projections. It had a section on computer programming and software where they list several programming languages and so on. I think I got some interest to study more." But only a small minority found it useful in studying for tests and exams.

Sections of the tutorial dealing with binary arithmetic and algorithms were cited by 88% of the participants as enhancing their interest and improving their understanding of the topic. The tutorial was also thought by 75% to be an aid in practicing skills that might not be as secure as the students would like them to be. One student explained it this way: "You actually get to try it out whereas when you're writing, there are so many different mistakes you can make and you don't know where you've made the mistake and the computer helps you to figure out where your mistake was and guides you step by step through the process."

When asked about the prospect of substituting the tutorial for part or all of the traditional lectures, all of the students said that this was not desirable, although there was no clear rationale given for preferring to stick with the lecture format. The great majority (88%) thought the tutorial would serve as an effective supplement that would aid their learning. Three quarters of the group appreciated the individualization the tutorial made possible, citing the ability to work with it "at their own rate." They felt that sometimes the class lectures went too fast for their ability to intake information. The tutorial allowed the student to go over material more than once. In addition, two thirds of the participants felt that the online tutorial was less boring than listening to a professor speak for long periods of time.

All of the students thought that the tutorial was "a good idea" and that it had great potential as a learning tool. One student said, "I wish all my classes had something like this. It's really a new way of teaching and I think its very exciting and there [are] a lot of things that this could lead into and improve teaching."

The generally positive feedback the tutorial received from the focus group participants must be balanced against the usage data, which indicates that few users made more than brief forays into the tutorial. Aside from the title page, only 10 pages received more than one visit per student user, and large numbers of pages were visited by only a minority of those accessing the tutorials. It would seem that most students felt that the time they spent attending lectures and labs, reading the text, and completing assignments was sufficient to prepare them well for tests and exams. The logistical difficulties imposed by having to go to a special lab to access the tutorial undoubtedly reduced its use. Students clamored for dialup access. The convenience of residential access should greatly enhance the educational utility of these types of tutorial programs. Other changes that the students themselves thought would foster greater use involved increasing the relevance of the tutorial to performance in the course, and they suggested several ways this could be done: having lecturers make direct reference to tutorial elements addressing curriculum being presented in class on a week-to-week basis; having lecturers explain the tutorial more fully in class and demonstrate its use; and have the tutorial itself "indexed" in some manner to the course and/or the textbook chapters so that users could quickly access resources relevant to their study needs.

D. Lessons Learned: Implications for Practitioners

The findings from our three case studies have implications for any teacher thinking about how best to utilize ICT in their practice. Based upon these cases, we have developed a set of suggestions and questions to keep in mind when you are considering bringing ICT-based activities of any type into your classroom.

Closely examine the type of ICT application or project you are considering and how it relates to your own and your students' ICT skill levels. Will you and/or your students face a steep learning curve in order to successfully use the application or complete the project? If so, do the potential outcomes make the necessary time investment worthwhile? If possible, talk to other teachers who have used the application or participated in the project to get a better sense of the possible benefits and limitations that could arise. Also investigate the available training and support resources that will be available to you. Will you have the types of support necessary to attain the needed competencies without undue stress or time pressure? Keep in mind that implementations that are large in scope and technologically complex, like the SNS project, will require a proportionately greater commitment of resources.

If you are considering participating in an ongoing project with an established pedagogical orientation and set form of practice, carefully evaluate its fit with your own approach to teaching. Be mindful that a program requiring you to adopt a new pedagogical direction will likely take some time to master and will require far more support than one that is fully congruent with your ongoing practices. You may conclude that pursuing a given project will open up more rewarding and fruitful approaches to teaching and learning; but considered deliberation will help you avoid those ICT initiatives which would prove frustrating and unproductive.

Caution is necessary if the technology or software to be used in the ICT project has just recently been brought to market. As the experience with the video-on-demand project vividly illustrates, many commercially released products initially contain substantial bugs which can derail efforts to use them in the classroom. Try to arrange for a pilot test of any technology you wish to use, and see that any available patches or upgrades have been applied to software or firmware – companies typically post these to the Web in order to fix bugs in shipping products, usually within a few months of their initial release.

If you are intending to pursue an independent project, such as the creation of a class Web site, it is important to keep some perspective on what will be possible in terms of production values and capabilities. Efforts like that undertaken by the CulTech group for the Introduction to Computers course cost upwards of $100 000 and take hundreds if not thousands of person-hours of highly skilled work to complete. Keep your curricular goals to a manageable scale – for example, developing a Web page for a specific project rather than attempting to incorporate a whole term's curriculum in an initial endeavor. And design your site so that buttons, links, and navigation aids such as menus are simple and their function obvious. Complex series of nested drop-down menus such as those used in the computer studies tutorial may look elegant, but they are hard to develop and can be confusing to use, especially for younger, less experienced students.

Rather than you as the teacher assuming sole responsibility for a Web site's development, the task might be better distributed by making the project a shared class learning endeavor. Or if you feel that the students in your class are too young to be a major part of the development process, you could work collectively with other teachers in your school to develop a school Web site.

When it comes to incorporating ICT in education, there is truth to that old saw, "forewarned is forearmed." By keeping the above points in mind as you begin to explore the use of ICT in your teaching, you can avoid wasting considerable time and energy, minimize the frustrations that are an inevitable part of implementing any innovation, and increase your chances for success.

CHAPTER 8
THE INTEGRATION OF ROBOTICS INTO A GRADE 2 CURRICULUM
MAKING SPACE FOR ROBERT
MARY M. CAMERON AND BARRIE R. C. BARRELL

Across Canada the integration of technology is now mandated in all grades and for all core subjects. For classroom teachers this means reading the nation's newly revised curricula documents in ways that are more inclusive of technology. In the English language arts (ELA) curriculum, the identified key strands have recently expanded from four to six in number. Now viewing and other ways of representing knowledge and information are to share equal instructional time with the traditional strands of read, writing, listening and speaking. This disciplinary expansion, when combined with provincial and territorial mandates for the inclusion and integration of various digital technologies, reconfigure both the nature and the work ELA teachers are expected to do in schools (see Barrell, 2000).

In the primary grades, the essential question is how best to engage with technological initiatives and curricula expansions while at the same time taking note of the new literacies that are surfacing within electronically enhanced environments and genres. For primary teachers and the parents of primary age children, an eye must be focused on what it will mean to be literate in the coming decades and what educational experiences young students will need to encounter earlier on in their schooling. What are the changes we can make in the way schooling is conducted that will better prepare children for a rapidly changing world?

Starting from the assumption that technology is not to be taught as a discrete subject in the primary grades, teachers and researchers are focusing on the specific details and models of technology integration that benefit young children. They want to investigate how the use of technology amplifies student knowledge, representations and textual constructions. Specifically, how does technology help represent student learnings, beliefs, perspectives, arguments and encounters with the world? Clear articulations are sought as to how information and communication technologies (ICT) come to affect the worldviews of children. How does ICT act as a partner with children in support of their reflections, articulations, internal negotiations, and meaning making processes and practices? Details are sought as to how ICT fosters collaboration and engages learners while helping to build consensus.

This chapter gives two views of a grade two class engaged in the use of technology at Banded Peak School in the Rocky View School Division in Alberta. One perspective comes from a teacher committed to the integration of technology directly into her classroom practice; the second view comes from an experienced teacher and university professor who spent time observing the children engage with technology.

THE SCHOOL

Opened in 1996, Banded Peak School (http://www.rockyview.ab.ca/bpeak/) is a public school located in the foothills of the Canadian Rockies. The K-8 school offers a technologically rich environment for teachers wishing to engage and explore new curriculum initiatives. Its open plan architecture and collective philosophy encourages and supports constructivist teaching practices in the belief that technology, if it is to be used most wisely, cannot be strapped onto traditional teaching methods and practices. Thus a variety of digital technologies are openly available in the school to help students represent their thinking and learning. It is understood that students will learn incidentally about digital technologies and bundled applications as they go about their work. Technological skill acquisition by students is a subtext to the intended theoretical aims of the school's incorporation of technology. It is what is done with and through technology that is of greater interest to the school community.

The founders of the school were not necessarily interested in if students learned particular things more effectively and efficiently with technology. Rather it was contended that the students would have to learn different skill sets and develop different research attributes as they engaged in complex, co-operative, authentic and collaborative work situated around essential questions and grounded investigations. Banded Peak School's philosophy seeks and foregrounds an intellectual partnership with technology in order to amplify and leverage the potential of student actions and engagements. The school does not advocate computer-assisted instruction (CAI) in the traditional drill and practice or in the tutorial senses, nor does it use many commercial computer programs. Rather, it seeks an alliance with technology in the *meaning making in partnership* sense. Succinctly, ICT is used in a constructivist environment that is in harmony with Jonassen's (1993; 2000) theoretical position and extensive work. As Jonassen (2000) points out, students learn *with* technology when computers: 1) support knowledge constructions, 2) support exploration, 3) support learning by doing, 4) support learning by conversing and communicating and 5) are intellectual partners that support learning by reflection (p. 9).

THE GRADE 2 CLASSROOM

An unusual space was given over to the grade 2s. Besides having enough room for desks and chairs, the room was open on one side. Here an all-purpose room containing several large banks of computers, a SMARTBoard and video editing equipment were kept. These technologies were for the collective use of the school. Sony digital cameras were also stored in this room for everyone's use. Directly outside the classroom was a pod of eight computers arranged on a carpeted area next to a small conference room. Across the hall was an art room and another conference space. All computers in the school were networked and used by all students. Thus a grade 2 student sitting at a computer could be found flanked by a grade 8, grade 5 or a grade 1 student. In addition to these computers, the classroom itself contained three networked machines. The grade 2s had access to a variety of bundled Microsoft applications similar to those found in business and associated with productivity tools. Databases, spreadsheets, visualization tools, computer concept maps, multimedia publishing tools, word processing applications and infrared applications were all available. The class also had access to instructional materials like white boards, VCRs, digital cameras and Lego robotics kits. As well as the usual furnishings of bookcases and shelving, the class had the remains of a castle chamber that had been built the previous year inside the classroom while the same students went about studying the Middle Ages. Theoretically, this structure stood as a reminder to both the scale and intellectual pursuits of the previous year. The classroom was not the only learning environment for the students. In fact, students often worked in the hallways, the conference room, the student gathering area or any space that lent itself to meeting the purpose of the students' needs.

MARS PROJECT

The Mars project arose out of the children's questions about space travel and the establishment of community in space. After visiting the NASA web site and following the ongoing coverage of the exploration of Mars, the students had a number of essential questions they thought needed investigating in order to go about setting up a colony on the red planet. The questions were situated around acquiring information that would lead to sustaining life. Thus together the students decided that they needed to find out if the planet had breathable gases, a reasonable temperature suitable to human life and needs, water, its own life forms and soil suitable for growing crops. They wanted to be able to collect soil and air samples for comparison to Earth's soil and air. They desired to be able to dig underground to see what is underneath the surface of the planet. They wanted to search for plants and water, any sign of life from bacteria to "alien life forms." In order to find answers to these questions, the students decided they would need to have robots land on the planet and look for evidence that would answer their questions, as it would be impossible for people to do such dangerous work.

Their questions led to more and more questions. The more they found out the more they realized they needed to find out. Their robotic work led to a study of structures. The guiding question was what robotic structure(s) would best suit the discovery of evidence for each guiding question about Mars.

The students divided into groups with the aim of discovering what structure would best suit the gathering of particular evidence for a particular question. During the discovery stage, students voiced their frustrations in building robots to do various tasks in daily class meetings. After each frustration was identified, solutions were sought from the group or answers where provided by those who had run into a similar problem or problems. Questions constantly arose and the Internet was often engaged to solve or give information that would help in the solving of a problem. Pictures of the Martian surface were sought that would give evidence as to what kind of terrain the robots would have to navigate. This led to the discovery of Olympus Mons, the largest volcano in the solar system, and the building of part of the Martian surface out of chicken wire and papier-mache complete with the volcano. Other questions led to the laying out of the Martian night sky on black material hung from the ceiling of the classroom and above the mock-up of the red landscape. Earth stood off in the distance. Land on Mars was purchased over the Internet near the volcano. Newspaper coverage and NASA news releases were followed and brought in by the children during the course of the project.

Using the SMARTBoard, a whiteboard that becomes a large interactive computer screen, the class began to study the programming of their robots. They were given just a few key ideas and then they began to figure out the programming together. The first assignment was to program a robot that would go forward, turn around and come back to its starting position. The children learned the specific 'grammar' for achieving this task, wrote it and downloaded it into their robots via an infrared data transfer system. There were constant frustrations and failures expressed during class meetings. However, when problems were overcome, the class often shared the solution. At these times learning was a community success and event. With practice, the students began to make the robots do the various tasks they felt were required to gather scientific evidence. Robotic structures varied; some had six wheels, other had four, some two wheels with a slider. Structurally the robots where tested for soundness and their ability to complete assigned tasks. They were then placed on the constructed Martian surface and under the Martian sky.

This project took up large chunks of time and was interdisciplinary most of the time. Art, ELA, science, geography and elements of the social sciences came together in a woven tapestry of discovery. Technology allowed these students to experiment with the specific grammars required to communicate one's wish to a robot. The grammar was very precise and not very forgiving. The children edited for clarity of purpose. Obviously there were many indirect lessons learned when doing this authentic work. This robotics project was a substantive model of school based technology integration. It moves well beyond simple word processing or key boarding skill acquisition to demonstrating how both learning and teaching are extended through the appropriate use of new technologies.

Cameron's Observations: Making Space

Our goal in grade two was simple: we wanted to learn more about the world(s) around us and to figure out more about ourselves in the process. This was a goal I shared with the 28 boys and girls. However, the roles of the members of our classroom community were often blurred. I was as much a student as they the teachers. For some educators, this giving up or freeing of the power of the tallest person in the classroom is unnerving; but in my mind it is completely necessary. It allows for magical things to happen when space is created for those students that traditional schooling often fails. This construction of schooling allows students to have more control over both the direction and the depth of their learning.

I was a good student in the public school system of the 70s and 80s. I received glowing accolades for my many academic successes. I took the notes, listened to the lectures and spit it all back to my teachers in their testing of my "learning." This was the way schooling was constructed for me. I loved to learn and thought that I was. On reflection however, I really was just honing an already acute short-term memory. In fact, I feel like I remember nothing from my grade school experiences. It seems to me that the only snippets of school that got lodged in my long-term memory were the few instances when I had a say in what I was learning.

I knew, as a classroom teacher, two decades later, I *had* to do things differently. I knew that society had moved beyond the assembly-line industrial world of work. I knew that the world my students were inheriting was radically changing. I knew that my classroom would need to reflect their world and prepare them for a world that would cherish critical thinking and lively engagement with the arts and sciences.

Technology was a natural tool to use, as part of our teaching and learning, to make school more closely resemble the real world, and in turn help the students make meaning from the world around them. While I have experience as a software evaluator, a network administrator and a provider of technology support, by no means does my teaching surround the use of technology. You might say technology surrounds my teaching. When the work students do is authentic and meaningful work, there are many natural places for technology to fit into the mix. In my teaching the integration of technology seems to happen because of the tasks the students perform. This is key. What is necessary for technology to seamlessly become incorporated into a student's classroom experience is for it to be available for use in real and meaningful ways. The work the students were doing in my classroom was almost identical to the work that teams of researchers at NASA and the Jet Propulsion Laboratory (JPL) were doing. This was evident in the interest the students took in reading and seeing NASA's exploration unfold.

I was struck with the way the class became a knowledge-building community. Each day the students would get together in their teams, depending on their robots' purposes, and would decide on how to best achieve the work that needed to be done in the time given. A representative would report to me on the team's plan. For the next hour or so I would circulate between the five teams, probing them as to what they were doing and why, and always noting who was doing and saying what. The teams would often break into smaller teams depending on the group's size and purpose for that particular day. For example, the team that was searching for proof of water and plants had nine students. A typical plan and work day for this group might have been to have two students looking for the latest research on what plants need to survive, while four students might be working on the actual structures of the robots. The rest might be on NASA's Website finding out what scientists were discovering about water and ice on Mars.

The students had access to the Internet, to books from the library, to software to gather written notes and images, to pencils and paper, to programming software and their robots. The grade two researchers were also encouraged to connect with real experts through the telephone, email or in person. After the end of a work session, the class would come together as a collective to share learnings, frustrations and future strategies. I would take notes on chart paper to be placed on the wall for future referral. It was during these conversations that something magical would often happen. As a rule we sat in a circle around our Round Table (painted by the students with Greek astrological symbols surrounding a superimposed sun and moon) facing one another. It was known that when you came to the table, your job was to share your thinking and be respectful of the ideas of others.

As the facilitator of the discussions, I would simply help them decide who would start and then away they would go into conversation. An example of a "learning" would be when they figured out that electricity had a direction. The robots were battery operated and when the motors were connected to the wheels with the motor attachments flipped in the opposite directions, then the wheels spun in opposite directions. The frustrations were very interesting to hear. They were not always about the robots or the research, but many times about teamwork. The students would almost always have a strategy for one another when they collectively shared their frustrations. Often they would ask each other questions like, "did you try this..." or they shared how they overcame the same problem. During the discussion I often became involved simply because I too had questions. The difference between my questions and those that were asked of me when I was in grade two was that my questions were real, authentic. I asked questions of the students for which I did not necessarily have the answers. The students knew that I was a part of their learning community. I recall one day we were trying to figure out how to program the robots so that they would remain on the "Martian surface." We tossed a few ideas around, and then Robert gave the answer. He suggested we paint the outside edge of the platform black. We were then to make sure each robot had a light sensor that would detect darkness. Each team/group would have to program their robot to turn the motors off when the light sensor detected darkness. Then they were to program the motors to go in reverse for a few seconds. Next one motor would have to turn on while the other turned off for a few seconds so that the robot would turn and once again go forward. I would never have thought up the black edge solution. This type and level of thinking constantly exceeded my expectations of the children.

The sharing of information was freely given. There was no hoarding of knowledge, no competitiveness to outperform one another. The feeling and demonstrations of collaboration were sensational. At some point in the day, I had the students journal about their work to get them to further reflect on their learning. I asked them to write about what they had accomplished that day, what their frustrations were, how they planned to overcome the frustrations and what they planned to do next with their work. I found that their frustrations almost always informed their next step.

When educators speak of engaging the minds of children and their limited attention spans, I think of Robert. Robert is a delightful boy who marches to a different drummer. In order to understand the level of his engagement in a piece of work, I need to give context to a situation. Picture over twenty-five seven year olds wearing splattered painting smocks. Containers of red paint mixed with mud are sporadically placed around the edge of the 8 ft by 8 ft replica of the Martian surface. The children are dipping their brushes and painting the surface with care, chatting excitedly about being so close to completing the terrain. A stereo is playing dance music and many children are singing and swaying. The entire afternoon is dedicated to our work. I too am painting, singing and swaying to the music. Everyone is engaged, except Robert. Despite the loud music, the painting, the chatting and dancing around the terrain, Robert is working with his robot. He is attempting to get it to perform a very particular task. He would program it, download the program into the robot, march out to the hallway and test out his work on the smooth flooring and then return to adjust the program. He was bound and determined to figure out the problem in his construction. For two hours Robert problem solved amid the mayhem of the afternoon's activities until I made him catch the bus to go home. I will forever remember the diligence and the drive he had to bring his robot into alliance with his thinking. Robert was given the space to experiment and to work independently with a sustained determination. What is significant here to me is valuing and encouraging deep engaged work. Robert had all the true attributes of a problem solver, adult or child.

June brought a winding down of our work. Our desks had been shoved to the outer edges of the classroom. They had been simply in the way for a lot of our work. Our terrain and night sky filled the room. Our Round Table ended up tucked underneath the papier-mache terrain. Students pleaded to stay in for recess (even on sunny days) to continue their work. They would groan when I'd tell them that time was up, that it was recess, that it was the end of the day. When Alexis told me that school felt like "home" to her and that our class was like a family, I knew exactly what she meant.

BARRELL'S VIEW AND OBSERVATIONS

I was a sabbaticant and visiting scholar at the University of Calgary and very much interested in a sustained period of classroom observation. I wanted to see, first hand, the new Canadian curriculum initiatives and the role(s) technology was playing in constructivist classroom practices. I had the opportunity to spend five months as a participant observer with Mary Cameron and the children in her class. Among other things, I was looking for classroom events that I could classify "new." That is, having unique and individual characteristics that could be considered significant enough to be seen as a departure from previously observed classroom experiences and practices. To the students in the grade two classroom, however, I was "Just Barrie," someone who was willing to discover the world alongside them. Mary Cameron is aware, like Spiro (1991), of the many understandings and notions of constructivism. She uses Spiro's theory of "ill structured knowledge domains" to transfer school learning to real-life authentic problem solving situations and explorations. True to constructivist ideals, she requires students to be responsible about learning and to teach themselves. She asks students to make choices about the methods they employ to solve problems and resolve conflicts. What Ms. Cameron insists students do is to identify particular frustrations they have with their ongoing work. In doing so, and in requiring students to talk about various road blocks that impinge upon their learning, she gets her class to see that in solving any scientific or social or artistic problem, things do not necessarily go smoothly. Children get the chance to understand that things do not necessarily run smoothly for adult scientists, economists, or artists either. What is more, "failure" is seen as a very natural part of experimentation. Hence, frustrations are seen as a natural part of the problem solving process. I observed that students were very tolerant of "frustrations." They accepted the fact that the learning process was often long and that plans often need revision and (re)visioning along the way. The class was often helped in learning about various methods for going about solving particular problems, and in the case of stopping robots from leaving the Martian landscape, came up with unique solutions. They seemed to expect that successes came from long periods of effort. A week's work was seen as just a part of a month's work in the assembling of materials or the constructing of plans to bring an investigation to a conclusion. This attitude must have been gained from building the castle antechamber, drawbridge and round table inside the classroom during the previous school year. Possibly sitting and working amongst the castle walls was a concrete way of tacitly feeling and understanding the possibilities of sustained effort and experimentation. Once on his way to show me a Power Point presentation his puppets were going to use to present information for his choice for class pet, Robert showed me pictures of a catapult. This was from work done in grade one. "Off topic," he explained to me about the levers and pulleys the machine used to deliver its payload. He had seen no reason to discard his work from the previous year. The images were just there, reminding him of past work. (I did classify puppets using Power Point as "new.")

The children did not have another model of schooling to fall back on. Ms Cameron did not have to bring students to understand a 'new' way of schooling or to contest traditional practices. Rather, collaborative group work and co-operative learning etiquettes were carried over from her work the previous year.

The grade two class offered richer learning environments for its children, set within a realistic understanding of Gardner's work on multiple intelligences (Gardner, 1983; Gardner and Hatch, 1989). In this classroom it was hypothesized that children needed exposure to the different requirements and strengths highlighted by Gardner's work. Further, it was felt that students needed opportunities to represent their engagements with the class questions and goals through their various intelligences. Thus spatial, musical, linguistic, interpersonal, etc., skills were often sought out and given opportunities to be displayed by all members of the learning community. Several times before class began, I observed children listening to classical music. However, one student had chosen to act as conductor while others pretended to play various instruments. This kind of inventive play and engagement was observed many times.

Authentic learning assessment methods were used at various places during the term. New student knowledge was always linked to the children's existing understandings in a way that emphasized the transfer of knowledge to real-life situations. The use of technology was always integrated into constructivist principles and linked constantly to the children's personal knowledge and understanding. Ms Cameron demanded that links between the work done in schools and that done in the outside world were always made visible. Thus classroom inquiry developed in ways that required authentic experiences (i.e., required and developed behaviors that emulate the behavior of experts in any of the areas under study). The NASA web site was used to follow the latest news and posted updates of their work. Naturally flowing from this was the students' deeper understanding of the work behind planetary exploration.

Following on from the previous year's work, in which students studied life in the Middle Ages in order to understand various elements of community, the children decided that they wished to think about the human habitation of Mars. They wanted to know what a community set in a Martian landscape would need in order to be able to sustain the life of the colony. This investigation scaffolds authentic experiences (built on the previous year's work with a medieval community) into a new area of research. It extended, expanded, leveraged and cemented notions of community and the requirements for collective human participation and co-operation. Observable evidence that greater student ownership of problems and the quest for solutions was demonstrated by increased student enthusiasm and persistence to complete tasks, to stay focused and to extend learning beyond the task at hand. I observed a genuine willingness for revising, improving and updating plans, procedures and task objectives. Technology allowed for greater access to information and knowledge. It allowed student representation of their work in a manner that often wove digital images, sound and print into a composition. These texts were sometimes linear in their construction, but at other times they were multifaceted. Overwhelmingly it was apparent to this observer that technology was opaque in this connected classroom. It was reached for much as past kids have reached for books or encyclopedias.

DISCUSSION

Typically at Banded Peak School information and communication technologies such as WWW authoring tools, databases, digital cameras and multimedia authoring programs are used to fulfill mandated curriculum requirements. The grade two class at Banded Peak worked together to conceive, build, encode and test robots to perform particular tasks and assignments devised by the students within a constructivist classroom environment. Technology allowed the collective and ongoing work of students to be made public and shared in both the school community and on the World Wide Web. Student work, which in the past has often been done in private or in isolation, found an audience outside the school.

Such electronic publishing can have unforeseen consequences. An example of this comes from other students at Banded Peak School who studied Homer's *Odyssey*. The students drew detailed depictions of events in the story. These pictures, with their expressive colors and imaginative lines, were posted on the class web site. Paul S. Lykoudis, a professor of Greek in Athens, found the site while finishing up a new translation of the *Odyssey*. He emailed the class asking for permission to use one of the pictures for the cover of his new book. A copy of his book, complete with a rendered scene on the cover, and a letter of thanks addressed to the students, sits in the school's foyer. They are a testament to the unforeseen consequences of technology being able to mesh two independent entities involved in authentic academic work and study.

We have moved into a new era in which young students chat electronically outside of school using ICQ or in chat rooms (see Cohen, this text). Their writing mixes acronyms, canned sounds, with iconographic images into grammatical structures unique and as ordered as any evolving language. Inside Robert's classroom, children learn how to write HTML code and weave digital images and sounds into their global communications and explorations. Their classroom reading stretched from traditional books to electronic texts. Students moved from NASA's latest findings posted on the web to robotics' manuals and celestial maps. They wrote with pencils, double tapped on SMARTBoards, communicated with keyboards or beamed information via infrared technologies. This generation is moving well beyond didactic models of instruction. They are also in need of new provincial assessment practices that incorporate some of the new ways of teaching and learning. Individual pencil and paper tests are not sufficient instruments to capture the group learnings of these children. And without changes in assessment practices, we run the risk of new technologies being used, as Stone Wiske warns, to "enact traditional practices" (p. 73).

For many young people, novelty now lies in older electronic technologies. Robert was quite capable of downloading images from a digital camera into his electronic portfolio, but thrilled when his Dad taught him how to load film into an older technology, a 35mm camera. Given a choice, a family friend once excitedly chose to use the 'dial telephone' over the digital one to call home. The point here is that many of the nation's students already know how to use a wide variety of technologies; they are simply awaiting their arrival in classrooms. In a very real sense, second graders could have been doing "professional development" with some of their school or district's teachers. They could have been guiding and giving demonstrations to teachers on how to manipulate electronic texts and edit digital images. The work done by the students demonstrates that we have reached a point where the community of learners within a school can, in a very real sense, include teachers.

REFERENCES

Barrell, B. (2000). "A Discipline in Metamorphosis," in Barrell, B. and Hammett R. *Advocating Change: Contemporary Issues in Subject English*. Toronto: Irwin Publishing.

Gardner, H. (1983). *Frames of Mind*. New York: Basic Books.

Gardner, H. & Hatch, T. (1989). "Multiple Intelligences Go to School: Educational Implications of the Theory of Multiple Intelligence." *Educational Researcher, 18* (11). 4-10.

Jonassen, D. (2000). *Computers as Mindtools for Schools*, 2nd edition. Upper Saddle River. NJ: Merrill.

Jonassen, D., Beissner, K. & Yacci, M.A. (1993). *Structuring Knowledge for Representation, Conveying, and Acquiring Structual Knowledge*. Hillside, NJ: Lawrence Erlbaum Associates.

Perkins, D. (2001). "The Big Question is How to Show Up Without Showing Up." In *The Digital Classroom: How Technology is Changing the Way We Teach and Learn*, edited by David T. Gordon. Cambridge, MA: Harvard Education Letter, c2000.

Spiro, R.J., Feltovich, P.J., Jacobson, M.J. & Coulson, R.L. (1991). "Cognitive Flexibility, Constructivism, and Hypertext: Random Access Instruction for Advanced Knowledge Acquisition in Ill-Structured Domains," *Educational Technology*, May, pp. 24-33.

CHAPTER 9
VIRTUAL SCHOOLING
INTEGRATING SCHOOLING INTO TECHNOLOGY
WILLIAM J. HUNTER AND ROSINA SMITH

INTRODUCTION

Virtual schooling is a remarkable innovation in the history of schooling – not simply because it uses online teaching and learning environments, or even because it is an educational alternative that has the potential to change conventional learning contexts. The remarkable thing about virtual schooling is that it is a major innovation in delivery that has been adopted by the school boards of public school systems. Because of this, we have become accustomed to predictions that virtual schooling will bring about major changes in schooling overall. It is certainly possible that this will come to pass, but our purpose here is to examine the ways in which our traditional conceptions of schooling are shaping the ways we develop online schools. We want to raise the question, "Is virtual schooling a matter of integrating technology into schooling or is it the other way around?"

Virtual schooling has introduced notions of "anytime/anyplace" learning, developed new opportunities for independent learning and dramatically reconfigured the work of both teachers and learners. But since these effects reflect broader social changes (i.e., the use of electronic communication in both corporate and personal communication, e-commerce, and new forms of political discourse) virtual schools may simply be indicating the ways in which a school system designed for the industrial economy is adapting to the demands of an information economy. That is to say, the changes we are seeing may be more evolutionary that revolutionary. They might be regarded as constituting a kind of minimalist change to new electronic work places and spaces. This change may be important, but it would not constitute the kind of fundamental change that many advocates of school reform (or of integration of technology into education) would advocate.

Online on the Prairies

The growth of virtual schools in Alberta, Canada, over the last five years has been impressive. From one school in 1995, the province now has 19 virtual schools. Despite substantial reductions in provincial funding for education during much of this time, virtual schools have been enthusiastically developed under existing public and separate school boards and have seen consistent growth in enrollment.

The development of online education in Alberta is a continuation of a long history of attempts to deliver quality schooling to citizens in remote locations (Muirhead, 1999) that include correspondence schools, educational radio and television, very early approval of home schooling and an experiment with fax-based delivery. This chapter draws on data collected by one of the authors in her doctoral dissertation (Smith, 2000). It may be that this data source, the province's history, and other elements of the Alberta environment (e.g., very favorable attitudes toward entrepeneurship and school choice) restrict the generalizability of some of the observations here, but we expect that readers will find much commonality in any large North American jurisdiction that includes substantial sparsely populated remote areas.

The Ways It Has Worked: Different Approaches

The variety of ways in which Alberta's virtual schools work makes it extraordinarily difficult to even think about such broad questions as "Do virtual schools improve students' learning?" There are schools that rely (or have relied) almost entirely on email for communication between teachers and students. Some make extensive use of print resources. Some are using WebCT or other course delivery tools. Some require occasional face-to-face meetings. Some focus on elite athletes, others on home schoolers. It is a dazzling array of options, but all make some regular use of computer-mediated communication as a fundamental part of their educational program.

Oblinger & Maruyama (1996) argue that distributed learning systems permit a variety of educational approaches based on student needs and provide for "anytime/anyplace" learning. The inclusion of a variety of approaches seems to be an attractive feature of online learning and may be the means by which school districts can attract greater numbers of students. Further, with the decline in government funding to education, the virtual school may provide a variety of course offerings in a more creative and flexible manner by collaborating and by sharing resources. Since funding for Alberta school systems is substantially driven by enrollments, incorporating a virtual school provides them with a competitive edge that may help to attract students.

However, school districts do not seem to regard the mere availability of a virtual school as enough 'innovation'; they also use a variety of approaches to structure the schools. There are blended programs, full virtual programs and dual registration programs. The range of choices enables students to take online courses that may not be available in their "base" school or to take additional courses online while attending a conventional school.

Blended programs combine online education with home schooling and create opportunities for students to benefit from professionally-guided learning while allowing parents to retain control over their child's schooling experience. These virtual programs are designed for students who prefer to learn using computer-mediated communication and who may have felt that the conventional school was not meeting their cognitive and/or affective needs.

The full virtual school program offers everything online and, therefore, does not require the physical structure of conventional schools. Even if students are provided with face-to-face opportunities, the venue need not be a school facility. The possibilities for reduced capital costs are certainly one of the attractions of full virtual schools, but virtual school advocates rarely mention this, focusing their arguments instead on learning issues.

Dual registration programs permit students to attend conventional school and also take classes online (for example, they may take courses required for post-secondary registration which are not offered by their conventional school). These dual registrations provide balance between online and face-to-face socialization, interaction, communication and collaboration and may also constitute the kind of responsiveness to different learning styles advocated in the research literature (e.g., in William and Brown, 1990). Both blended and dual registration programs permit students to register in part-time online offerings.

DIFFERENT VIEWS OF STUDENT LEARNING

Historically, distance education emphasized curricular content and instructional design. This approach meant attempting to anticipate learner needs in general and overlooking the characteristics of individual learners as they engaged with the materials. Smith (2000) describes virtual schools as a fourth generation of distance learning that combines such third generation innovations as e-mail, audiotape, bulletin board systems, Internet, videotape, fax, voice mail and other asynchronous and synchronous communication tools with a greater responsiveness to the affective needs of students and parents.

PARENT SATISFACTION

Research has shown that parents choose virtual schools because they value flexibility in time and space and opportunities for autonomous learning (e.g., Holmberg, 1989; Smith, 2000; and Flinck, 1989). In Smith's study, parents indicated that they would continue to register their children in a virtual school despite discouraging results for virtual students on provincial achievement tests. Students taking online courses also want to continue to take courses using this delivery system (58% in a 1996 study by Hiltz, Johnson and Turoff.). Parents, teachers and students in these studies seem more concerned about students being active participants in their learning and becoming autonomous learners than about students doing well on achievement tests. In fact, acquiring autonomous learning skills is an important factor that draws students and parents to online learning (Moore and Kearsley, 1996).

Parents in Smith's study also believed that having children in a virtual school environment would decrease their exposure to bullying and violence and might, therefore, provide the potential for greater learning. Parents, teachers and students were interested in what they saw as growth in student motivation. Students working in online educational settings are reported to be more highly motivated than those in conventionally taught courses (Baker, Hale and Gifford, 1997).

Smith found that Alberta parents believed that the involvement of a 'key parent' in some models of online learning provides students with individualized learning opportunities and promotes growth in the self-concepts of students who might have learned to devalue themselves in the conventional school setting.

It seems clear that parents who choose to send their children to Alberta virtual schools tend to be pleased with the results. However, it is worth noting that for many such parents, the choice of a virtual school is, in some way, an attempt to recapture the school of bygone days – smaller schools closer to home with parents actively involved. Despite the trappings of technology, virtual schools seem to satisfy this fundamentally conservative longing for a simpler, safer time.

Teacher Satisfaction

Teacher satisfaction, on the other hand, was rooted in the use of a new approach to delivery and the opportunity to work in an innovative, creative environment. Teachers reported that they valued the collaboration and communication with the students this environment made possible. They also appreciated the potential for developing stronger skills in the integration of technology in teaching. They felt that they were seeing growth in student motivation and behavior. The model of professional work in these environments gave them more flexibility in the use of time and space and they felt that this was part of a changing role for teachers. They valued the camaraderie they experienced with other teachers (in contrast to the isolation many teachers report in traditional schools).

For teachers, then, virtual schools do seem to represent some kind of transformation of the profession; i.e., something fundamentally different about how we deliver education. For some, this would be amply reflected in longer work hours that are more directly under their personal control. For many, it has much more to do with the way their relationship to students is changed, especially in that they have more direct academic communication with individual students.

We need to ask whether the teachers' satisfaction reflects a new model of teaching and learning or a delivery system that better enables them to make their existing models work. This may be a specific example of a general observation made by Weizenbaum (1976) who argued that computers do not change how we do things; rather, their speed allows us to persist in doing them the same way after our procedures have become too cumbersome. (Weizenbaum's example was the banking industry which he claimed was so encumbered by paperwork that it was on the verge of a collapse when computers made it possible to exchange and store information electronically rather than on paper. Bankers did not change their processes; they just moved them to the computer environment.) It is likely that we will not have a clear sense of an answer to this question until there is a generation of teachers who have grown up learning with computers. In that kind of environment, it may be easier for teachers to rethink the whole of the teaching and learning process with the importance of technology declining as it is taken-for-granted.

Student Satisfaction

Smith's students reported satisfaction with their virtual school and with the innovative approach to learning that it made possible. They also reported satisfaction with the changing role of teachers, the safe environment online education offers, the reduced number of distractions and the opportunities for interaction, collaboration and socialization permitted by virtual school.

When students reflect the same kinds of attitudes the parents reported, it is more difficult to attribute the attitudes to a longing for bygone days. Though they may well be reflecting their parents' values and standards, we must also consider the possibility that what we have is an indication that these parents have made the right choice for these students. At the very least, that would suggest that virtual schools represent an important shift insofar as they do indeed give parents a choice.

However, it is difficult to judge the overall level of student satisfaction with virtual schools since studies so far have not tracked the perceptions of students who leave virtual schools. Even if all students currently enrolled in virtual schools were to be supremely satisfied, questions would remain about whether this self-selected group was representative of students in general. That is, if students who currently choose to attend traditional schools were required to attend virtual schools, they would not necessarily share the opinions of those currently attending virtual schools.

REDEFINING TEACHER AND STUDENT ROLES

Participants in Smith's study reported that the union between teacher and learner in the virtual school permits a role reversal. This exchange of responsibilities is constantly shifting, triggering ongoing role changes for the student and teacher. Kaufman (1989) argues that this ongoing support between teacher and student permits open dialogue among learners and that this dialogue allows "the learner" to be defined as both student and teacher. The authors have noted this phenomenon in other virtual schools. Students frequently comment that they feel they get more personal attention from virtual school teachers because they get personal emails from them several times each week.

Many virtual school teachers refer to their role as being a guide or coach to autonomous learners, many of whom have been immersed in a technological environment. Both teachers and students reported satisfaction with the reconstruction that "anytime/anyplace" learning permits. Students are able to learn in their homes, community or workplace when they feel the time is right, and they say that they experience quality learning through the guidance and support of qualified teachers (Garrison, 1990). When teachers accept this reconstruction, they can no longer be an unquestioned authority on the subject matter. Since students are not physically present with them when they work, teachers also cease to function as managers of classroom behavior. The students accept some of the responsibility for learning independently and they learn to govern their own learning. Baker, Hale, and Gifford (1997) argue that online students develop more positive attitudes toward the discipline under inquiry. Jonassen (1992) indicates that the current model of distance education, in which virtual schools can be classified, has the students assuming more control over their learning than the teacher does. However, one Alberta virtual school administrator has confided to the authors that students are sometimes "inappropriately" drawn to virtual schools because they come with the expectation that the work will be easier or that "someone else will do the thinking for them."

What does it mean to say that online students take more control of their learning? Students have reported that it took less time for them to do their work online, thus, increasing learner efficiency (Baker, Hale &

Gifford, 1997). They have also reported that they would return to the virtual school in the next school year, as did the study by Hiltz, Johnson, and Turoff (1996), which reported that 58% of online students would choose to take another online course. Students often work from a "home office" environment, lending a touch of seriousness to their studies. Teachers report that online students are more likely to negotiate the terms of their assignments and that they succeed in this because they make a good academic case for what they want to do.

These kinds of changes do promise that online education opens the way to rethinking how we approach teaching and learning. With data from a survey of 4000 teacher leaders, Riel and Becker (2000) report that teachers who integrate technology into their teaching become more constructivist in their thinking about learning (and in their reported practice). Interestingly, Reeves (2001) has made a case that while students benefit from the changes online education introduces, teachers pay the price in the form of longer hours, more demanding work and reduced control over course content. For the risk-takers who sign up early, these changes may be just the price of innovation; but if the price remains that high, it is unlikely that the system will accept this reform with enthusiasm.

Student Enrollment, Retention, and Attrition

Since the 1996-1997 school year, when Alberta virtual school student numbers were first recorded, it has become evident that there has been a substantial annual increase in student enrollment. Steady enrollment increases have been evident in all grades, but the highest growth occurred in grades 4-6, followed by 10-12, K-3, and finally 7-9. It should be noted that the least amount of growth has been consistently from grades 7-9 and that there was actually an 8% decline in enrollment at this level in the 1999-2000 school year. To date, retention and attrition rates have not been formally reported by school districts and/or Alberta Learning.

Possible Effect on Public Education

It is becoming apparent through the data recorded in the school profiles that virtual schools were created in an effort to not lose students to other jurisdictions and to offer alternatives that might attract students both from within and outside their school jurisdictions. This has led to some competition among virtual schools which, in turn, has led to structuring "fee-for-service" plans to accommodate part-time students. They also permit "anytime/anyplace" learning which is attractive to many students and parents. Clearly, the introduction of new delivery mechanisms and the creation of a competitive environment have the potential to broadly affect public education, but it is probably equally true that the existence of virtual schools as a service provided by public education will place some constraints on the degree to which the virtual schools depart from normal school practice – e.g., thus far, it appears that "anytime/anyplace" does not mean that students may complete courses in the summer more readily in virtual schools. Many of the virtual schools courses have definite start dates and finish dates that correspond to the usual school calendar. In short, there seems to be at least as much give as take in the exchange between virtual school and traditional school.

Pre-Service and In-service Teacher Opportunities

Online courses could provide unique pre-service and in-service opportunities for teachers; for example, a pre-service teacher working with a virtual school might have exposure to a full year of teaching in a subject area in the compressed time of a semester of student teaching. Likewise, since online teaching tends to produce artifacts (email messages, discussion logs, web pages, etc.), there will be more opportunity for experienced teachers to see the products of novice's efforts and to comment both critically and supportively. For the same reason, the environment is rich with opportunities for collaboration between novice and master teachers. Of course, these opportunities are not limited to novices and there are exciting possibilities for practicing teachers interested in creating or delivering online courses collaboratively. The very possibility of separating the course creation and course delivery functions (as has been done to some degree at Chinook College in Calgary) is itself an opportunity for teachers to hone particular skill sets or to capitalize on the strengths of colleagues. To date, literature on the online development of online teachers is very limited, but there is a hint of the possibilities in one report of a pilot study of student teachers working with practicing online teachers (Bulls, Brown, Hunter & Fryatt, 1996).

CHOICES

The theme of choices was apparent in the discussion relating to parent satisfaction. Parents registered their children in the virtual school because they sought another alternative to the educational context their children had previously attended. Parents who had students registered in a conventional school setting prior to attending the virtual school reported that the negative social element, the promise of more relevant, meaningful learning opportunities, and the independent learning skills that the virtual school offered were the reasons for selecting this alternative.

The parents indicated they were satisfied with the flexible, "anytime/anyplace" learning opportunities that this choice offered and that socially and emotionally their children were happier. Both parents and students stated that the positive change in their social and emotional growth had a positive impact on their grades.

Students also felt that the virtual school was a safer choice as they were no longer open to being criticized, embarrassed, or made to feel less worthy by other classmates. Students did, however, acknowledge that there are some aspects to online learning that are "frightening," such as issues of being stalked online or of entering an inappropriate site.

Students perceived that their academic achievement had improved since registering in the virtual school because this choice helped them feel better about themselves and because they were more accepted by their online peers than they had been in the conventional school setting.

Teachers also reported that this was an alternative choice that they selected because they wanted to teach in an innovative environment and because issues of class management were different. Although teachers argued that they spent less time on behavioral issues, there were still some behavioral issues that existed, but they were different from the ones in conventional classroom settings.

For parents who are proponents of the home schooling context, the virtual school is a choice that offers them direct control over their child's affective and cognitive growth while permitting guided learning by certified teachers. These parents feel that the conventional school context is not appropriate and that the virtual school offers a choice which provides them assistance with the day-to-day learning requirements, without the parent-perceived negative factors of conventional school settings (Mayberry, 1991). These perceived negative factors include inappropriate peer relationships and inappropriate behavior that may be distracting and may negatively influence their child's behavior.

Since the home schooling population continues to grow and since this is one of the groups from which virtual schools draw, it is likely that virtual schools, through their blended programs, will continue to see an increase in student enrollment. Garrison (1990) confirms this trend by arguing that students need the choice of studying in their homes, community, and workplace while still experiencing a quality learning experience through guided learning and support from a qualified teacher.

STUDENT ACCEPTANCE AND PARTICIPATION

Students reported that the elimination of any concern for appearance, race, gender and/or age made them feel accepted and increased their grades as they were no longer occupied with how they felt about themselves and what others thought about them. Students also reported feeling more at ease to ask questions without getting embarrassed and were less likely to worry about their physical image. Parents, students and teachers felt that this environment was beneficial for those students perceived to be socially incongruent within their conventional school settings due to physical or affective differences. In the virtual school, students are known through their text-based dialogues, not through their physical and/or affective characteristics.

Teachers also saw merit in this approach in its potential to enhance independent learning skills, since students were required to assume more responsibility for their own learning. Further, parents, teachers and students reported improvements in student motivation, a decline in distractibility factors and improved student ability to communicate ideas because it eliminated the physical presence which made certain students feel less worthy, awkward or embarrassed and made them less likely to communicate in conventional classroom contexts. It was the parental perception that the elimination of many of these factors improved their child's academic standing.

WHY IT SOMETIMES DOESN'T: CHANGES TO REGULATORY AND ADMINISTRATIVE FRAMEWORKS

Presently, Alberta school administrators are assuming an innovative role as they adapt and interpret the School Act to address the virtual school context. The theme of administrators and the regulatory framework in education requiring changes emerged from an analysis of the data relating to the regulation and administration of virtual schools and illustrates the change in regulatory and administrative roles.

The School Act governs virtual schools, but there are no specific regulations that pertain to virtual schools. Administrators are required to evaluate teacher performance, but if teachers work from home offices, it is not clear yet how their work is assessed. Principals cannot visit classrooms or be present in the hallways in making an evaluation of teachers' performance. Different methods of evaluation must be employed. In the virtual school context, the principal may review the teachers' online communication in attempting to understand how much time a teacher spends on teaching or related duties, and through online lessons. Certainly "an electronic trail" (email records, discussion groups, web pages, etc.) of a teacher's work is available but we do not know the extent to which administrators use this information in assessing teacher performance. Assuming that they do use it, we do not know what evaluative practices and standards are being applied.

Administrators report that their duties shift from engaging in the regular day-to-day management required in the conventional school context to focusing on a role of advocate for the virtual school. Advocating for continued support from the school district, parents and teachers was one of the major reasons identified by administrators for the sustainability of student enrollment. The administrative advocacy role, then, is in reality about marketing the virtual school program.

The role of virtual school administrator requires adaptability to change, which may make stakeholders feel uneasy, insecure and at-risk because roles and requirements are altered, changed and interpreted. How their work fits with the requirements of the School Act and/or the expectations of a conventional school context may not be clear. Teachers may be concerned about how to replicate classroom learning in this new environment or they may lack confidence in their skills with the technology. Parents may have very different expectations regarding the control they have over what and how their children learn. Administrators must also be mindful that this uneasiness, insecurity and risk also extend to the staff, students and parents (Anderson and Lavid, 1986).

The time will no doubt come when the province will begin to have questions about how best to manage virtual or online schooling. At present, a substantial portion of the students receiving virtual schooling in the province are enrolled in the Alberta Distance Learning Centre, which emerged from the Alberta Correspondence School, a provincial initiative. Although the Alberta Distance Learning Centre is now administered through a local school jurisdiction, it is fair to say that the provincial ministry has maintained an active involvement in its development to date. From this experience and from research that the government has sponsored, it may become clear that standards need to be set for such things as assessment practices or teacher workloads. While many will be happy to have such guidance and direction, it may also reduce the extent to which the virtual schools can continue to function as an exploration of new options.

CHALLENGING TEACHER EXPECTATIONS

Virtual school teachers are concerned about the workloads they endure, many of them regard the workload as too onerous to be sustained long term. They reported that keeping current with changes in technology, keeping up with a larger marking load (since they only "see" students through the students' work), developing and revising online courses, communicating with parents and students, and engaging in professional development required exceptional time commitments. The "intensification" of teaching has also been a concern in the conventional teaching context within the past two decades, but online teachers feel they carry an even greater burden. As one spouse of a virtual school teacher said to one of the authors, "I knew I should worry when she didn't come back from the bathroom in the middle of the night and I found her answering email." Novelty and a sense of mission justifies the involvement of many current teachers, but the model will not grow if the workload is perceived as too demanding for the typical teacher.

Some teachers in Smith's study found that they had difficulty adjusting to the variability in student's progress through material. This is not just the normal variation due to ability or study habits, it is also a matter of students entering and completing at different times. While the model of "anytime/anywhere" learning would suggest that this is an acceptable, or even desirable, feature of online schooling, some virtual schools have limited the extent to which teachers must deal with this issue by imposing strict starting and ending dates for courses.

Teachers in Smith's study also expressed concern about lacking time for professional development, but teachers in another virtual school (not part of the study) where teachers are hired on part-time contracts, reported that the opportunities the virtual school provided for professional development was a rewarding feature of the position. Clearly, this is not such an easy option for full-time teachers, but it is an indication that when the time is available, online teachers avail themselves of the opportunities and value them. In an even more recent case, an online school contracted with a university to provide a graduate course online during normal working hours because 1) the teachers had the flexibility with their time due to the amount of evening work they did and 2) the school could make attendance at the course an expectation for employees. This situation seemed to work out very well and may be a valuable model for future professional development for full time teachers in online settings.

Virtual school teachers do not have regular daily schedules, so some feel that marking and preparation for classes was on their own time, outside of regular school hours. Teachers in regular classrooms do have "prep" time, but most would say that they spend many additional hours on these tasks. We really don't have a basis for assessing the total workload, but teachers with experience in both settings consistently say that online teaching demands more time, as do university faculty involved in distance education (estimates run from 50% to 100% more time).

Online teachers work at computers on desks at school or work. They sit still for long hours, rarely in ergonomically designed chairs. Some virtual school teachers in Smith's study indicated that they had medical confirmation that they had injuries and ailments directly attributable to their working environments.

THE BOTTOM LINE

Although the Provincial Achievement Tests (PAT) indicated that virtual school student achievement was, on average, below the Provincial Acceptable, parents were still satisfied with the virtual school. A provincial official has indicated that testing of virtual school students is highly problematic, since the range of enrolment patterns varies so greatly (including students who are in regular school full time and take additional courses online). The fact that the number of students tested was a small fraction of those believed to be attending virtual schools and the variation in types of virtual schooling offered also combine to make it impossible to have any overall sense of how well students in these schools are doing on the PAT.

Online students express concern about writing the PAT because they are required to write them in a conventional school setting. Since they may have found conventional school contexts somehow disadvantageous, they also feel disadvantaged by being tested in a setting that differs from the setting in which they learned (in this, the students are supported by testing research). In short, the bottom line for online student achievement is both dotted and curvy.

ISOLATION AND COMMUNICATION

Anyone familiar with the hustle and bustle of a typical school hallway, lunchroom or playground would realize that the vision of kids working quietly on computers in their own homes creates confused reactions. On the one hand, many parents have chosen virtual schools to avoid bullying, rough play or other negative social influences they see present in regular schools. On the other, we generally expect that schools are the place where children learn to get along with others in large and small groups and we expect that to be an enjoyable experience for the most part. Virtual school students have nearly all of their school communication in text form. The reader of this text will recognize that text-based communication is usually a pretty lonely business for both writer and reader.

Traditional home schooling parents report that they find alternative ways to achieve the ends of socialization: students have part-time jobs, they work with others in study groups, participate in social and recreational programs, etc. Virtual school students told Smith that they needed to be outgoing individuals, ensuring that socialization, collaboration, interaction and communication did occur both within and outside of the virtual school. Indeed, though the research on the topic is limited and the researchers often acknowledge a home schooling bias, the more careful studies, like Thomas Smedley's master's thesis, conclude, "the home educated children in this sample were significantly better socialized and more mature than those in public school." At the very least, we must say that questions about isolation and communication in virtual school environments remain open.

FOR WHOM ONLINE EDUCATION TOLLS

It seems clear to those involved that virtual schools are not for everyone. To succeed, students must have intrinsic motivation and independent learning skills; they must enjoy working with computers, read and write reasonably well, have consistent parental support and guidance and have very good time management skills. Kauffman (1989) and Flinck (1980) confirm these findings and support the need for these characteristics if a student is to be successful in an online educational environment.

The issue of "parental support and guidance" deserves elaboration. In the context of online education, this is not a matter of dinner table conversations on the topic, "how did school go today?" Parents need to be actively monitoring their child's work and engaging with them as they work their way through new materials. Online teachers can provide the academic content, but the parent is often responsible for informal assessments of progress, for frequent encouragement, and for supervision to ensure that work is done in a timely manner.

THE OTHER BOTTOM LINE

In Alberta, the provincial government funds virtual schools through per-pupil grants to the school districts. Many of the schools also accept "outside" students on a fee-for-service basis. For example, other schools may pay for the online courses that the student registers in – for example, if the student is taking a physics course that her own school does not offer. Some students pay for their own online courses – for example, students past the age of 19 seeking to complete high school or students from out-of-province. Parents of elite athletes may pay additional fees for virtual schools that accommodate their child's travel, competition and practice schedules.

Perelman (1993) argues that the proliferation of schooling alternatives will result in a greater need for restructuring educational bureaucracies to manage the differences. Similarly, Webber (1995) argues, "Educational consumerism is a characteristic of the era in which Albertans live and...this competition might lead to a healthy transformation of public education." This transformation may see school districts ensuring that all of their educational contexts are pedagogically sound so as to draw as many customers to their districts as they can.

A relatively unexamined funding question is the cost of technology for teachers and students. At least to some extent, the reliance on home computers may constitute a subsidy for the schools by reducing other capital costs. Some virtual schools have purchased computers for their students, some lease computers, some require the student to obtain access on their own. Some online schools subsidize the cost of an Internet connection; others expect the family to pick up the cost. In all of this, the question of equitable access to public schooling looms large and the answers are elusive.

Administrators at the four virtual schools in Smith's study reported that they must have open access and cannot discriminate because these schools are publicly funded institutions. The virtual schools can only advise and recommend characteristics of students who would most benefit or find success in the virtual school. The promotional materials of other virtual schools make clear that this is a general pattern.

"WHAT WE HAVE HERE IS A PROBLEM IN COMMUNICATION"

In an online environment, students spend more time working with course content independently, leading teachers and administrators to see the environment as friendly to the kind of constructivist teaching that encourages students to actively develop their own mental organizations for material rather than passively accepting teachers' dictates. For example, as early as 1987, Harasim reported that 10 to 15 percent of online class time was directed by teacher talk as opposed to 80 percent of the class time in a conventional setting. This increased role of student-based communication, combined with the now hackneyed observation that "on the Internet no one knows you are a dog," may be leading to a more equal form of exchange between teachers and students. Some virtual school students talked about it this way:

> *Mike: One thing that I find that my teacher does that's different is that when you e-mail. Your teacher or when you talk to your teacher, you don't have to call them Mr. Perkins or Mr. Something, you can call them by their first name. Like hey Jean, you don't have to talk to them like they're some adult that's not approachable. They're completely approachable because they are someone who is at your level. Like to me calling a teacher, like I mean if it's an adult, it's like a person you don't know or it someone you're going to meet then you'd call them Mr. or Mrs. But when it's a teacher you see every day that you know and stuff I'm more prone to not wanting to call them, because to me that's kind of impersonal. But when I can call the teacher by their first name which is just a nice thing to be able to do because you don't do it often. It helps me to create a personal relationship, which doesn't happen with all the teachers. It's just a very personal relationship.*
>
> *Alice: I'm still uneasy when it comes to calling a teacher by their first name. I don't know why I've just always been. I like to call them mister or missus.*
>
> *Jason: I find with e-mails and what not that the teacher gets to know you more on a more personal bases than in an regular school because they're responding solely to you, you don't have a crowd of people there wanting to ask the exact same thing. It's you talking to the teacher not a whole group of people. What I've noticed is they're not as up-tight with using their Mr. and Mrs. because well, by the way I look at it, you have to write out their last name and what not but their first name could be easier because you might not know how to spell their last name and really, I wouldn't want to insult somebody by spelling their last name wrong.*

Teachers did have concerns, however, about the issue of not being able to actually see the reactions of their students. Both teachers and students indicate that occasional telephone or in-person meetings add to the quality of their interaction.

Although Szabo (1998) suggests that the human need to understand the world and have a mental model of it may imply a need to be physically present with other human beings, it is clear that there are positive patterns of socialization, interaction, collaboration and communication in online schools. It may be, as Tapscott might argue, that new models of interaction will emerge in a generation raised with interactive computing. To again borrow from an online student:

> *Jen: (What) I like the best about it is that the teachers that you have are so willing, no matter, like if their busy they don't complain to you that they're busy. You have their undivided attention because you email them or you ask them a question and they will respond to you. But you know that they, it's not like they can say, "I'm busy right now."...they will reply to you within two days of school. I have the teacher's undivided attention when I need it. And then that's good because I don't have to fight with them. When I need them they'll answer me and I'll get a very good answer.*

CONCUSSION

Virtual schooling is off to a good start. Teachers are using technology effectively to reach students that might otherwise be missed. Parents, students and teachers report positive experiences with their online schools. But then, so do parents, students and teachers in most public schools in Canada. When people express discontent, it is with "schools," not "my school." It often seems like it must be "other people's schools" that are the problem, but we can understand it better than that. In the particular, people believe their schools work well; the problem is with some general notion of "schooling." For virtual schools, at this point in time, the generalities are elusive. They are new and varied and experimental. In the entrepreneurial climate in which they are emerging, we can reasonably expect that market forces will shape their destinies: the fit will survive.

Fitness will no doubt be determined in part by the students' success on some form of provincial or standardized testing, since policy-makers like numbers. Preparing to establish credibility in this format may mean that the schools will have to be deliberate about preparing students for a kind of assessment they rarely encounter in online learning. As a matter of survival, that is often what happens in regular schools as well – days and weeks are given over to preparing for examinations rather than working with the course content in creative and constructive ways.

Fitness will likely also rest on the ability of virtual school leaders to convey the message that online education is not "correspondence school." Too many people, including many school leaders and teachers' union officials, live with the unexamined belief that anything that involves distance education can be equated with an image of an isolated student struggling unaided through piles of paperwork, basically become self-educated with the help of recommended readings. People who have never participated in an online forum, who do not make regular use of email in their work, who forget that teachers and students can use telephones, are inclined to brand virtual schools with this image and to assume that no meaningful learning can take place in these environments. Confronting and correcting that perception may be a more difficult challenge than raising achievement test scores.

The big questions, however, have not to do with the success or survival of individual virtual schools but of the impact of the virtual school movement on schooling in general. At present, the virtual school bag is as mixed or more mixed than the regular school bag. Apart from reliance on technologies that are also available to regular school teachers and students (and which students are increasingly required to learn in any event), are there lessons and directions for "schooling" from the virtual school experience? They use the same teaching methods, the same curricula, similar teaching materials (sometimes more electronic media) and they seek to engage learners in the same ways even though they must do it through computer-mediated communication. So, are they sheep in wolf's clothing? Is there anything there to be alarmed about or excited about?

There is. While the expectation that students are engaged in constructivist learning simply because they are working independently is naïve, the very fact that online teachers are working toward a different model of learning is important. That they are frequently working toward this model of learning with a clientele that is more-than-normally predisposed to favor the conservatism of a back-to-basics schooling (and being well-received doing so) is worthy of note. It is also noteworthy that the integration of technology is pretty much a foregone conclusion in virtual schools. These students will likely find that notions like "information society," "knowledge management," and "single-source documentation" make sense to them intuitively. They will learn and work in computer rich environments as if that is the way it is supposed to be.

Can we look to a time when all education will be virtual education? Well, maybe, but we can't look forward to it with optimism or enthusiasm. Part of what we are learning from virtual schools is that the whole notion of "school choice" may have merit and that its merits may be played out within the contexts of a more responsive public education system. If we now steer a path toward a completely online educational system, we will be ignoring that lesson. Just as there are kids that are distressed by roughhousing that others enjoy in physical schools, there are students who would wither in the absence of daily face-to-face contact with other students. There are kids who desperately need direct contact with a caring, compassionate adult who values learning in general and who fosters it in them personally. There are kids who will always need "Jiminy Cricket" reminding them of what must be done and when. What we need to learn is how to respond to this diversity sensitively and fairly and to recognize that equity lies not in giving everyone the same education, but in helping everyone to get the education that they need.

References

Anderson, R.E. & Lavid, J.S. (1986). "The Effective Principal: Leader or Manager?" *NASSP Bulletin*, April, 82-84.

Baker, W., Hale, T. & Gifford, B.R. (1997). "From Theory to Implementation: The Mediated Learning Approach to Computer-Mediated Instruction, Learning and Assessment." *Educom Review, 32*(5), 1-10.

Bulls, M., Brown, M., Hunter, W.J. & Fryatt, M. (1996). "Virtual Teaching in the Information Age: Preservice Teacher Perceptions." *Computers in New Zealand Schools. 8*(3) 12-15.

Garrison, D.R. (1990). "Communications Technology". In D.R. Garrison & D. Shale (Eds.), *Education at a Distance: From Issues to Practice* (pp. 41-52). Malabar, FL: Robert E. Krieger Publishing Company.

Harasim, L. (1987). "Computer-Mediated Cooperation in Education: Group Learning Networks." In *Proceedings of the Second Guelph Symposium on Computer Conferencing*. Guelph, ON: University of Guelph.

Hiltz, R., Johnson, K. & Turoff, M. (1996). "Experiments in Group Decision Making." *Human Communication Research, 13*(2), 225-235.

Holmberg, B. (1989). *Theory and Practice of Distance Education.* London: Routledge.

Jonassen, D. (1992). "Evaluating Constructivist Learning." In T. Duffy & D. Jonassen (Eds.), *Constructivism and the Technology of Instruction: A Conversation* (pp. 112-127). Hillsdale, NJ: Lawrence Erlbaum.

Kaufman, D. (1989). "Third Generation Course Design in Distance Education." In R. Sweet, (Ed.), *Post-secondary Distance Education in Canada* (pp. 61-78). Athabasca, AB: Athabasca University.

Logan, R. (1995). *The Fifth Language.* Toronto, ON: Stoddart Publishing Co. Limited.

Mayberry, M. (1991). *Conflict and Social Determinism. The Reprivatization of Education.* Paper presented at the American Educational Research Association Meeting, Chicago. (ERIC Reproduction Service No. 330 107).

Muirhead, W. (2000). *Teachers' Perspectives of Online Education in Alberta.* Unpublished doctoral dissertation, The University of Alberta, Edmonton.

Oblinger, D. & Maruyama, M. (1996). *Distributed Learning.* Cause Professional Paper Series, #14. Boulder, CO: Cause.

Perelman, L. (1993). *School's Out.* NY: Morrow.

Reeves, T. (2001). *E-Learning and the Professorate: The Issue of Productivity.* Invited address, EDMEDIA 2001, Tampere, Finland.

Riel, M. & Becker, H. J. (2000). *The Beliefs, Practices, and Computer Use of Teacher Leaders.* Presented to the AERA conference, New Orleans. Available online: http://www.crito.uci.edu/tlc/findings/aera/start-page.html

Smedley, T.C. (1992). *Socialization of Home School Children: A Communication Approach.* Unpublished masters thesis. Radford University. Available online: http://members.aol.com/tomsmedley/smedleys.htm#chap4

Smith, R. (2000) *Virtual Schools in the K-12 Context.* Unpublished doctoral dissertation, The University of Calgary, Calgary.

Szabo, M. (1998) "Updating Our Mental Models to Take Advantage of Modern Communication Technology." In Z. Berge & M. Collins (Eds.), *Wired Together: Volume 1* (pp. 155-173). Cresskill, NJ: Hampton Press.

Tapscott, D. (1998). *Growing Up Digital: The Rise of the Net Generation.* McGraw-Hill: New York.

Webber, C. (1995). "Educational Change in Alberta, Canada: An Analysis of Recent Events." *Education Policy Analysis Archives*, Vol. 3, No. 12, July 9. 1995, ISSN 1068-2341.

Weizenbaum, J. (1976). *Computer Power and Human Reason: From Judgment to Calculation.* San Francisco: W.H. Freeman.

William, C.J. & Brown, S.W. (1990). "A Review of the Research Issues in the Use Computer-related Technologies for Instruction: What Do We Know? *International Journal of Instructional Media, 17*(3), 213-225.

Zellhofer, S., Collins, M. & Berge, Z. (1998). "Why Use Computer-mediated Communication?" In Z. Berge & M. Collins (Eds.), *Wired Together: Volume 2* (pp. 1-14). Cresskill, NJ: Hampton Press.

Part III

Technology Leadership and Teacher Education

CHAPTER 10
THE MANY FACES OF ICT LEADERSHIP FOR DIGITAL TECHNOLOGY AND <u>CANADIAN PEDAGOGY</u>

DIANNE YEE

MY VENTURES INTO ICT LEADERSHIP

I have been wrestling with the concept of information and communication technology (ICT) leadership since the early 1990's when I became principal of an ICT project school in "small-town" Saskatchewan. I was blessed with a newly-renovated facility equipped with one computer for every two students, a considerable budget for teacher professional development, and the expert assistance of an advisory committee from the Saskatchewan universities, the Saskatchewan Teachers' Federation, the Saskatchewan School Trustees' Association, Apple Canada, SaskTel, and Northern Telecom Canada. In the everyday world of a school principal, there is little time for professional reflection or research. Fortunately, the university professors who were part of our project team assisted us in using action research to document our journey into the unfamiliar territory of using ICT as a teaching and learning tool within a middle school environment. Our experienced staff members had come from a variety of traditionally structured elementary or junior high schools and most of us had little or no computer skills. As a newly formed group, we were expected to experiment, to collaborate, and to restructure. We were encouraged to ask the difficult questions about how we learned, how we interacted with our students and each other, how we structured our daily routines, and how ICT could assist us with the work of teaching and learning.

As a result of this experience, I had many questions regarding the responsibility of principals to foster appropriate ICT use in their schools. In 1997, I began a doctoral program with the hope of re-examining the roles of the principal, the nature of effective professional development, and the competencies required of educational leaders in current ICT contexts. I believed that principals who advocated using ICT to enhance learning and teaching faced a myriad of leadership challenges. But, the ICT leadership of principals remained a topic that rarely was considered when educators or academics discussed the unfulfilled promise of ICT in schools. In response, I decided to investigate ICT leadership by exploring the lived experiences of principals in ten carefully selected ICT-enriched schools in Canada, the United States, and New Zealand (Yee, 1999). The principals who participated in the study were recommended by university professors from the fields of educational technology and educational leadership who perceived the principals to be competent ICT users, working in ICT-enriched schools. Because of my previous research regarding ICT-enriched schools, I also knew of several principals and schools that I hoped to include in my study. In order to be considered "ICT-enriched," I selected schools with a significant number of networked computers – at least one computer in each classroom supplemented by computers in the office, library, labs, instructional pods, or common areas. The schools had Internet access, and there was evidence of multiple information and communication technologies in use, e.g., computers, laser disks, CD-ROM, fax, telephone and Polycom, television and video, digital cameras. The schools also were or had been involved in higher education partnerships or corporate sponsorships. Finally, the schools had developed an explicit ICT mission statement, vision, or strategic plan.

My study examined how principals in these schools used ICT in their daily work, and it outlined their perceptions of ICT leadership. The study traced the experiences of the principals as they developed personal competence with ICT while at the same time assisting staff members and students to acquire their own knowledge and skills. In addition, the study examined the perceptions of staff members, students, and parents regarding the responsibility of the principals for personal competence with ICT and for the overall ICT use in their schools.

ICT Leadership in Practice – So, Who Should be Responsible for What?

Because of my research and my work experiences, I have come to believe that a variety of people share responsibility for ICT leadership in our schools. In this chapter I attempt to consider the ICT leadership of principals, of ICT specialist teachers, and of classroom teachers in ICT-enriched schools. Choosing to discuss principals first does not imply a hierarchy of responsibility – only the place where I have spent most of my time working with educational technology. However, during my work as a school administrator, I have always chosen to keep my job as a classroom teacher. And, because of my interest and skill in working with ICT, at times I have worn the hat of "computer teacher." It is interesting to note that ICT leadership roles also overlapped for most of the principals in my study. As examples, one assistant principal had a media specialist background; another assistant principal shared the job of school media coordinator; and one principal was previously an ICT coordinator for the school district.

THE ICT LEADERSHIP OF PRINCIPALS

I hoped my study of ICT leadership would present the rich descriptions of each case – each principal and each ICT-enriched school – that would document its uniqueness, but I was also searching for shared patterns that appeared across cases and derived their significance as generic processes or constructs. The principals in the study were certainly a heterogeneous sample. They were located in three countries, each with varying educational governance structures. The principals, both men and women, were at different stages of their administrative and teaching careers. Their schools, varying in size from 250 to 850 students, were located in rural areas, small cities, and the suburbs of large urban areas. The schools also were at varying stages in the cycle of ICT planning, implementation, and evaluation. Despite their personal differences and the differences in their school contexts, the principals shared unwavering visions that ICT had the potential to improve student learning. The principals also portrayed a passionate commitment to providing appropriate ICT professional development opportunities for staff members. Finally, each principal was a very skilful entrepreneur who used a carefully constructed social network to locate creative sources of ICT hardware, software, and expertise.

In the leadership framework that arose from my study, I suggested that ICT leadership as demonstrated by these principals might be organized into eight categories – each with specific characteristics or properties. Using descriptors that I selected from the language of the participants, the categories of ICT leadership that emerged were: equitable providing, learning-focussed envisioning, adventurous learning, patient teaching, protective enabling, constant monitoring, entrepreneurial networking, and careful challenging. In my study, there was no intent to create a rating scale for principals or to suggest that an exemplary principal should, or even could, possess strong characteristics associated with each one of the ICT leadership categories.

(In the following descriptions of the leadership categories and in the remainder of the chapter, the phrases in quotation marks indicate the specific language of the study participants.) It is interesting to speculate why the ICT leadership characteristics and practices outlined in this study resonate with a number of the transformational leadership factors (e.g., charisma, inspiration, individualized consideration, intellectual stimulation), dimensions, and practices described by Burns (1978), Bass and Avolio (1990) Leithwood (1994) and others. This is an area of inquiry that I believe warrants further attention.

Equitable providing. In this ICT leadership category the principal was the source of the school ICT hardware, software, and complementary resources:

> *"The teachers believe it's my job to find ways for us to do things [with ICT]. I never take no for an answer...even if I run into a dead end. If it's really important to us, they know I'll make it happen." (Principal interview, January 1999)*

The descriptor *equitable* indicated the importance that the principals, staff members, and students placed on the principal "providing access" to the ICT for all staff members and students, not only for select "techie" teachers and students. A teacher explained that, "It's not hard to get the computers because of the way the school is laid out. It's not a lab you have to go into in a formal sense. The physical layout allows that [flexible access] to happen." In one school, the principal mentioned that "any student from any room [could] use any of the computers on demand," and he employed a computer desktop messaging system to ensure that "students [could] be easily found when necessary." Associated with *equitable providing* was the value placed on the principal securing the technical support to keep the ICT "infrastructure robust":

> *[Teachers] get their students out there to research something or to do math, and [an ICT failure] happens two or three times, and they*

don't try it again. With students twirling around and poking one another, [teachers] are going to give up. They're willing to give this a try, but if they have too many glitches, they'll just give up. (Classroom teacher interview, January 1999)

Often the principals readjusted staffing formulas to provide "small parcels of time" for interested staff members to do important ICT work:

In many schools [creating a school website] is another task that is added on to the technologically competent teacher in the school after the rest of the day is complete. If something is of value, then you need to give time and resources to do that. That is something that we probably do more than many other school environments do. (Principal interview, February 1999)

Learning-focussed envisioning. The principal also was the "keeper of the [school ICT] vision." A specialist teacher indicated that most principals were not able to "hold the vision and support people towards that vision." She explained that:

...the rest of them deek out all of the time. Their images of teaching and learning have not progressed...because they are not fluent enough or comfortable enough with the technology. They can spout the words of teaching and learning changing, but when you start to make some of those changes they are really uncomfortable with it. (ICT specialist teacher interview, January 1999)

Learning-focussed described the value that the principals, staff members, and parents placed on the principal keeping student learning at the centre of ICT decision making. Another teacher reiterated the importance of the principal's clear vision and "personal investment in the idea of using technology" for teaching and learning: "There has to be a passion in the principal's mindset that this is something that is going to improve the achievement, the education, of students." One principal explained his focus on authentic student learning with ICT:

A big part of what I think technology enables us to do is to allow students to be able to make the work their own. We've all seen classrooms where all of the kids are doing the same worksheet at the same time. We've seen the art projects where all the students are pasting tissue paper onto the same picture the same way. [ICT] allows us to go beyond that paradigm and enable students, not to do school work, but to do their own work. That's what makes the difference in our school. If you look at the way the kids are working and you talk to them about their work, they're not doing schoolwork any longer. It's not the teacher's work; it's their work. (Principal interview, February 1999)

Another principal reinforced the importance of continually examining the value of ICT in student learning:

[ICT] is a recent addition to the [teacher's] toolbox that we need to examine and explore and look at what the possibilities are. I don't think we know what all of the possibilities are yet. But, if we keep asking questions about how does it impact, or how could it impact [on student learning], we will have a better understanding of how we might use technology [skilfully]. (Principal interview, February 1999)

Adventurous learning. In this category the principal was someone who demonstrated a desire to be an ICT learner along with staff members and students. *Adventurous* indicated the value that the principals and staff members placed on the principal developing personal competence with ICT and being willing to experiment with new technologies and learning strategies. A principal indicated that all principals should be expected to have some degree of skill with ICT: "If you don't use it and have an understanding of what is possible; how can you possibly have any vision of how [ICT] can add value [to teaching and learning]." Although most staff members did not expect their principals to be ICT experts, they did expect principals to make learning ICT "a big part of their professional improvement every year" so that they would be able "to imagine the possibilities that technology might offer" to schools. One teacher expressed concern that the principal "wouldn't know what the opportunities [with ICT] were," and he "wouldn't know how to mentor or work with the teachers" if he did not have the experience of learning how to work with ICT himself. Another teacher believed that a principal's ICT experiences and skills often determined the school's financial allocation for ICT: "Unless you have had experience with technology yourself, you don't tend to recognise what the capabilities are. The budget doesn't allow for it because the budget is not seen as needing to allow for it."

Patient teaching. In this category the principal was "close to the classroom" and was willing to teach students, staff members, and parents. These principals often were "very keen to teach" staff members, and they attempted to create many flexible learning opportunities. *Patient* indicated the importance that staff members placed on the principal being non-judgmental when they requested assistance to learn ICT. A teacher explained:

> *He made [ICT instruction] very available to absolutely everyone that wanted it, and if you couldn't come at those times he would sit down with you at noon hours and show you how to do these things. ...He will take the time. He's one of those people who will not ask you to do anything he can't do or that he does not have the time to help you with. (Classroom teacher interview, January 1999)*

Associated with *patient teaching* was the value placed on the principal encouraging all staff members to participate in appropriate ICT professional development activities.

Protective enabling. The principal also was someone who created shared leadership activities for staff members and students. Although these principals understood that they possessed "positional power," often they valued shared leadership because it allowed for creation of "energized and committed" staff members:

> *When you help people to pursue their passions you're going to have tremendous commitment [from staff members]...because you have two things running in alignment, the personal and professional goals and aspirations of the teacher and the organisational goals that we have set collectively. (Principal interview, February 1999)*

According to a principal, his "enabling leadership [allowed] leadership to emerge in various places in the school," and as a result he had "the enviable role of being a leader of leaders." *Protective* described the value that the principals and staff members placed on the principal being willing to "remove the roadblocks" that were characteristic of educational bureaucracies. A teacher described the necessity for the principal to support innovative teaching practice:

> *Even if colleagues line up against you, somehow that administrator conveys to you that they believe you're on the right track and will support you even if you don't fill all of the papers out or attend to all of the details...so we don't have to spend all of our time deflecting arrows. (Classroom teacher interview, January 1999)*

Associated with *protective enabling* was the importance placed on the principal advocating ICT as a learning tool and being willing to defend the school ICT vision when it was threatened by public or school district forces. A parent explained that, "The teachers that we really value highly would never do what they're doing or be supported in another school. Their hands would be slapped, to put it mildly, for doing what they're trying to do here."

Constant monitoring. In this ICT leadership category the principal was someone who ensured that staff members and students were using the ICT according to the vision of the school, the district, the province/state, or the country. A principal explained, "I expect teachers to use technology here. They know that. They're really clear on that. If it is true that it is a powerful tool…then why wouldn't they be using it?" If the district had not mandated teacher ICT competency, then the principals and staff members often developed their own standards or "benchmarks" based on the outcomes articulated for students. *Constant* illustrated the value that the principals, staff members, and parents placed on the principal providing appropriate supervision for teaching staff. According to several staff members, the principal communicated a focus on classroom practice and accountability for their ICT professional development:

It's one thing to just say, "Here is someone who's going to teach you this particular technology. Have a good day!" It's another thing to say, "This person is going to give you the technology tools. Once you have the information you need to report back with what you've learned and how you can use it [in your classroom]." (Classroom teacher interview, January 1999)

Another teacher summarized the principal's ICT supervisory competencies and highlighted her ability for "multi-tasking":

I see here with ____ an excellent model of a principal who supports the use of technology because she's so good at supervising people and programs. She provides a structure and a support to really encourage the use of technology. She makes sure we get the people to come in and trouble shoot. She's great at making sure committees run well, and we have a really strong technology committee. She's excellent at being on top of budget and in finding resources to make things happen. She's great at delegating, but she's there supervising making sure the work gets done. She's always doing several things simultaneously…It's the structures that are in place and her constant supervision, constant monitoring, to make sure things are happening. *(Classroom teacher interview, January 1999)*

Entrepreneurial networking. The principals also were skilful "partnership builders" with school district administrators, ICT vendors, and higher education personnel. One principal described the importance of developing "ethical partnerships" in education:

We have tried to define clearly what the values and benefits are in advance of implementing any kind of partnership, and we've talked about the benefits for us and for potential partners. We've learned how best to capitalise on these relationships, but it's been through identifying and adhering to what we said was really important [about student learning]. (Principal interview, January 1999)

Entrepreneurial indicated the value that the principals, staff members, and parents placed on the principal being able to "groom relationships" and develop a support network in order to find the necessary ICT resources for the school. Another principal explained that, "Some of my dearest colleagues are the maintenance workers for the district, and they know that I respect them for what they do." As a result, she consistently received positive responses regarding ICT infrastructure issues. Still, these principals had "to scrounge and to be in the right spot at the right time . . . always looking for opportunities" in order to find the necessary ICT resources for their schools:

I guess I've always believed that if you want something, and you know that it's right to want [it], it's okay to ask...If I know that the ____ Center is remodelling and giving away desks and chairs, I'll make a contact and see what I can do about it...We just cut deals with everyone. (Principal interview, January 1999)

Careful challenging. In this category the principal was an innovative educator – someone "on the edge of knowledge" regarding ICT and learning. A principal compared the "commitment and passion" associated with learning both in kindergarten and in graduate school to explain his desire to create a similar learning environment:

So what happens in between [kindergarten and graduate school]? We do something totally different. A big part of it is historical. That's just the way things have evolved in our educational system. It's based on a time that no longer exists and needs that are no longer present, yet we continue to live out that legacy. We really need to change. (Principal interview, February 1999)

These principals often valued opportunities to "challenge [educational] assumptions" and found inspiration "in breaking those barriers that are so traditionally entrenched" in school bureaucracies. One principal explained that for him, "Leadership doesn't set the limits...It helps people break limits." This type of leadership often required that he did not limit his thinking to "what we have conventionally seen the roles [of principals] to be." Another principal especially valued developing business and higher education partners as allies in order "to break through some of the constraints of the forces that exist in the district." *Careful* described the importance that the principals and parents placed on the principal having enough political sophistication to understand how much risk-taking would be accepted or tolerated within the educational organisation, without jeopardising her career or creating difficulties for his school. For several principals there was an underlying sense that their "butts are out on a line" and that ICT leadership could be "a very uncomfortable place" at times.

The ICT Leadership of Specialist Teachers. As part of my study I also interviewed and observed ICT specialist teachers in the schools. Depending on the location and the ICT vision of their school, these teachers described themselves as technology facilitators, media co-ordinators, information specialists, technology lab teachers, information skills teachers, or information technology specialist teachers.

The specialist teachers definitely demonstrated some of the ICT leadership characteristics found in the principals. As a reflection of *equitable providing*, although the specialist teachers did not possess the final budget control, many of them were very influential in acquiring appropriate ICT hardware, software, and complementary resources for their schools. They frequently expressed concern that there was equitable access to the ICT for all staff members and students. The specialist teachers who were responsible for media centres or "Information Stations" often developed flexible loan procedures to encourage students and staff members to use the available technologies. A number of these teachers helped provide valuable technical support—the onsite trouble shooting that kept the ICT infrastructure operating well.

Learning-focussed envisioning. Specialist teachers also were very influential in creating the school ICT vision and were concerned with maintaining student learning as a focus of ICT decision making.

According to a specialist teacher, "meaningful use" of ICT depended on the individual student:

> For some students, the best thing might be learning how to word process because that is where they want to go. For other students, it might be challenging them at the higher-level thinking skills. We have some programs that have no set answers, and they really just have to go in and explore. For others, it might be the ELF club where they're doing science research on how to best enhance fishes' reproductive cycles. Or the video announcements every morning. Or using the digital camera. There are so many different facets, and every kid is different. (ICT specialist teacher interview, January 1999)

They were active members of the school ICT committees and frequently sought ICT professional development opportunities.

Adventurous learning. All of the specialist teachers in the study had a history of developing personal competence with ICT. One specialist teacher had developed her technology skill because she was "willing to spend some time exploring" with ICT: "I just kind of make myself available for opportunities to learn more about education and technology." Another specialist explained that ICT had become an integral part of her daily work: "I think you can look forward but once you have the bells and whistles…I would find it really hard not to have an automated library. Or how could I go back to doing weekly announcements over the intercom?" when she had become used to working with their Kids News Network video announcements.

Patient teaching. All of the specialist teachers were responsible for instructing students – in classroom groupings, in small groups, or as individuals. Sometimes they worked as partners with classroom teachers providing the ICT expertise or teaching specific ICT skills to students. One specialist teacher explained that her ICT leadership role was "working alongside teachers who want[ed] to push their own thinking, [working] with them in the context of their own classrooms." A number of the specialist teachers also accepted a leadership role in ICT professional development of staff. One specialist teacher explained that she needed to be "one step ahead" of the staff members to anticipate their ICT questions and needs. Staff members valued the assistance of the specialist teachers as "teaching partners," but also placed importance on the specialist teacher being non-judgmental when they requested assistance to learn to use the ICT.

Entrepreneurial networking. Many of the specialist teachers also were skilful "partnership builders" with school district administrators, ICT vendors, and higher education personnel. They often were given opportunities by their principals to attend meetings, workshops, and conferences where they developed collegial networks.

THE ICT LEADERSHIP OF CLASSROOM TEACHERS

In addition, I interviewed and observed several classroom teachers in each of the ICT-enriched schools, and these teachers also demonstrated ICT leadership. In reference to *equitable providing*, although the classroom teachers did not possess as much influence as the principals or the ICT specialists, many were very eager to locate appropriate ICT hardware, software, and complementary resources for their classrooms. They also expressed concern that there was equitable access to the ICT for all of their students. Several classroom teachers were concerned with gender issues related to ICT access for students, and they created structures within their classrooms to ensure that both girls and boys were allowed appropriate access to the technology. A number of the classroom teachers were skilled in doing minor ICT repairs in their classrooms and in their colleagues' classrooms in order to keep the whole system operating smoothly.

Learning-focussed envisioning. A number of classroom teachers also were very influential in creating the school ICT vision and were concerned with maintaining student learning as a focus of all ICT decision making. They served on the school ICT committees and frequently sought professional development opportunities related to ICT in their classrooms. Their ICT professional development took various formats: presentations during faculty meetings, informal workshops which arose from emergent ICT issues, ongoing "technology support groups," formal district training sessions on specific topics for teachers and their student representatives, and ICT conferences.

Adventurous learning. All of the classroom teachers in the study demonstrated a desire to be an ICT learner. In these ICT-enriched environments, teachers developed an acceptance of learning ICT skills with their students. One teacher explained: "A third of my students will know more about technology than me, but my students don't think any less of me. They say, 'Oh let's show this to Mrs.____,' and they get excited about it." Several teachers revealed that, because they were competent and confident teachers who were open to change and to taking risks, "learning alongside students" did not worry them.

They were willing to experiment with new technologies and learning strategies. Many of the classroom teachers used computers daily with their students for writing process activities, for research, for alternate presentation of difficult concepts, or as a motivational device. They indicated that one of the most valuable uses of ICT was accessing "difficult-to-find" information, "straight answers," or information written by students. They also valued ICT for meeting individual student needs in multilevel classrooms and for "allowing non-traditional learners to achieve success." In addition to using ICT for student reporting and classroom organization tasks, teachers used the Internet and email as vehicles for distributing information to students and parents.

Patient teaching. Obviously, all of the classroom teachers were responsible for student instruction. For many teachers, using ICT had been a catalyst to create "learning communities" with a shift in traditional classroom power structures. They often promoted peer learning with ICT because they believed that "the most powerful learning with technology came from students teaching other students." And, their teaching often extended to their colleagues as they worked in teams with other classroom teachers on interdisciplinary projects. A number of the classroom teachers also accepted a formal leadership role in ICT professional development by sharing their ICT "success stories" with colleagues or providing skill-based workshops. A culture of ICT information exploration and sharing developed at the schools such that staff members who found promising strategies, projects, technology, or software made other staff members aware through the use of voice mail or email.

As a final note regarding the ICT leadership of classroom teachers, it is important to understand that there are considerable differences in the ways that ministries of education delineate the requirements for teacher competence with ICT. For example, Alberta Learning has been very explicit about the ICT outcomes expected for students at grades 3, 6, 9, and 12 and that these outcomes be developed through the core subject areas (Alberta Education, 1998), but it has made only passing reference to the ICT competencies of classroom teachers. Other ministries of education, a number of them in the United States, have been very explicit about teacher ICT competencies and have included those competencies in the teacher certification process (e.g., ISTE, 2000). These anomalies remind us of the importance of considering ICT leadership in its local context.

THE IMPACT OF ICT LEADERSHIP

So, how do the experiences of principals, specialist teachers, and classroom teachers in ICT-enriched schools apply to Canadian schools in general? Why should educators pause to consider ICT leadership? Governments in many countries, Canada included, view ICT as instrumental in creating a highly skilled workforce capable of coping with the rapid technological change of the 21st century. Many educators also believe that students will need both content knowledge and fluency with ICT in order to be successful workers and continual learners in a fluid, expanding global economy (Sparks, 1998). And, ministries of education have placed an emphasis on ICT to ensure that students develop the abilities to make informed choices about ICT, to use ICT skilfully, and to become technological innovators (Alberta Education, 1998; Bitter, Thomas, Knezek, Friske, Taylor, Wiebe, & Kelly, 1997; Learning Media, 1995). Thus, use of ICT in our schools has become both a pedagogical and a political issue. As one of the teachers in the study suggested, "It's an obligation now. We just have to accept that [ICT] is all around us."

As an educator, I know that information and communication technologies may be used in a variety of ways in schools. But, not all current ICT use in schools is meaningful, pedagogically sound, fiscally responsible, or ethical.

As a principal, I need to ensure that the limited human and financial resources of my school are being used wisely. When ICT is purchased I must be confident that I have enough ICT skill and knowledge to make decisions that will allow my staff members and students access to the most appropriate ICT tools for teaching and learning. I have learned that I must shift my personal vision to value ICT as a learning tool rather than as a course to be taught in isolation. I also need to accept that a shared leadership style will help me to manage my workload and will foster staff member commitment to developing a school vision for ICT in teaching and learning. I will promote "any technology at any time for any learning purpose" access to ICT by students and staff members. I know that I must "put the best machines in the hands of teachers" rather than in computer labs, and it is important that I deploy computers in "easy-access, high-use areas" such as classrooms, libraries, or hallways. In addition, I will remove the singular "computer teacher" position from my staff roster, and be clear about my expectations for all teachers to learn to use ICT in their classrooms. But, I will provide "appropriate training and adequate time" so that several staff members can assist with on-site network administration and troubleshooting. I know that neither principals, nor teachers, develop comfort or skill with ICT by listening to experts talk; instead, I will support "hands-on, needs-based, just-in-time" professional development for all staff members. I also need to follow up with appropriate supervision – so teachers know I really care about whether or not they use ICT in teaching and learning. I will continue to "groom a network" of people who can help me find answers to ICT questions; and those individuals might be teachers, students, parents, ICT vendors, "switched on" principals, university faculty, maintenance workers, or technical support people – I will "cast a wide net." I also need to actively search for "ethical partnerships with credible organizations" outside of my school to provide additional sources of ICT equipment and expertise. But most importantly, I must continue to be ICT learner along with my staff members and students.

As an ICT specialist teacher, I must have easy access to appropriate ICT infrastructure and resources for my daily work with teachers and students. I need my principal to be respectful of my ICT competence related to purchasing appropriate ICT hardware and software and to ICT policy development. I also need my principal to support my ICT professional development initiatives so that I am able to develop a network of ICT colleagues and so that I am equipped to assist classroom teachers to use ICT tools in pedagogically sound ways. Most importantly, I must continue to model appropriate teaching and learning with ICT alongside classroom teachers and students.

And as a classroom teacher, I must have appropriate ICT infrastructure in my classroom and easily accessible ICT resources throughout my school. I need a supportive principal and ICT specialist teachers to assist me in using ICT tools in a manner consistent with our school and provincial vision for ICT in teaching and learning. Finally, I also must be an eager learner and a patient teacher, assisting my students and colleagues as we learn to use ICT, with wisdom, in our daily work.

REFERENCES

Alberta Education (1998). *Information and Communication Technology, Kindergarten to Grade 12: An Interim Program of Studies*. Edmonton, AB: Author.

Bass, B.M. & Avolio, B.J. (1990). *Transformational Leadership Development: Manual for the Multifactor Leadership Questionnaire*. Palo Alto, CA: Consulting Psychologists Press, Inc.

Bitter, G., Thomas, L., Knezek, D.G., Friske, J., Taylor, H., Wiebe. J. & Kelly, P. (1997). "National Educational Technology Standards: Developing New Learning Environments for Today's Classrooms." *NASSP Bulletin, 81*(592), 52-58.

Burns, J.M. (1978). *Leadership*. New York: Harper & Row, Publishers, Inc.

International Society for Technology in Education (2000). *ISTE National Educational Technology Standards (NETS) and Performance Indicators: Educational Technology Foundations for All Teachers* [Online]. Available: http://cnets.iste.org/teachstand.html

Learning Media (1995). *Technology in the New Zealand Curriculum*. Wellington, NZ: Author.

Leithwood, K. (1994). "Leadership for School Restructuring." *Educational Administration Quarterly, 30*(4), 498-518.

Sparks, D. (1998). "Using Technology to Improve Teaching and Staff Development: An Interview with Kathleen Fulton." *Journal of Staff Development, 19*(1), 18-21.

Yee, D.L. (1999). *Leading, Learning, and Thinking with Information and Communication Technology (ICT): Images of Principals' ICT Leadership*. Unpublished doctoral dissertation, University of Calgary, Calgary, AB.

CHAPTER 11

INVERTED HOLLYWOOD

THE PITCH FOR e-KNOWLEDGE MEETS PRE-SERVICE TEACHER EDUCATION

LISA KORTEWEG

To open this chapter, I begin with a confession. While I have learned enormously from research articles and scholarly texts, I have also learned a lot from movies. Like most typical pre-service teachers, when I entered my teacher education program, I had ingested more celluloid than I had academic articles. To frame this chapter, I am going to fuse the theme of increasing the use of online resources in teacher education with movie making: I am going to give you a movie pitch for the Public Knowledge Project – The First Installment. I am intentionally choosing a movie pitch script for this chapter to illustrate several points, not the least of which is that scholarly communication in general (through online or any means) has a problem of Inverted Hollywood. Scholars or academics have wonderfully substantial content to deliver but we often lack the means to motivate users to visit our web sites and to read our articles. Hollywood, on the other hand, can motivate high interest amongst the public but can rarely deliver any substantial content (Norman, 1993, p.5). In this chapter, I intend to make the analysis of the Public Knowledge Project more 'Hollywood' and, in the process, hopefully motivate a few readers to visit the Public Knowledge Project website (http://pkp.ubc.ca).

THE MOVIE PITCH STRUCTURE

A movie pitch structure usually contains the following bolded elements. In order to demonstrate how this structure applies to movies, I draw upon the example of a recent academy award nominee movie, *Chocolat*. A movie begins with a **hero who has a motivation**. For example, Vianne, the heroine in the movie *Chocolat*, is a single mother in the 1950s who wishes to open a chocolate shop in a small conservative French town. She wishes to make this town her home by having a successful business and putting down roots. **But, the clock is ticking and the time is beginning to run out for the achievement of the goal.** In *Chocolat*, Vianne is being boycotted by the town's mayor, Comte de

Reynaud. To the nobleman-mayor, the chocolaterie's vendor represents desire and lust, grave sins that are to be especially resisted during the pious season of Lent. Vianne's time is running out for her business to take hold and for this town to accept her. **Or else** – if Vianne does not befriend the mayor, the strongest leader in the community, he will continue to dissuade the townsfolk from frequenting her shop or accepting her as a community member. **But luckily**, the heroine befriends other members of the community and they buy her chocolate and enjoy her company. **But luckily**, the mayor realizes the sensual pleasure of chocolate and is willing to accept Vianne into the community. And, **our heroine realized that** she wanted to stay in this community and make it her permanent home. So, **just in the nick of time**, just as Vianne was ready to declare defeat and move on to another town, the mayor begins to tolerate her and stops his active campaign against her. The heroine and the town have learned to compromise and accept one another. **The forces of GOOD prevail** and all is returned to harmonious order.

The Public Knowledge Project (PKP) movie is not as romantic as *Chocolat* nor is it fictional. PKP portrays an educational quest, not an Epicurean one. However, PKP and *Chocolat* both strive to convert communities: PKP wishes to demonstrate the rich merits of educational research resources available online to practitioners, beginning or established in their careers, just as the heroine of *Chocolat* wishes to demonstrate the liberating pleasures of chocolate to a repressed and fearful community. PKP strives to make research an actualized public good just as Vianne in *Chocolat* strives to make chocolate an acceptable and pleasurable public commodity.

THE PKP MOVIE PITCH

The PKP story begins with a team of researchers, our so-called **"heroes"** in the Faculty of Education, University of British Columbia, Vancouver, Canada. **The motivation of the heroes:** we want to make academic research and scholarly literature more accessible to the public, integrating it with other sources of understanding and information to which people turn. We want to make university-produced knowledge, public knowledge. We want to contribute more scholarly knowledge for the public's good. In this particular case, we want to contribute more scholarly knowledge to the education of pre-service teachers. We want pre-service teachers to know the value of public access to this knowledge to prepare and assist them for their in-service lives. We want the public and pre-service teachers to know that their tax dollar funding of academic research is going to good use, applicable use.

But, the clock is ticking and our time is beginning to run out for the achievement of our goal. The Public Knowledge Project, our team of researchers, has to learn how best to support the learning needs and interests of educators (e.g., in-service teachers, pre-service teachers, teacher union members, educational researchers) before our research funding runs out.

Or else, the public will continue to see futility, for the most part, when they see academic research. Teachers will view educational research as inapplicable to their professional lives. **Or else,** scholarly texts will be seen as useless and outdated. **Or else,** the Great Gap will widen between theory and practice, abstractions and experiences. **Or else,** someone else will fulfill the public's needs for research. Someone, like a private corporation, will fulfill student teachers' needs for research and the corporation will do so for a price, for profit. Then the goals of research will be of a private company, not those of a public institution.

But, luckily, PKP has assembled a team of researchers and website designers who are ready to experiment and work at this dilemma. **And, our heroic team realized that** we should use available technologies to create an online repository of filtered texts. **And, our heroic team realized that** we should make a tool that permits many different types of users (e.g., teachers, pre-service teachers, administrators, parents, scholars) to access many different types of knowledge texts. **And, our heroic team realized that** we should demonstrate how to connect different types of knowledge such as research articles and reports, classroom practices and tips, policy documents, organizations working to promote change, and, editorial texts reviewing issues. We realized that these knowledges could inform and introduce public users to a breadth and depth of knowledge on one topic that they probably never imagined existed. **And, our heroic team realized that** we had some ideas that we should shape into website prototypes. So, our heroic team, PKP, made the first prototype of the Public Knowledge Project, the PKP-*Vancouver Sun* website (http://www.pkp.ubc.ca/sun/index.html).

THE SET-UP: THE PKP-*VANCOUVER SUN* PROTOTYPE

The first collaborative experiment of the Public Knowledge Project was to electronically complement a series of journalistic articles appearing in the *Vancouver Sun* newspaper over the course of a week in the spring of 1999. The *Vancouver Sun* believed it was a critical time for the public to be exposed to the complex issues pertaining to education and technology in British Columbia schools. On each day of the newspaper's coverage, a different issue was explored. The five main issues covered by the journalists and mined for online resources by the PKP team included 1) the impact of technology on curriculum and teachers, 2) funding issues, 3) gender and technology, 4) the dangers and advantages of the internet and 5) equity of access. In our first repository of web documents, the PKP team wanted to motivate newspaper readers to go deeper into the issues raised by the journalists and to make connections across these issues. We endeavored to organize a web architecture of knowledge domains related to each issue that would permit this type of cross-pollination of connections. We created and filled with web resources five knowledge domains entitled Research (academic articles and reports), Practices (classroom practices and tips), Policy (examples of policies from different locations and levels of government), Organizations (non-profit groups working on the topic), and Issues (an editorial approach to the topic).

We attempted to encourage and achieve connections for users by offering overview pages under each issue and for each of these knowledge domains. These overview pages summarized each document with a quotation or chunk that encapsulated its intent, stated the bibliographic information; and, hyperlinked the title to the actual document. The user received the document in its entirety inside the PKP frame, thus, PKP acted as a portal or gateway to a contained set of internet resources. We realized that we could offer our view of the best of the web on these newspaper topics concerning technology's impact on education. During the five days in which the *Sun* article series ran, we averaged close to 100 visitors per day. After six weeks of being on the web, the PKP-*Vancouver Sun* site received 1881 hits in total with a quarter of these hits coming from visitors outside of Canada.

So, our heroic team now had a sophisticated prototype and we realized that we were not certain as to what the public had gained from our web site. **We realized that** we had something to offer a more specific audience, such as educators, who might be investigating issues of technology and education. **We realized** we needed to find a purpose and a test group for our team to observe more closely. **We realized that** we needed an empirical example of how this online experiment in scholarly communication would work in practice. **Or else,** our web site would lay unused and unvisited. **Or else,** educational research would remain inaccessible to those it is meant to inform. Important research findings and probing questions would remain isolated and in applicable for teachers and pre-service teachers. **Or else,** as teachers are overwhelmed by a plethora of difficult educational decisions in their classrooms, research findings lay dormant and purpose-less.

THE SEQUEL:
THE CITE EMPIRICAL EXAMPLE

So, our heroic team sought a situation where we could test the utility of our filtered database. We sought a situation where teachers would confront and discuss issues of educational technology. A sequel to any movie or any web site is always difficult. We decided to continue with the same PKP-*Vancouver Sun* database but configure it into a different situation. Basically, PKP was the same but instead of setting it inside a newspaper context, we set it inside the context of a university class. And, **luckily,** we found a rich empirical location, the CITE Teacher Education program at the University of British Columbia. The acronym CITE stands for Community of Inquiry for Teacher Education. It is a one-year program of studies for prospective elementary teachers where the students are actively encouraged to analyze and reflect upon "how learning is personally constructed, socially mediated, and inherently situated" (UBC, CITE, 2001). The central quality that distinguishes CITE from other teacher education programs is "a conceptually and experientially coherent program that encourages: full participation by all CITE community members in all aspects of program design and implementation; and integration of all curriculum areas within and across two distinct learning contexts (campus-based instruction and practica experiences)" (UBC, CITE, 2001).

There are roughly 36 pre-service students who take their courses together as a CITE cohort. One of the required courses is entitled Education Studies. The course examines how social relations of class, gender, ethnicity, sexuality, and poverty influence educational opportunities. With the leadership of Jane Mitchell (the CITE technology coordinator) and the participation of Linda Darling (the instructor of the Education Studies course), we developed a unit entitled Education Studies Online.

In my work with PKP discussion forums and in Jane Mitchell's work with CITE discussions, we had both witnessed a tendency by users to remain in an exchange of opinions and anecdotal experiences inside discussions. In this PKP-CITE experiment, we wanted to move academic knowledge (or formal abstractions) into the pre-service teachers' online discussions. We wanted them to cite sources from the PKP repository to inform their positions and incorporate hyperlinks into their statements. In short, we wanted to motivate the pre-service teachers to incorporate academic conventions of discourse into their online chat. We wanted to help students achieve a virtual discussion where it was no longer as experience or anecdotally driven as a chat room but not as solitary or static as a term paper. We wanted to arrive in a new in-between place where students would employ academic discourse to exchange and build upon ideas with one another and with other teachers. But we didn't want the students to become overwhelmed by the morass of documents that appears when conducting web searches. We wanted them to have easy access to a range of texts and knowledge documents that they would probably be unable to find on their own and that they could integrate into their learning and their talking about learning to teaching.

To attain these goals, we designed a task or purpose that required the students to use our PKP prototype for an assignment. We developed a Webquest project outline, located on a WebCT bulletin board, where we asked the students to consider how social relations influence the curriculum and implementation of computer technology in schools. In the Webquest, the students were first given the following question: "As a beginning teacher, what do you think are some crucial equity issues pertaining to technology and education and what action do you think schools and teachers can take in relation to these issues?" Secondly, students were encouraged to find accurate and reliable information on the internet to support their positions on the above question. They were encouraged to use the PKP-*Vancouver Sun* site and a list of links posted on the Education Library's page as these were two hyperlinked resources inside the Education Studies Webquest. Finally, the students were instructed to work in online groups to create a collective text on a WebCT discussion board concerning one equity issue. The students were also instructed to include hyperlinks inside their postings (at least two) to reference or footnote their statements. Each discussion group also included a guest external participant whose purpose was to connect the discussion to sources and people outside the CITE program and the university walls. Of the six external participants, five were university-based professors or graduate students. Only one of the six participants was a classroom teacher. Discussion groups and topics for the externals were designated by the CITE technology co-ordinator. None of the externals had working relationships or professional contact with the CITE pre-service teachers before this Education Studies forum.

This collaborative venture with Jane Mitchell and the Education Studies course was a field study of how pre-service teachers would use a PKP tool. We designed a task or purpose that required the students to employ the PKP-*Vancouver Sun* tool. We were testing our prototype with real educators to attempt to track how they acted on the website, what connections they were able to draw between texts and between practice and research, and, which PKP documents they found to be of value.

Generally speaking, the pre-service context of most universities is one marked by a culture of fragmentation between program parts; a perceived split between research and practice; and, a lack of communication and articulation between educators located in schools and educators in universities (Goodlad, 1994; Tom, 1997). For the Education Studies instructor (Linda Darling) and the CITE technology coordinator (Jane Mitchell), the appeal of integrating PKP into a course assignment was to countervail these fragmenting tendencies. The intent of the assignment was to help student teachers substantially engage with their colleagues, with the available web resources, and with guest participants (including school district personnel) from outside the B.Ed. program. Our goal was to help the pre-service teachers make intellectual connections between their course work and their school experiences, between theory and practice, between foundational and curriculum courses.

Movie Scenes: Connections in the Gender Discussion

Online discussions are the equivalent of movie scenes. They are the building blocks of the movie's story. Through connections, questions, and challenges, a good online discussion advances a story, builds community, explores an idea thoroughly, and challenges previously held notions. Exploring some of the key movie scenes or pivotal turning points in one group's discussion provides some important connections as well as dis-connections for the PKP movie pitch.

The discussion concerned with gender equity was the most richly connected of all the PKP-CITE group discussions. There were connections made between past experiences and future action, between conceptual ideas and implications for practice. And there were unique connections made between the pre-service teachers and their external participant, an elementary school computer lab teacher working in the same school district as the pre-service teachers' practicum experiences.

The Gender Equity online discussion began with the following statement by Claire, a pre-service teacher.

> *In the GenTech Research Findings Final Report by Mary Bryson and Suzanne de Castell, they stated "evidence from research on gender and access to, and uses of, new information technologies (NITs) indicates that in public schools, female staff and students (in comparison to male students) are: (a) disenfranchised with respect to access and kind of usage, (b) less likely to acquire technological competence, and (c) likely to be discouraged from assuming a leadership role in this domain." It is obvious from the references cited in this article that there is a lot of research out there regarding this statement. I think it would be interesting if we discussed any one of the three areas mentioned. A question that comes to mind is are female and male users of technology using technology for the same purposes?*
>
> *If you would like to read the final report before responding, here it is: http://www.educ.sfu.ca/gentech/research.html*

This is a model opening statement for the requirements of the assignment. It begins with a citation that is referenced with the hyperlink. The citation comes from a web resource that had been filtered by the PKP repository. Claire then posits a question for her group to participate in. She is actively attempting to make connections with her online colleagues and she refers them to more literature on the issue. As she was the first participant to make a statement, Claire helped model a type of inquiry (of citation, question, leading reference) for the rest of her group to follow.

The external participant, Caroline, a teacher working primarily in an elementary computer lab, responds to Claire's statement.

Dr. Mary Bryson worked closely with our school to help us identify goals for technology and then to select appropriate software and hardware to achieve them. Conversations with Dr. Bryson helped me to acknowledge the power imbalance that exists around girls and technology, and I tried to ensure that this imbalance did not prevail in my classroom.

By chance, the external participant, Caroline, has had Mary Bryson in her school and in her lab. Mary Bryson is the researcher that Claire's statement quoted and referenced. Not only did Caroline make a connection to Claire's question, she also connected the researcher back to Claire with a real life, practical encounter.

Claire then asks Caroline to extend the equity discussion into more concrete examples and strategies. She specifically wants to know from Caroline how she would judge and recognize power imbalances in the lab and then what the ensuing strategies for action would be. The preservice teacher, Claire, is asking a theoretically laden question – how does one recognize power imbalance – with an appeal to Caroline for specific instances of practice to address issues of power.

Caroline, I am also interested in hearing about the specific changes you made to your teaching style and the selection of models and mentors you made in your classroom. Also who did you allow access to in the computer lab at lunch and recess? Did you permit those students who showed initiative and productive working habits, or did you allow access to those who did not have computers at home? What were your strategies because as a pre-service teacher, I am not all that confident I would recognize the power imbalance you are talking about.

Key Movie Scenes: Disconnections in the Gender Discussion

Every posting in a discussion group sets up the next set of communications like movie scenes in a dramatic chain of action. The movie scenes or communication exchanges between Caroline, the teacher, and the student participants demonstrates some key disconnections for the PKP movie pitch. These disconnections are important dilemmas of scholarly communication and knowledge management projects in a pre-service context.

Caroline did indeed respond to the first student Claire with a continuation of the link of Mary Bryson. However, Caroline did not make this link explicit to the first student of the thread, Claire, nor did she make it explicit to the other members of the discussion. Caroline did not say, "Claire, Dr. Bryson is the researcher who you have referred to in your opening statement." The connection is not clearly established and, given the lapse of three days and the addition of three other comments in the thread, it is questionable to presume that the forum participants have made the connection.

It is also important to note that Caroline, the teacher-participant, did not reveal any specific ideas of Mary Bryson nor did she list any citations or references to Bryson's work. She did not directly relate to the citation that Claire had posted by stating her support of this position or this particular idea's impact on her thinking as a teacher. However, Caroline did state that Bryson changed her thinking, that in talking to Bryson, not in reading her articles, Bryson convinced Caroline of the power imbalances that occur in a school lab, through both the organization of equipment and the use of certain software. Caroline did demonstrate another facet of how research and researchers serve the schools and how the online resources can serve as a point of connection.

The fact that Bryson worked in a school with a group of teachers to develop a technology plan and organize a computer lab for greater gender equity is advantageous enough. The fact that a computer lab teacher could name a scholar as someone who had changed her practices through conversation is an inspirational model of scholarly impact for new teachers. However, Claire's response to Caroline was a question for specific strategies or tips. It was not a desire for closer examination and discussion of Dr. Bryson's central ideas or theories. Ironically, once the teacher Caroline entered the discussion, the overall rate of citations and references in the forum dropped to almost nil. The students became focussed on Caroline's personal experiences, her professional practices and classroom observations. Still, here were signs of at least an initial integration of teacher experience and research knowledge working in close proximity.

This instance of Caroline's participation, its anecdotal and personal account discourse was not a unique stance in this online discussion. Unlike the students fulfilling the requirements of the assignment, most of the other external participants did not use quotations or cite resources from PKP nor did many externals refer students to other web resources outside PKP. For the most part, the external participants tried to push broader thinking for the pre-service teachers by asking the students more questions that sought to expand the examination of the issues. They served as another order of knowledge to complement the site's other resources. The externals would respond to the pre-service teachers' statements with more questions rather than experiential examples from classroom observations. The gender discussion was unique in that the questions originated with the pre-service teachers and they were directed almost entirely at the external teacher, Caroline. These questions were focussed on the practical implications of what had been well established in the research literature, helping the participants to focus on and identify the problem in need of strategic interventions.

The external participants fulfilled the role of expanding and enlarging the university classroom walls to include more than just the pre-service teachers and their instructor in this community of inquiry. But, in this experiment, five out of six of the externals were university-based professors or graduate students. The externals did not represent an active perspective from inside a classroom or school. For the most part, the externals represented other institutional spaces of the university rather than this particular course or degree program. The externals were in other university locations, pursuing other disciplines of inquiry in education, or graduate students establishing their academic identities. But, the externals did validate the discussion of this topic and validated the use of an electronic forum. In their positions as professors and graduate students, they were also in the best position to validate the use of citations and references to web documents. The effect was a much richer information environment in which to consider the process of becoming a teacher than what was occurring in the typical teacher education classroom.

In any movie or story, the heroes usually receive help in their quest. This help often comes from external sources such as a gypsy, a magical wind (such as appeared in *Chocolat*), an elder of the community or a mentor. The external mediators in the PKP-CITE experiment were "helper" characters. A helper character is a person who has special knowledge and special skills that can assist the heroes. In the story of PKP-CITE, we knew that the externals had mentor type qualities that would help the pre-service teachers' in their understanding of the complicated implications of technology's integration into education. However, we didn't fully comprehend the extent to which the externals could assist us, the PKP team, with our goal of making academic research more accessible and meaningful to the pre-service teachers.

Assistants to the Heroes: The Pivotal Role of the External Mediators

In one topic group inside the Education Studies discussion, a different dynamic existed between the external mediator and the pre-service teachers than the one that developed in the Gender Equity group. I was the external participant in a group discussing the role of big business and corporate sponsorship for technology in schools through technology initiatives and funding technology's high costs. The group was debating the futility of using corporate funds to buy equipment when there was a greater need to support teachers to become more comfortable with computers.

In my role as external and researcher, I was curious to see how other groups were progressing in their intellectual engagement and use of web resources in the chosen topics. In one of the other Education Studies discussion groups, I observed an exchange between three or four pre-service teachers where they excitedly exchanged information about a new corporate program of environmental education. I felt it was an important example to bring back to my group's attention as it concerned corporate sponsorship and a delivery of curriculum for teachers and schools, and so I wrote to the group about a program that was much admired:

Subject: re: This may be off topic but...

In speaking about big business involvement with schools, I was struck by an example right here in the CITE forum. I noticed one group excitedly discussing the Grizzlies' [Vancouver's NBA team] Environmental Education curriculum for classrooms. I went to the Grizzlies site to check it out as I wrote my MA thesis on environmental education. Go take a look at it INCITE people and tell me what you think. http://www.nba.com/Grizzlies/grizz_ed_index.html.

As I gave the free corporate offering my critical reading, I was struck by a few things...

I asked my discussion group, the INCITE group, to investigate the situation for themselves by visiting the Grizzlies website address and giving me their opinions. My comments and questions were then intellectually amplified by Brenda Trofanenko, another graduate student external participant in the Education Studies discussion.

Public sites of knowledge, including the actual sites such as aquariums and museums along with the virtual sites offered on the web, posit themselves as educational. Yes, they certainly are. But you need to ask yourself what is it that they want you to learn and why is it being presented in such a way?...

Certainly, each corporation has a mandate for financial viability. My concern is how education is being employed as one way in which to show a profit. While it may be great to have the learning packages each corporation provides, I would advocate you be critical of the package, the intended learning, and the ways in which it has come into your classroom.

Whew! Who knew I could get so incensed about a grizzly bear, real or otherwise. Brenda, on Denman.

At this stage in the discussion, the pre-service teachers were placed in a position of response to an example that had incited enthusiasm by their cohort members but had now evolved into a forum of intellectual criticism by two externals. As the external responsible for the corporate sponsorship discussion, I had put my participants in a position of heightened response. I was no longer on the spot to answer their questions or interpret the reality of schools in conjunction with theoretical ideas or academic frameworks. Instead, I had put the students on the spot asking them to visit specific websites and respond to my critical interpretation of an education program. Bravely, four out of the six pre-service participants did respond and they responded in a similar fashion.

> *In response to the issues that Lisa raises in her comments on the Grizzlies' environmental ed program. I was working for the Green team when the B.C. Ministry of Environment was in negotiations to create a Grizzlies environmental ed team and we discussed the pros and cons fo working for and with the Grizzlies…In my mind, corporate sponsorship cannot exist in blatant opposition to an educational system that it funds. What is the point of an environmentally unsustainable company funding an environmental education program? Should we use the word hypocrisy here?*

The pre-service students recognized the "hypocrisy" of the Grizzlies program but they found this position of critique "disturbing." A couple of them still believed the Grizzlies' environmental program to be valid and inspirational for students' exposure to and thinking about environmental issues. The pre-service teachers understood their cohort members' enthusiasm for the program, but they were also confronted with academics critically reading this enthusiasm inside an assigned discussion. It must have been a difficult and precarious position where cohort members are looking for affirmation of a curricular idea while academics are simultaneously criticizing it. The position did force my group's members to think, but, perhaps it was uncomfortable thinking coerced by my chosen type of participation and intellectual engagement. In this instance, the external was taking control of the discussion's direction and the discussion's agenda. My use of citations and URLs was meant to challenge the pre-service teachers to form an opinion of their own accord on a topic of my choosing.

In the gender equities discussion, a dynamic developed whereby the pre-service teachers were more in control of the thread's agenda and direction. Cohesion between participants developed with the introduction of the external, Caroline. All the pre-service students in the gender thread wanted to specifically hear Caroline describe and analyze her classroom observations. Alongside this external, the pre-service teachers wanted to actively participate in the interpretations of classroom observations and strategies to recognize and promote gender equity. The gender thread's pre-service participants immediately and intuitively recognized Caroline as their bridge between classroom experience and strategic interpretations. They directed Caroline to speak by asking her specific questions. They also directed her to give them practical pedagogical interpretations of gender equity for classroom application. This advice was an extension of the concept of gender with which the students found themselves unfamiliar. They understood the complexity of the issues involved with gender and technology but they did not know where to begin to address it inside a classroom as a teacher. Whenever Caroline answered the pre-service teachers' questions with tips, strategies or practical interpretations, the pre-service teachers were greatly appreciative.

When Brenda and I challenged the pre-service teachers' enthusiasm, we were guided by a similar bridge metaphor. We were searching for ways of making our critique a point of connection for practice in a classroom. Asking students to examine the environmental costs and balance in order to develop ethical criteria for corporate participation in educational programs appeared to be a practical, pedagogical interpretation of corporate sponsorship. However, the pre-service teachers' responses to our critique were cautious, whereas, the responses to Caroline in the Gender online discussion were overwhelmingly positive.

> *Caroline, Thank you so much for responding to all my questions. Your ideas and strategies are amazing, and I know I will remember them when I am teaching. I am going to be teaching computers in my practicum starting next week, so I will be conscious of the power struggles that may be going on, and how I can help facilitate a more equitable environment...*
>
> *Caroline, I want to thank you again for being such an inspiration, and for contributing to our discussion in such a meaningful way. I can't wait to see what else everyone else has to say.*
>
> *Caroline, Wow! Thank you for all the information. I especially appreciated all your real life experience. It is very obvious that you have serious thought about gender equity and technology. Do girls struggle more in technology or is this just a myth? If girls do struggle more, what do you think contributes to this?*

It is apparent from these responses that the users, the pre-service teacher participants, had greater need for Caroline's classroom experiences than for the PKP document hyperlinks. Or at least, the documents only provided a starting point that Caroline could help extend through its relevance to the classroom. Caroline, the only in-service teacher in the Education Studies discussion, provided a bridge between the students' academic work on the topic of gender inequities. She provided practical interpretations and strategies for making technologies more equitable in the classroom. After a minimum of five years in the university with myriad essay assignments demanding a certain number of citations, the pre-service teachers seemed saturated with certain academic conventions (e.g., academic sources of refereed journals, citations in a particular style, citations to support an argument). But, the pre-service teachers did not readily transfer these conventions of scholarly discourse into their online discussion. The students' primary criteria for referring to web documents and incorporating hyperlinks were to fulfill the requirements of the assignment. What appeared novel and inspirational to them was an insider, a classroom teacher, revealing conventions of classroom practice and identity formation as a teacher.

It was only after all the discussions had closed that the collaborative research team, PKP-CITE, realized the pivotal and powerful role the externals such as Caroline could have in the discussions. In hindsight, I realized how we, the assignment designers, could have helped instruct the externals to model qualities that would have helped us attain our research goals and motivate the students to integrate PKP as an important knowledge source in their teaching. If the goal of this experiment had been to create an electronic essay or a collaborative writing piece, we needed to communicate to the externals the need to model and direct that type of writing for the discussion participants. If the goal had been to help students internalize norms of academic discourse, then we needed to emphasize to the externals to link references inside their statements (i.e., continually refer to web documents in PKP with full footnotes of the title, author, and publisher). If the PKP research goal had been to link different types of knowledge together to more fully inform the PKP user, then we needed to incorporate criteria into the assignment to make two or more citations, each representing a different type of knowledge. We also needed to ensure that the external mediators stated the types of knowledge they were drawing upon and they needed to defend how this knowledge worked to answer the student's or the collective's questions.

To summarize, the collaborative research team needed to make its goals more explicit and transparent to both the external participants and to the pre-service teachers. We needed to distinguish what type of a discussion we envisioned through this assignment, as it moved between documents and people, and as the integration of themes from these different sources could have been encouraged. In the online and asynchronous forum, participants can go beyond simply sharing their experiences to sharing them reinforced with sources of information. Not only can they build upon each other's ideas, applying the ideas of a larger research community, but they can also develop an interpretive framework with the external mediator for future experiences. "For it is not shared stories or shared information so much as shared *interpretation* that binds people together" (Brown & Duguid, 2000, p.107, emphasis mine).

The Difficulty of Shifting Knowledge Needs

What I am attempting to point out with the example of Caroline and the gender discussion is that technological tools and their particular features can be easy to modify, but culture, or the specific knowledge needs of a particular group, is much harder to define or change or shift. In the culture of teacher preparation programs, pre-service teachers are highly motivated to learn from practical classroom tips and from established teachers. In the context of the Education Studies assignment, the pre-service teachers were highly motivated to learn from practical ideas and strategies for the classroom developed in response to scholarly notions. The bridging work between the domains of scholarly research and classroom practices was one that we did not actively design the PKP tool to develop. We did not realize this Hollywood factor of motivation, of connecting the students' academic experience with a practitioner actively working to translate the academic into practical strategies for the classroom.

For the PKP design team, we believed the user would make those connections and bridges for themselves in moving among the various knowledge domains. However, the act of bridging and connecting between types of knowledge was one not successfully facilitated by the PKP site for various reasons. The site *did* indeed offer a knowledge typology including research and practices repositories. But, the irony is that the pre-service teachers never realized the content of the Practices section. For example, the gender equity discussion had a total of 32 messages with 11 containing hyperlinks. Six hyperlinks referred to research articles, three referred to issues (a more editorial approach to reviewing issues), and two referred to organizations (non-profit groups working on the particular issue). As the researcher, I am the one who has categorized these texts into these knowledge types because the pre-service teachers did not refer to the typology in their statements. Surprisingly, consistent in all of the discussion threads, there was a predominant tendency to refer to research documents located in PKP, not to practices documents.

When I interviewed a group of five CITE pre-service teachers, representing different discussion groups and topics, I discovered that the students had had no idea that there existed on PKP a whole category of filtered documents that focussed on teacher and classroom practices. When I presented them with photocopies of the Gender-Practices Overview (Appendix II), they were stunned that they had not realized that the site contained this type of practical knowledge.

THE FRAILTY OF THE PKP PROTOTYPE

At this point, I can attempt to hypothesize a few factors to explain the tendency on all the pre-service teachers' parts to have predominantly used research citations. The nature of the CITE discussion was one of an assignment where students were required to make two citations. They were also aware that their instructor, the external participants, and their cohort members would be reading the messages. No qualifier was given as to what kind of knowledge would be valid for this assignment. As the normative requirement for most university essay assignments in the social sciences and humanities is refereed journal citations, it is understandable that the pre-service teachers would presume this is the category that would best suit the discussion requirements.

Another hypothesis for understanding the pre-service teachers' reliance on research documents is due to a design feature of the PKP-*Vancouver Sun* site. In the line of knowledge buttons located beside the topic title, the Research button appears first in the line. In this case, a design issue could have interfered with the utilization of the knowledge typology. Even though there were buttons that indicated a range of knowledge types and even though the heading on the abstract/summaries page would read Practices, more steps could have been taken to reinforce the knowledge typology. More design features could have been strategically situated to continually reinforce the different knowledge categories available through the PKP site. But, perhaps, the problem in realizing the potential range of knowledges available in PKP was not a navigational or design frailty of the site. Perhaps the pre-service teachers did not find the Practices section of PKP because they couldn't conceive of a Practices or classroom tips domain inside a university endorsed and university created website.

In hindsight, it is easy to see that the pre-service teachers were not motivated to peruse all the knowledge categories. We at PKP had taken a website tool that was not user-driven, not driven to understand what would motivate users to enlist our site as one of their regular sources of web-based information. The PKP-*Vancouver Sun* site was a tool for which we had imagined a group or a public of users. It was not a tool specifically designed for or tested with a group of pre-service teachers and their experiential needs. We at PKP are what Donald Norman refers to as "early adopters" (1998), meaning that we are regularly reading and interpreting websites and foraging and retrieving knowledge from web based tools. We also have different needs in pursuing technological tools from our position of researchers. We are making tools for public knowledge and we consider them important. Whereas our users, pre-service teachers in the context of a university course, wanted a website that was convenient to use, with technology that had already proven itself. They wanted a good and easy experience in the confines of this course to serve their particular course requirement needs at a particular time. They did not want a Swiss Army knife experience of too many blades with too many purposes that do not serve the immediate task at hand.

THE FINAL PITCH

To conclude, I return to the Public Knowledge Project movie pitch to determine if we, the research team, had reached our goals with the CITE experiment. Our PKP team has made a first attempt at electronically delivering substantive knowledge to a group of pre-service teachers. However, we have done so without asking or understanding what these users want or what would motivate them to use this type of tool outside the confines of an assignment. We realized our PKP-*Vancouver Sun* tool is great on providing substantial content, but lacked motivation for these users. Our research has culminated in a Hollywood inversion: we have substantial content to support the professional working lives of teachers, but they are not yet enticed to thoroughly investigate it. We failed in convincing these educators to see its full potential, its application to their teaching, or to integrate our site into their favorites' list as an important source of knowledge.

But, **just in the nick of time,** we have learned important lessons. Our research confirms that teachers are the critical link or bridge for the success of technology's implementation in the classroom (Pea, 1998). And we confirmed that teachers need a collaborative community of educators to share, connect and confront ideas on how best to make that implementation serve students' learning (Grant, 1996). PKP is committed to the idea that the internet and our website prototypes can serve teachers in their professional development by our offering them both a contained library of filtered resources as well as a tool of inquiry and collaboration to put the resources to the test of the classroom context.

We discovered that the role of the externals (the mentor, experienced professional peer, or academic) is crucial in the creation and cohesion of an online community of inquiry for teachers examining new issues. They are the participants who can bridge different worlds: experienced with novice, academic with practical. We now know that the sequels of the Public Knowledge Project need to address this role of the 'helper' or mentor. Like many academic research projects, we are in the process of creating the conditions for sequels. We are committed to reiterative design and the participation of our users. We are confident that we will be able to demonstrate to educators our prototypes' contributions, and, along with other contributing scholars, we will win the prize of the Public's continued support and endorsement for research.

Acknowledgements

The author wishes to thank and acknowledge the comments and contributions made by the following readers of drafts of this chapter: John Willinsky, Brenda Trofanenko, Vivian Forssman, Jane Mitchell, Suzanne de Castell, Barrie Barrell and David Peerla.

REFERENCES

Brown, J.S. and Duguid, B. (2000). *The Social Life of Information.* Cambridge, MA: Harvard Business School Press.

Goodlad, J. (1994). *Educational Renewal: Better Teachers, Better Schools.* San Francisco: Jossey-Bass.

Grant, C.M. (1996). *Professional Development in a Technological Age: New Definitions, Old Challenges, New Resources. Model Schools Partnership.* Cambridge, MA: TERC. (http://ra.terc.edu/publications/TERC_pubs/tech-infusion/prof_dev/prof_dev_frame.html)

Norman, D.A. (1993). *Things That Make Us Smart.* Reading, MA: Addison-Wesley.

Norman, D.A. (1998). *The Life Cycle of a Technology: Why It Is So Difficult for Large Companies to Innovate.* Nielsen Norman Group. (http://www.nngroup.com/reports/life_cycle_of_tech.html)

Pea, R. (1998). *The Pros and Cons of Technology in the Classroom. Bay Area School Reform Collaborative Funders' Learning Community Meeting.* Palo Alto. (http://www.tappedin.org/info/teachers/debate.html)

Tom, A. (1997). *Redesigning Teacher Education.* New York: State University of New York Press.

University of British Columbia (2001). *Community and Inquiry in Teacher Education Program Description.* (http://www.curricstudies.educ.ubc.ca/projects/cite.html)

CHAPTER 12

COMPUTERS IN HUMANITIES EDUCATION

FIVE TEACHERS EXAMINE THE ISSUES

JIM GREENLAW, NATASHA BOUDREAU, JILL BURRY, MARILYN MACLEAN AND MARY MURRIN,

INTRODUCTION: THE TEACHERS

In this chapter you will read a sampling of the discussions which took place among four graduate students who participated in an online Computers in Humanities Education course offered by Jim Greenlaw at St. Francis Xavier University. The purpose of the course was to examine the new teaching approaches and philosophies that are emerging because of the introduction of computers into elementary and secondary school courses in English language arts, social studies and arts education. This was primarily an issues-based course in which we considered a variety of problems and challenges that are associated with the current paradigm shift in humanities education which the new technologies have precipitated. Each Monday evening for twelve weeks, we met online together to discuss, in conferences and chat rooms, topics such as the following: Beyond Classroom Boundaries, Creating Literature Theme Units with the Help of Children's Literature Web Sites, The Effects of Technology on Students' Writing and Research Abilities, Using Multimedia in Arts Education and Visiting Virtual Museums and Art Galleries. The course culminated in the sharing of web lessons that we created for use with our students.

What follows is a selection of some of our discussions from the course. It is hoped that, as you read these conversations, you will ask yourself how you feel about the new technological literacy paradigm that we have been attempting to introduce into our teaching. If you feel, as we do, that these new approaches to teaching the humanities have merit, then we hope that the descriptions of web lessons which we offer at the end of this chapter will provide you with possible models for your own use of computers in humanities courses.

BEYOND CLASSROOM BOUNDARIES

Jim: What do you think literacy involves in a post-typographic world? Do you think you need to teach your students how to do chat, email, web navigation, etc. as part of their literacy training?

Jill: Literacy in a post-typographic world is much the same as it always was – reading information, assessing and evaluating it, then applying it. The only difference today is the resources we use to gather this information. In a post-typographic world this includes not only books, magazines, newspapers, encyclopedias and the like, but also the vast amount of information available on the World Wide Web and through communication vehicles such as email and chatrooms. It is becoming essential for students to learn how to use this resource if they are to become totally literate. This is becoming evident as more and more school boards are devising or adopting technology curricula.

Jim: To what extent do you agree that it is your job as a teacher to help your students to construct meaning from text through interactions with each other and the world? How does this differ from the way we have traditionally taught children to interpret text?

Jill: I agree to a point that it is a teacher's job to create an environment where students can, through social interaction, construct knowledge. I say "to a point," because I still see a place in the classroom for the teacher to impart knowledge to students in the form of advanced organizers and through stories that students can use to build their own knowledge from and around. The role of the teacher is definitely changing. No longer are we to be "transmitters" of knowledge but "facilitators" and creators of situations that take students beyond their current level of learning. The Internet provides students with the ability to interact with each other and others around the world and through this interaction and discovery of information, they build new knowledge and apply it in different ways. No longer are students limited by what the teacher says or what is in a textbook. No longer do they have to just listen, read and then regurgitate information.

Jim: As you venture into the Internet to construct your own knowledge in our course each Monday night, how do your reading and writing processes differ from those you normally employ in a face-to-face course?

Jill: In preparation for each Monday night's class I have altered the way and the amount of time I spend to prepare. I not only read a text and assigned articles but read digital articles on the Internet and surf web sites for hours. I turn on the computer with the intention of looking at a particular site but often get sidetracked as my "curiosity" becomes aroused. I know that with each link and screen I read or skim, I am altering old knowledge to construct new. This new knowledge I then use to answer questions for class or share in chatrooms. If this course were face-to-face (and on a different subject, of course) I do not think that I would be so inclined to check out other sources listed at the end of a chapter or even look up recommended sites on the computer. With Windows applications it is so easy to be composing an answer to a question and to then quickly go to another window where the web site I am discussing is open and the information is at my fingertips. In a classroom situation I would not have this luxury. I could probably talk in generalities about something I had read previously, but not be specific. The only disadvantage with the Internet supporting a learner's natural curiosity is the amount of time I spend feeding my curiousness. But then again, I am constructing new knowledge. What better use of time is there?

Jim: What will this new paradigm for constructing knowledge mean for your students, if you engage them in the kind of learning experience that you are having in our course, that the kids are having in the Real Kids Real Adventures site, etc.?

Jill: The use of the Internet opens so many doors for everyone. Students socially interact with other students from around the world, as well as with professional writers and mentors, and they can also interact with web site activities. In the process, they create new knowledge by building on existing knowledge already in their cognitive structures. So many adventures and learning experiences await students as they venture into the post-typographic world. Teachers have a responsibility to become familiar with and utilize this phenomenal resource so that students can produce new knowledge.

Creating Literature Theme Units with the Help of Children's Literature Web Sites

Jim: If you had the opportunity to create a literature unit for children or young adults, how might you make use of some of the information which can be accessed by visiting the Children's Literature Web Guide and some of the other major children's literature sites which are linked to it, such as Carol Hurst's site and Kay Vandergrift's?

Mary: A theme unit I might like to construct for my grade nine Language Arts class would be about mystery writers. The general outline would be as follows. Students would visit the site, The House of Usher: Edgar Allan Poe, to examine the short story, "The Purloined Letter." This selection is said by some to be the forefather of the mystery genre. Poe's detective is the first to use deductive reasoning to solve a crime. Next, the class would go to the Sherlockian homepage. They would examine short story selections as examples of the classic mystery refined and made popular by Arthur Conan Doyle. The Sherlockian homepage contains many interesting links that would provide ideas for research projects and writing activities. For example, students could research and present facts on England and the Victorian era, or write a summary of Arthur Conan Doyle's biography, find out about stage and screen productions or research other famous masters of crime writing.

Then I would have the class look at an example of a contemporary mystery novel, such as one of the novels of Lois Duncan. Her web page is available through the Children's Literature Web Guide. Duncan's novels, such as *Killing Mr. Griffin* and *I Know What You Did Last Summer*, are more than just examples of thrilling suspense. They also provide opportunities for stimulating class discussion around issues such as acceptance, peer pressure, revenge, responsibility and leadership.

Finally, we would compare and contrast selected stories of Arthur Conan Doyle and Lois Duncan in terms of writing style, character development, plot, creation of suspense, intended audience and the historical context. The students would give possible reasons for the popular appeal of both the Sherlock Holmes detective series and the novels of Lois Duncan. We could also do a film study, since many of Doyle's works and Duncan's novels have been adapted to the screen.

There are so many possibilities. The major challenge with this unit would be to zero in on specific selections from each author to accomplish specific goals in various skill levels of literary criticism, composition, the use of language, etc. As with any thematic unit, I would have to collect and make available for students the works of many different mystery writers. There are some full texts available online, but actual book copies would be required for students to choose from as well.

Jill: After hours of surfing the Internet to find novels that I was somewhat familiar with that had similar themes, I decided to explore the theme of war and the profound moral decisions that are made in the name of family and friendships. One novel that I would definitely use in this unit would be Lois Lowry's *Number the Stars*. In this novel, Anne Marie helps her friend Ellen and Ellen's family escape to another country before the Nazis annihilated them. Carol Hurst's Children's Literature Site offers a review of the book, suggestions on how to introduce the book to students and detailed descriptions of five activities that can be used as is or adapted to meet individual or group needs. They include researching a country that was under Nazi occupation, studying statues that were erected after WWII and designing your own statue, studying maps and identifying escape routes that Jews might have taken, singing Jewish folk songs or cooking traditional Jewish food, and studying pictures of Tivoli Gardens and other landmarks in Denmark to make a travelogue. I would also have students write a response to the novel describing what they would have done had they found themselves in the same situation as Anne Marie. Another activity would be to have students pretend to be Anne Marie and Ellen and exchange letters or postcards after they knew their escape plan worked and they knew they were out of danger.

This theme has so many possibilities and the Internet offers such a wealth of ideas, information and resources, that I could easily develop it much further. This theme could be built around the Remembrance Day holiday and students could write peace poetry, diary entries from the perspective of a soldier, or letters to family back home. There are many more books, novels, web sites and resources related to this theme of war and the profound sacrifices people make in the name of friendship and family. It is a theme that I will certainly develop further and use in the future.

The Effects of Technology on Students' Writing and Research Abilities

Jim: How can the approaches to teaching writing and research, not only in the English classroom but also in all other humanities classrooms, be transformed through the application of new technologies, whether you are teaching grade 3 history or a university level course in French Literature?

Mary: I think many teachers are caught in the middle of the transition between tradition and technology. Distribution of and access to hardware and computer time is a major problem, at least at my school. Therefore, you have many students in class who wish to abstain from in-class writing assignments because they can do it faster at home, or they already have their first draft saved on disc.

The use of the Internet for research assignments has made life a lot easier for many students. Yes, they spend hours surfing for the right information, which, they say, is preferable to sifting through books and articles at the library, but pictures, diagrams, charts and maps can be saved and pasted into the final copy or printed out and added to the assignment. I have watched my 12 year old complete all his projects this way. His teacher has not been the one to instruct him on how to use the technology; he is self-taught.

So, how can a teacher such as myself participate in this transformation of pedagogy and student role? Teachers in the humanities must be given opportunities for inservice and they must have access to computers for their students. At our school, the lab is mainly used by senior high for specific computer courses. At the grade 9 level, students have 40 minutes three times a week in the lab with an instructor who teaches computer literacy. The language arts and other subject teachers are left out of the equation. The students are getting the skills and the classroom teachers are not. The old paradigm has to change. Teaching computer skills in isolation is no longer feasible. Give those humanities teachers, who are ready, willing and able, the opportunity to integrate technology into their curricula.

Marilyn: I agree totally, Mary. The paradigm has got to change. The key is to integrate technology into the curriculum, not to create separate courses. Our school operates our lab on a flexible schedule. There are very few scheduled times and teachers book in their classes based on what projects they have going on in the classroom.

Natasha: I also agree with you, Mary. I think that the teachers who are willing to learn should be given the opportunity to do so. Hopefully, this will have a snowball effect and we will all ask for inservicing that means something! I believe that, in order to keep students motivated to write for pleasure, we have to ensure that they are getting authentic experiences and what better way to do this than with computers and the Internet? The Internet offers endless possibilities as far as approaches to writing go (email, ePals, Webquests, etc). Students are generally motivated to do these tasks, and they enjoy them as well. There are also other approaches to teaching writing that are emerging. We are including a variety of media in classrooms to help students write. Using other types of technology is helping us to motivate students. The use of digital video cameras, digital cameras, CDs, etc. is allowing students to go beyond the limits of the physical classroom.

Jill: We need a middle ground between traditional instruction and instruction that is totally computer based. A multimedia lab is probably what most teachers long for, but they still need to learn to make use of what they already have. Word processing and the Internet are really all that is necessary in order to have rich literacy experiences with technology. Given these two additional features of the writing and research classroom, students no longer have to write their stories and reports manually. Nor do they any longer need to recopy during revisions. On a computer screen students can easily delete words and passages, insert new information and manipulate paragraphs without having to rewrite their material. This alone saves time and motivates students to complete a piece of writing to the publication stage. Assignments in language arts, French, or social studies can be completed on a word processor with relative ease. Using a word processor alleviates a lot of frustration for students who struggle with the writing process. Not only has the actual writing of a report been made easier, but the Internet has made finding information for that report easier for some students as well. No longer do students have to rely on bound encyclopedias or the lone book in the library on a specific topic for a research paper. The World Wide Web and email offer a wealth of information to students in today's classrooms. Sifting through and evaluating information on the web enhances a student's critical thinking skills as well. Corresponding with students in another country via email also provides valuable information to students about that person's country and culture. WebQuests and other interactive sites on the Internet provide students with a wealth of facts. No longer do students have to wait for a conference with the teacher to figure out the next step in writing a biography, for example. The steps are all provided in The Biography Maker site. This project can then be presented through PowerPoint or Corel Presentations packages.

Writing and research are definitely being transformed! It is now up to teachers to take advantage of what is available to them. They will probably find that students become more creative once engaged in such a collaborative and student-centered environment.

Marilyn: Learning how to learn within this information and technology-rich environment requires skill and experience. Learners need educators who understand this and are willing to learn with their students. Today's and tomorrow's teachers are also learning new strategies and skills, and are developing a new understanding of what it means to be "literate" in this new world. As our society has shifted from an industrial age, based on the production of goods and the exploitation of resources, to an information age, more frequently termed a "knowledge-based economy" or "knowledge society," our economy has come to rely upon service and the exchange or use of information. Implications for educators are clear. Students can no longer be limited to learning a finite body of knowledge.

With the so-called "information explosion," there is more data available than ever before. Knowing how to ask the right questions has become the essence of the learning process. The principal task for educators is to teach young minds how to deal with ideas. They need to understand how to evaluate and analyze, then apply, and synthesize these new ideas into knowledge. One way of transforming the traditional approaches of teaching writing and research is through resource-based learning. Resource-base learning is student-centered. Students are actively involved and more accountable for their own learning. Classroom teachers and their partners in education need to do much more than simply ensure access or provide the wide range of appropriate learning resources; they must also ensure that the students' learning environment is properly structured, so that independent learning will occur.

I believe that WebQuests are becoming a favored approach to moving resource-based learning into the electronic learning environment. WebQuests need not exclude information in other formats. In fact, the best WebQuests are those that scaffold or structure students' learning to ensure they access, evaluate and use appropriate information, regardless of the format or source!

In addition, doing "research" may not be new, but its importance in today's classrooms is unquestioned. There is a renewed emphasis on inquiry or problem-based learning activities. A great deal has been learned about properly structuring this type of resource-based learning for success, and students and their teachers will only make optimal use of this approach when time is taken to plan and implement truly "authentic" and meaningful projects.

Using Multimedia in Arts Education

Jim: What are some of the multimedia software packages and projects that you have encountered in your teaching and research? How have sites such as ArtsEdNet helped you to appreciate the role of multimedia in arts education?

Marilyn: I have had my students do many multimedia projects using a variety of programs. Just this year, we had our students do radio dramas. We went into our local radio station and had their dramas recorded with sound effects added in and put on the Internet. Back at school, we had other students listen to the radio dramas via computer and critique them. This worked out really well.

Currently, I have my grade 8 students working collaboratively to examine the themes of a novel and to present these using multimedia. Students are also adding in either a poem they have written or a letter to the author of the book. We used programs such as Corel WebMaster Suite, HTML Assistant Pro, FrontPage, etc., for creating web pages. Our students are really good at this now. They have created lots of projects on the net with these programs. Last year we had our band students video taped and we converted the video to a RealVideo file which we put on the Internet. This allowed people to view a short clip of our band students playing. We have a video cam at our school, so we have also used it to create short video clips to add into web pages, etc. We have also used programs that allow us to create interactive online activities such as quizzes, word puzzles, etc. Some of our students have become very good at using technology and have a lot to offer and teach us as educators. They are a wonderful source for us.

Really, the topics for multimedia projects are endless. Multimedia projects are beneficial for a variety of reasons: students are motivated to learn, they like the interactivity and hands-on experience, and they seem to retain the material better. In reality, multimedia presentations by students are not just beneficial for the students who created them, but, once published, they then become a resource for other students and teachers.

Jill: I have often heard teachers (myself included) ask for suggestions or ponder about what to do for an upcoming art lesson. From my experience, generalist teachers are not expected to teach specialist areas such as French, physical education or music, but they are expected to teach art. Many teachers, unfortunately, have very little (if any) formal art training, yet we are expected to teach artistic techniques, art history and an appreciation for various art forms. As a grade six teacher for five years, I used the approved art textbook for our school board. Even though many of the concepts and techniques were unfamiliar to me, I worked very hard in planning lessons that I could use with my students in rural Newfoundland. To search for other resources such as those provided by the ArtsEdNet site just never occurred to me.

The ArtsEdNet site provides high quality, detailed lesson plans that any teacher can follow. Lesson plans are available for all grade levels and are connected to the National Standards for Art Education. Many of the lesson plans are theme related (such as "Space Art through the Ages") or identify related subject areas. Often a summary or context for the lesson is given, followed by a focus and objectives. Resources, materials, vocabulary, preparation, procedure, and assessment are all outlined for the teacher. Sometimes background information is provided for the teacher as well as extension activities and references.

ArtsEdNet offers numerous lesson plans that I would certainly consider for future use, but the lesson that intrigued me most was "Teaching Across the Curriculum: An Aesthetic Experience for Grade Six" by Evelyn Sonnichsen. This lesson is designed to take 2-3 sessions (but I could see it taking longer). Students, through presentation and discussion, learn about the different functions of art and how art in public places can sometimes cause controversy. Students study and identify the function of various works of art (pleasure, economic worth, power or position, to record history or other functional purposes), write about a piece of art in their journals, read and discuss an article with a controversial art issue, then take on roles of the various people involved in the issue and in groups plan and perform a skit highlighting their ideas about the problem. After all performances, a discussion/debate will be held to clarify issues. A second performance will be videotaped, then students will write in their journals, summarizing their ideas about public art. The lesson plan for this is very detailed and offers the teacher support materials. I can identify with this lesson as Newfoundland (my former home) has numerous examples of public art. Much of it is to record history and is painted on water towers, concrete walls surrounding cemeteries and sides of buildings. In any school, lesson plans from ArtsEdNet can be adapted to meet the art education objectives outlined by the province.

VISITING VIRTUAL MUSEUMS AND ART GALLERIES

Jim: Visit two online art galleries/museums such as the Royal Ontario Museum in Toronto and the Metropolitan Museum of Art in New York. How might you make use of sites such as these to include some art history and appreciation in your teaching?

Marilyn: Online museums offer wonderful opportunities for teachers and students. Sites such as the Royal Ontario Museum and the Metropolitan Museum of Art can be used to improve students' creative writing, social studies and critical thinking skills. Online art collections can also assist students to become divergent thinkers. Teachers can use online landscapes, pictures, and paintings to inspire their students to do some creative writing. They have to imagine the setting for the picture and then develop a story around it. This usually works out really well. It encourages students to think, write, research, and create their own works.

Online museums can also be used to help students to explain how artworks can tell stories about important historical events. Artworks also often express the personal and cultural identities of those who make them. Students can learn more about cultures by looking at paintings from different countries and in different eras. Online museums/galleries can allow teachers to bring the art and culture of different countries into their classroom. Students can come to understand the values and attitudes held by individuals and communities.

Students can make their own exhibition of a country's cultures by clicking on images and saving them. They can then create a presentation to show the rest of the class in which they talk about the art images they have selected for their exhibition and why they have chosen them. I believe arts education definitely has a place in our curriculum. It helps develop self-esteem and encourages students to become more self-expressive. The arts also enhance the development of multiple intelligences. They allow all students to become involved in areas of thought that they may have otherwise found too difficult or uninteresting. Although arts education is critical to include in our curriculum, I also believe that it too will be moving more and more into the technological realm. Students will need to learn graphic literacy and design skills in order to create the kinds of multimedia presentations we now require them to make. Students need to know how sound, music, video, images, backgrounds and animation communicate ideas. Students need to know not only how to produce these types of presentations, but also how to read them.

Jill: It is important that students of all ages develop an appreciation for art. This is particularly important within one's own culture because, with the appreciation of local artists' work comes a history lesson. As a Newfoundlander, I reflect on the work of Christopher Pratt, David Blackwood and Lloyd Pretty who, through their works of art, tell of Newfoundland traditions such as mummering, the seal fishery and the Canadian Railway train known as the Newfie Bullet.

Through the use of such sites as The Newfoundland Museum, the Royal Ontario Museum, New York's Metropolitan Museum of Art, and many others, teachers can invite students to share in the history of many cultures. For the thousands of students who live in rural Canada and cannot make actual visits to museums and art galleries, web sites such as these can be visited virtually.

Teachers can create treasure hunts on the web, and students, through their searches, can find information, graphics, artifacts and other treasures on such topics as The Newfoundland Mi'kmaq, the history of electricity in Ontario, Canada's native people and landscapes, Japanese arms and armor, Egyptian art, or early costumes and jewelry. Students could also study the theme of particular Canadian artists such as Paul Kane (Canada's natives and landscapes) or David Blackwood (Newfoundland's seal fishery and hardships) and present their findings in a slide show using Corel Presentations, PowerPoint or ClarisWorks Draw. Whatever the activity, web sites such as those mentioned above, open the doors to wondrous works of art and provide great opportunities for teachers to teach art history and appreciation.

Natasha: It would be easy to incorporate these sites into an art history and appreciation lesson. Some children will never have the opportunity to visit these museums "in real life," so to take a virtual tour is the next best thing…and it's free. It costs $15.00 for adult admission at the ROM! I thought the 360 degree picture of the Egypt exhibit was an excellent Virtual Reality tour. What students would benefit from the most, though, I think would be the Web Activities and Quizzes sections. This is where I spent most of my time. I think, through these activities, that students can be introduced to art appreciation.

CREATING WEB LESSONS FOR THE HUMANITIES

Jim: What topic have you chosen for your web lesson and how have you structured the activities? Why have you chosen the particular sites and multimedia formats which you have included in the lesson?

Mary: The topic I chose for a thematic multimedia project was a novel study of *Anne Frank: Diary of a Young Girl*. I plan to assign a variety of class projects with student groups being responsible for developing identified sub-topics. The sub-topics will be as follows. One group will examine the historical context of the novel by seeking sites which will provide information on Nazism, Hitler's rise to power and facts about WWII. One activity for students will be to construct a time line of significant political and economic events in Western Europe during the 30's and 40's. Another group will find sites which provide facts about the Holocaust and interviews with survivors. Students in this group will also research Judaism, particularly Jewish holidays and symbols. Students in a third group will be responsible for visiting sites which provide photos of the camps, the crematorium, selected entries of Anne's diary and perhaps a virtual visit to the Secret Annex. Students in a fourth group will research facts about Anne's life and include a photo scrapbook of Anne's family and the people who helped them while they were in hiding. Finally, in the fifth group, students will have an opportunity to express their own views on stereotyping, racism, local and global examples of injustice and other human rights issues. The student groups will rotate around each of the sub-topics so that all students would contribute to the research and gathering of sites.

Natasha: When I originally thought about my final web-based project for this course, I felt that I wanted to do a multimedia project that I would personally enjoy working on with my students. I wanted it to include the idea of a multimedia scrapbook activity similar to the 'Exploring China' one in Tom March's *Six Paths to China*. If I were teaching in the Maritimes, I would want to have Acadian students explore their origins in France. They could go on a virtual tour of the different cities where their ancestors lived. Here, with audio and video clips, they could see how dialects are different and trace the pattern of how they evolved and explain why they are continually changing. They could gather information on French music (mp3s or words), dance (video or instructions with music), the history of deportation (pictures), etc. They could also contrast Acadians then to Acadians now and research why Acadians are in a constant struggle to save their language. All of these artifacts could be gathered and arranged in a multimedia scrapbook to be presented to the class or to the school for everyone to enjoy. Students would definitely learn to use the tools not only of the net, but also of various software packages (Hyperstudio or Power Point, Hypertext Dictionary, Roget's Internet Thesaurus, Shareware.com, etc.).

Because I now live in Ontario, for my final project I chose to create a web-lesson on New France and the Acadians to meet the requirements of some of the Ontario Curriculum outcomes for Grade 7 History and English Language Arts and to introduce the culture of Acadians to Ontario children. Here is a quick overview. My goal was for students to learn a few basic concepts and gain a deeper appreciation for the Acadian culture. The general outcomes were for students to understand the concepts of why people came to live in New France, the impact of the Battle of the Plains of Abraham and the effects of the expulsion of Acadians. My lesson plan included one CD-Rom activity, seven web activities (including three enrichment activities) and one final evaluation. I also included a list of 10 teacher resource sites. The following is an example of one of the web activities.

At the following URLs you will learn about the Battle on the Plains of Abraham. At CBC's site devoted to the telecast, *Canada: A People's History*, you will read about how the British forces assembled, how the French forces mobilized, the battle, the French retreat and the abandoned battlefield. At The History Net you will read an article entitled "On the Plains of Abraham" written by Laura Byrne Paquet. After reading both texts, please prepare answers for the following questions. a) If Major General James Wolfe was alive today and you asked him to describe the impact of the battle of the Plains of Abraham, what do you think his answer would be? b) Imagine you are visiting the Plains of Abraham on the morning of September 13, 1759. Describe what you see. How do you feel? What are you hearing? Do you smell anything?

Marilyn: The initial idea that I had for my web lesson was to produce a multimedia project on Prince Edward Island. I wanted it to contain a page with a collection of links to appropriate sites on Prince Edward Island (from which a research activity could be developed). I also really liked the idea of an Internet-Based Treasure Hunt. I have therefore developed a page with a variety of activities for students to complete (i.e. local folklore, legends, weather sayings, origins of place names, famous Islanders, etc.). I included an "Island Trivia" page for students to test their knowledge on specific topics. In addition, I have developed a WebQuest (on tourism, history, geography, etc.) for students to complete.

One of the "paths" I decided to develop for my multimedia project on PEI was a research assignment called "The Islands Project." The purpose of this activity was to research the rural community of Vernon River, Prince Edward Island. The information gathered could then be shared with students from other Islands, resulting in interactive learning. Research topics included history, folklore and legends, transportation, maps, attractions, sports, the school calendar, the school community, businesses and weather. To complete each activity, students were required to use a variety of print and non-print resources and to publish their work online.

There is much more that I can add to this website and I hope to have it grow and expand. We do so many things on the Island at a variety of levels. My goal was to create a resource which could serve as a starting point for teachers in my school and across the province. To help me to do this web lesson work I have purchased a program that allows me to create and publish web pages. I used FrontPage to do the basic web page design. I used Swish 5.1 to do the animations on the first page. I just learned about this program from one of my grade 9 students. It is downloadable from the Internet. It is a great program. I had a lot of fun doing this project and reading about everyone else's web lessons. Sharing our ideas is really a way to build and integrate technology into our curriculums. Thanks!

Jill: In the activity I have created, the students are to learn more about their country of origin by using both email and Internet searches. If the children's families are unsure about their origins, then they can explore more about their province or about Canada. Once this is done, they present their findings in a Claris Works slide show presentation or any other presentation format with which they are familiar such as HyperStudio, Corel Presentations, or Microsoft Power Point.

The first step in this activity is for students to find an e-pal in their ancestors' country of origin, or in the case of First Nations students, to find an e-pal in another First Nations community in their province. One way to do this is by visiting the epals.com web site.

Once the children are registered and receive their first e-mail, then they will, in their communications with their new e-pal, gather information about that country our community.

Some questions they may want to ask their e-pal might include: What are your favorite foods? What do you do in your spare time? Describe a typical day in your school. What are some things that you learn about in your school? Are you involved in any sports? What holidays do you and your family celebrate? What is the weather like where you live? Other questions will surely evolve out of the students' conversations.

The second step in this activity (which will be simultaneous with their e-pal communications) is to find out as much information as possible about their country of origin through research. They will use books from their school (and community) libraries, encyclopedias (in both paper and electronic form) and sites on the Internet such as KidsClick!: Countries and The World Factbook. Students are to look for information in their searches about as many of the following topics as they wish: Capital City, Population, Life Expectancy, Languages, Religion, Location (continent, in relation to other countries, latitude and longitude), Maps, Flags, National Anthem, Size (area), Climate, Natural Resources, Major Industries, Modes of transportation, Holidays and Traditions, Currency, Government, Current Issues, and Other Interesting Facts. Once the children feel that they have enough information about their country of origin and have corresponded with their new e-pals, they are to present their findings to the class.

Overall, creating this web lesson, while challenging, was very rewarding. I already see areas that I could change and areas where I could expand it. I think that I will be designing more of these lessons as I continue familiarizing myself with the software.

Conclusion: Future Possibilities

Although the format of the online course on Computers in Humanities Education was not intended to serve as a teaching exemplar for the graduate students who took part in the weekly sessions, we learned a great deal about the power of virtual communication by interacting with each other in chat room discussions and conferences. One of the important priorities in any humanities course is to teach students how to communicate their ideas about art, literature, history and music as clearly and effectively as possible. Certainly, by participating in the above online discussions, we have learned how to express ourselves in a new medium. When we wanted to show each other interesting web sites, we included their URLs in the text of our messages and our classmates were able to click on the http addresses to then go directly to the image or sound clip under discussion. In the future, this kind of seamless environment will become even more powerful and comfortable as a space in which to work out common understandings across various boundaries. Our students will be able to not only type their sentences into chat rooms, but they will be able to talk with and view one another around the planet.

We are optimistic about the role of computers in humanities now and in the future. We believe, as we have demonstrated throughout this chapter, that the teacher is still a crucial partner in the learning process. We are certain that teachers will continue to need to collaborate and reflect with one another if we are to make the best use of the many new pedagogic digital environments and tools that will arise in the coming decades.

What have we gained and lost by tearing down the walls of our classrooms through the power of the Internet? Technology has enabled us to provide our students with new literatures, to hear the voices of different cultures, and to experience a wide range of artistic and musical forms. This has greatly enriched the literacy environment in which our students learn. But it has also greatly increased the amount of time and effort that we have had to devote to facilitating our students' quests for materials and construction of project presentations. The paradigm shift, which we have embraced, is not for everyone. Large class sizes, inadequate student-to-computer ratios and insufficient technical support are obstacles to overcome.

What happens to teaching that reaches out beyond the walls of the classroom and beyond the constraints of individual subject disciplines? Teachers have to give up some control and power in order to be challenged by the new experiences that we have been describing. Reading and writing hypertextually involves the employment of lateral thinking and multiple intelligences. Thus, we have described the kinds of adventures that we wish our students to experience as they follow complex and divergent paths in their quest for new ways to represent a historical problem or a literary theme.

How have we had to change in order to meet the challenges of the adventure we experienced during this course and how have our experiences changed the way we see teaching and learning in the digital age? The activities of the course have shown us how enjoyable online group work can be. Therefore, we have been anxious to involve our students in the similar kinds of respectful, collaborative ventures in so that they too may enjoy constructing knowledge with partners on the Internet. We have learned to be tolerant of the technical difficulties that are unavoidable in this type of enterprise. Finally, because of the possibilities inherent in the new technologies, we all gained a renewed enthusiasm for our teaching.

REFERENCES

ArtsEdNet. Retrieved August 31, 2001 from World Wide Web: http://www.getty.edu/artsednet/

Canada: A People's History. Retrieved August 31, 2001 from World Wide Web: http://cbc.ca/history/?Mival=ContentHome.html&series_id=1&episode_id=4&chapter_id+8&page_id=1&lang=E.

Carol Hurst. Children's Literature Site. Retrieved August 31, 2001 from World Wide Web: http://www.carolhurst.com/index.html.

Children's Literature Web Guide. Retrieved August 31, 2001 from World Wide Web: http://www.ucalgary.ca/~dkbrown/

Duncan, L. (1999). *I Know What You Did Last Summer*. New York: Laurel Leaf.

Duncan, L. (1990). *Killing Mr. Griffin*. New York: Dell Books for Young Readers.

epals.com. Retrieved August 31, 2001 from World Wide Web: http://www.epals.com/

Frank, A. (1996). *Anne Frank: Diary of a Young Girl*. New York: Doubleday.

Kay Vandergrift's Children's Literature Page. Retrieved August 31, 2001 from World Wide Web: http://www.scils.rutgers.edu/~kvander/ChildrenLit/index.html

KidsClick!: Countries. Retrieved August 31, 2001 from World Wide Web: http://sunsite.berkeley.edu/KidsClick!/midcoun.html

Lowry, L. 1998). *Number the Stars*. New York: Dell Books for Young Readers.

Metropolitan Museum of Art. Retrieved August 31, 2001 from World Wide Web: http://www.metmuseum.org/collections/index.asp

Real Kids Real Adventures. Retrieved August 31, 2001 from World Wide Web: http://www.realkids.com/

Royal Ontario Museum. Retrieved August 31, 2001 from World Wide Web: http://www.rom.on.ca/

Sherlockian.Net. Retrieved August 31, 2001 from World Wide Web: http://www.sherlockian.net/

Tom March's Six Paths to China. Retrieved August 31, 2001 from World Wide Web: http://www.kn.pacbell.com/wired/China/

The Biography Maker. Retrieved August 31, 2001 from World Wide Web: http://www.bham.wednet.edu/bio/biomaker.htm

The House of Usher: Edgar Allan Poe. Retrieved August 31, 2001 from World Wide Web: http://www.comnet.ca/~forrest/

The Newfoundland Museum. Retrieved August 31, 2001 from World Wide Web: http://www.nfmuseum.com/

The World Factbook. Retrieved August 31, 2001 from World Wide Web: http://www.cia.gov/cia/publications/factbook/

The History Net. Retrieved August 31, 2001 from World Wide Web: http://www.thehistorynet.com/HistoricTraveler/articles/1998/1198_cover.htm

CHAPTER 13

ISSUES OF EDUCATIONAL USES OF THE INTERNET

A Case Study of Pre-service Mathematics Teachers

Judy M. Iseke-Barnes

Introduction

Access to information and the ability to communicate nearly instantaneously through the Internet is changing the landscape of educational endeavors. As educators we are frequently challenged to pursue interactive activities for ourselves and our students using the Internet. This chapter addresses issues about the Internet in education through a study of pre-service teachers engaged in learning to use information technology in the presence of their growing pedagogic knowledge. This chapter examines concerns about Internet communications in e-mail and news groups, information searching on the Internet and pre-service teachers' search strategies and group techniques, hindrances to success in using the Internet, and ponders pre-service teachers' suggestions of what the Internet is to them.

The participants in the study were 29 pre-service teachers enrolled as students in a Faculty of Education in two sections of an 8-week, 36 hour, mathematics education course providing preparation for the teaching of secondary school mathematics. Participants had previous undergraduate degrees with either a major or minor focus in mathematics. In this mathematics education class students engaged in discussions of pedagogy in regard to mathematics education. As one of their course tasks they were to learn to use the Internet. Each student received an account on the provincial teachers' network with full text-based Internet access. They used this network to engage in communications and to search for information on the Internet in regard to mathematics education. One of the choices for class assignments was to find some mathematics software on the Internet, download it, and incorporate it into a lesson plan.

Many students used their time on the Internet to search for mathematics software or lesson plans. Students 'logged' their activities on the Internet using the script command in UNIX. They summarized their logs at the end of the course in preparation for writing a paper about their uses of the Internet. They were asked to describe their uses of communications and Internet searching and to respond to the statement "Present network users often liken themselves to pioneers on an electronic frontier: a virtual reality where learning, trial-and-error, and exploration are the norm" (Ryan, 1993, p.76). What follows are excerpts from students' summary papers about their uses of the Internet. Frameworks for looking at the Internet are provided both by students' writings and theoretical positions. Both are integrated in discussions of study results.

THE INTERNET AS A COMMUNICATION SPACE

The Internet offers a wide range of activities to educators and learners (who have access) including many communications possibilities. Internet communications can be considered as part of the study of computer-mediated communications (CMC) which is an interdisciplinary field incorporating computers, information, and communication systems. This field serves the objective of using computers to facilitate human communication. The ability to connect to other users is an essential element in understanding use of the Internet (Collis, 1992a, 1992b). Users of the Internet can engage in thousands of discussion groups on many topics. They can read news posted by users from around the world. Topics of discussion are diverse and the number of topics is growing. Personal communications can be shared via e-mail. Interactive messaging allows the sending and receiving of line-by-line or character-by-character messages between participants who are on-line at the same time. Multiple user domains create interactive, game-like contexts based upon narrative descriptions of environments. Users navigate through these environments while assuming characters and interacting with other users' characters. Research must determine the types of educational uses of CMC and the extent to which these uses can engage educators and learners in educational endeavors.

STUDENTS' COMMUNICATIONS THROUGH ELECTRONIC MAIL

Students' first in-class experience with the Internet was to send an e-mail to a classmate. Some students had used the Internet previously and so the only new activity in this event was to send to a classmate in the same room. For other students, this was their first use of the Internet in their academic programs. I was surprised by how few of these students with mathematics degrees had used computers (except for library searching) or the Internet in their previous undergraduate degrees.

During the course some students made regular use of electronic mail. Nora (all names used are pseudonyms. All students gave permission for their work to be used here) indicated that she checked her account "every morning for mail, not that I get mail everyday." She used e-mail to remind herself of things to do or recall by sending mail to herself. She was very willing to engage in use of e-mail. "I have always found letter writing to be a chore, but I would not hesitate to send someone a letter using e-mail." Nora's engagement in e-mail demonstrates the modifying effects of technology on people's lives. Technology is an environment that effects how we act in our worlds (Rheingold, 1991; Bowers, 1988; Ihde, 1979). As Ihde (1979) indicates, technology transforms experience. He explains that it amplifies certain possibilities while reducing others and thus technology imposes an "amplification-reduction-transformation" (p. 56). Interacting with a computer inclines particular types of activities and amplifies (e.g., electronic mail) and reduces these possibilities through interaction (Ihde, 1979). In the case of these students, interacting with the Internet amplified frequently sending and receiving electronic mail.

Technology also impacts upon how we interact with others (Rheingold, 1991; Bowers, 1988; Ihde, 1979). It both controls and limits discourse and determines the nature of content as well (Postman, 1992). Tracy, a student in the class, noted that after learning to use e-mail she contacted "former teachers of mine, my brother, uncle, and aunt who are all presently teaching…" She made use of this facility in preparing a unit plan for the course. The unit she had selected pertained to polynomials and factoring. She contacted her former high school mathematics teacher through e-mail. "He made the suggestion that I use algebra tiles." Using e-mail, they also arranged a meeting when she returned to her hometown during the mid-term break at which time he showed her "how to use algebra tiles" and "spreadsheets for various topics in math." Later in the course, Tracy shared her understanding of algebra tiles with the rest of the class. Tracy also used e-mail to contact her brother who was teaching at the time in a school in a small town. They kept in contact through the term. With his help, Tracy was able to get ideas from mathematics teachers in his school. Another student, Nick, was able to locate his cousin's e-mail address. Through this contact he was able to get teaching ideas as Tracy had done.

"As a medium of experience (discourse), technology effects our consciousness, our visions, and our expectations" (Muffoletto, 1994, p. 52). Adam indicated that he sent messages to classmates and to other people he wished to contact. "Some very important business was made through e-mail, especially frequent conversations with a member of the school board I was from. He was very encouraged and happy to see me using email and I think this type of thing could impress future employers." Allen expressed his commitment to the usefulness of e-mail for students during internship (a 12-week student teaching experience in local or distant schools) during the next term. He wrote that

> *there are bound to be moments where I'll probably feel as if I am adrift in a sea of administrative confusion. It is therefore the reason why the following quote by Henry Hardy in the article, "Life on the Net" by Z. Berge and M. Collins caught my attention. It says, "The Net is my culture, my tribe, if you would. In many ways its the only place where I feel at home." The significance of this statement is that after a hard day next term [in which pre-service teachers intern in schools throughout the province] I will be able to contact friends through e-mail or search sites for information or activities to improve my effectiveness as a teacher.*

In using the Internet these students also expanded the number of mathematics resource people available to them during their mathematics methods course. They perceived Internet communications to be potentially useful in the same way for student internships. Perhaps these same facilities and contacts will continue to be useful to them as they begin their teaching careers. This study did not track these pre-service teachers as they became practicing teachers, but that may well be an interesting follow-up study.

News Groups for Communications on the Internet

An episode of *The Nature of Things* (a television program produced by the Canadian Broadcasting Corporation) regarding the information superhighway was aired during the term of the course. The date and time of this CBC production was announced during the class. Many students 'tuned in' to the show from their homes on a Thursday evening and/or recorded it to video tape for later reviewing. In this show, Jack Capitzca described news groups and Internet communications as being "like a cocktail party, where 25 000 people have been invited, and your job is to go out and find the right conversation for you." The Internet conversations to which Capitzca referred take many forms including list servs, multiple user domains, and news groups. Nora, a student who provided this quote from Captizca, checked the news groups available to her on the teachers' network "on a regular basis." She wrote that she believed the news groups to likely be "an invaluable resource when I am teaching. It provides an excellent forum for discussions and debates on all aspects of teaching." In addition, she mentioned that all students in the teacher preparation program had accounts, and would continue to have them when they student interned and began to teach. She indicated that this access provides a "way for everyone to keep in touch."

Students posted messages asking for information to news groups for mathematics teachers. Tracy asked for information in regard to her teaching unit – polynomials and factoring. She had hoped to "receive a response from various teachers across the province" but did not receive any. However, she didn't seem to mind too much as she had assistance from her former high school teacher through e-mail. Michael asked for assistance in news groups and got a response from a teacher indicating software packages which "helped in developing an activity for my unit plan." Adam turned the tables when he "sent information on a history of mathematics book to a lady…who posted her request on the math bulletin board and I knew I could help her. I sent her the information I had on a book dealing with the subject and she was very grateful." In this case a pre-service teacher is accepted as a teacher prior to his enrollment in the profession by virtue of his account on the teachers network. It was only through this pre-service teacher's involvement in the pre-service program that he was able to get an account on the teacher's network.

Students' use of news groups was limited. They used them to look for information or to provide it. Many other news group conversations are potentially useful and interesting to teachers, but these students did not find any of these in their subject area. The short term of the study and the shortage of time to engage in activities that were not directly course related may have played a role in their lack of news group usage. This is unfortunate because a computer conference in a news group is a forum in which meaning is constantly, and rapidly, negotiated and re-negotiated (Myers, 1993). Computer conferencing can serve as an opening for stories – "A listening, communicating, translating process in which story informs theory, theory informs story, and story informs story" (Martel and Peteret, 1988, p. 94). The dialogic potential of hearing and sharing stories, or interactions within/between stories, is important in computer conferencing. Through computer conferencing participants can share stories of their lives, exploring ways in which their voices have been silenced and considering the voices of others and their alternative perspectives.

Educators and learners create ways of using the Internet for sharing ideas, exploring alternative perspectives, and creating meanings. Students and teachers influence the educational Internet by their use of it. They change the content of the network when they publish their ideas. They influence the ideas of others by presenting their own in news groups and alter interaction patterns in groups of communicators by their presence in these communications. Students found friends, family members, and communities of teachers with whom to communicate. They had a voice in the teachers' network in the province and therefore they were a part of a much larger educational community. Their interactions were far broader than might typically be expected in pre-service education. They interacted with teachers in distant locations, incorporated teachers' ideas into their plans and activities, and made suggestions to teachers.

The Internet influences pre-service teachers by its structure and content. They were provided certain kinds of environments in which to interact – news groups, list serves, mailing lists and e-mail. The news groups were perceived as an information resource and so were used in this way. If chat mode and less formal discussion in news groups had been available, then the interactions of these pre-service teachers in news groups might have been different. The choices of news groups were not large on the teachers network. These pre-service teachers were limited to these choices and so they found informational groups with whom to interact.

THE INTERNET AS A SPACE FOR INFORMATION SEARCHING

A common use of the Internet is for information searching. Knowing which information sites or information services are best to answer particular types of questions is a matter of experience. Experienced searchers see searching as a dynamic process, adding terms to a search, eliminating expressions, changing parameters as they search in order to find the information required (Basch, 1993).

Many factors affect search strategies and search success on the Internet. Features and functionality of the search tools used will partially determine the outcomes of searching. Some tools provide choices of Boolean logic operations to place between key words which may make searching more efficient. The extent of one's vocabulary can also determine search results. In text searching, knowing the terminology to use and using synonyms or related concepts aids in search success. More structured databases (which are available through the Internet) provide lists of searchable words, thesauri, and search structures (for example, search for author, title, or descriptor of a journal article in an on-line version of ERIC – Educational Resources Information Clearinghouse), assist the less experienced searcher. Searching in structured databases also limits the locations which can be searched and the kinds of information which can be found. The amplification-reduction transformation of technology (Ihde, 1979) is again evident.

The nature of a search partially determines the interaction patterns evident in Internet searching. Clarity of ideas about the nature of the search and a clear goal make searching most efficient provided the information one is searching for is actually available on the Internet. Given that there are no 'maps' of the Internet, it is hard to know whether what one is looking for is actually 'out there.' Browsing through a hypertext and determining the nature of its contents is another mode of interaction (Slatin, 1990). The objective is not to reach a clearly defined goal but to explore what is available.

In informational usage of the Internet for education, pre-service teachers explore ideas transmitted through the Internet. Their task is to search or browse through the vast amount of information available. Pre-service teachers may sometimes create 'trails' through the information (e.g., as UNIX logs), generate lists of ideas gleaned, collect software, gather lesson plans and teaching ideas, or find educational resources of many kinds.

Search Strategies and Group Techniques

Tony, a pre-service teacher who enjoys a good joke, stated "if the Internet is information's super highway then I do not have a license to drive." He clearly did not feel he had sufficient experiences with the Internet to become fully conversant. This is a challenge for all educators, whether they are pre-service or in-service teachers. What does it really mean to have a 'license to drive' on the Information Superhighway? What are the costs involved in gaining this 'license?'

Percy described his initial search strategies as "purely experimental." He initially logged on and searched "blindly from one menu to the next." He indicated that "it was easy to enter sites and 'get lost' for hours in the vast amount of information." Percy indicated that "eventually" his search techniques improved so that he was able to find information, download documents, and get hard copies. In addition to mathematics documents, Percy also found educational sites that "outlined some math activities and historical notes on mathematicians."

Percy indicated that "another technique I used to search was to ask my classmates if they [had] found anything interesting and where they found it. Most were quite willing to share their discoveries." Carl also mentioned this group technique. He indicated that after some frustration at not being able to find materials on his topic: "There was some light at the end of the tunnel when one of us came across a bunch of math unit plans one day, but alas, our spirits were dampened when we discovered that they were all encrypted in word perfect format and we didn't have access to the descrambling code."

Carl constructed searches using search engines, which provided "a whole new strategy. Rather than searching through directories randomly, we could specify our topic of interest and let the computer do the searching." Carl was unsuccessful in finding information for his unit of study. "Basically, at this stage of the game, time was short and so I aborted my desperate mission with the Internet and developed a few activities from the ideas I had bouncing around in my mind." How much time did it take to develop the materials versus how much time it took to try to find them? What was the nature of the learning in which Carl engaged by creating ideas for a lesson from his background knowledge versus finding someone else's ideas on the Internet?

Margaret also had difficulty finding mathematics learning activities despite the list of mathematics and education sites having been provided. She wrote, "It seems that success in using search engines requires either expertise at setting up the right search or a little luck." Perhaps both are beneficial. She indicated that

When I would finally get to the stage of FTPing a particular host, I would have trouble getting access to the files or the files would not contain the type of information I had expected. The whole process seemed to take more time than it was worth. I ended up inventing my own math activities for the most part, and enjoyed doing so; had I found helpful descriptions of someone else's ideas, I may have missed the opportunity to be creative.

Margaret reminds us that although information may be available, if it is decontextualized it may indeed limit our engagements and expression of ideas. If she had found the information she might have missed the expression.

Nick provided a concrete example of his search frustrations. He described his initial expectations that the Internet would provide "a wealth of information and activities that I could use." He became disappointed when his searches were unsuccessful:

Many of the sites that I had searched for mathematics activities and materials wound up being dead ends. This was not because of the fact that the sites had no math related material at all, but instead it had material which was either of no relevance to my topic or well beyond the scope of what I had wanted. For example, I had found what I thought was going to be an excellent program that I could use in a graphics application. However, when I had downloaded the file and unzipped it, I found that it was not what I had anticipated. Although it seemed like it would be a fairly good graphics program for me to use, I found that it was not very user friendly and fairly difficult to understand.

Nick suggested that the difficulty of the software interface and lack of documentation made the software inappropriate for use with students. However, Nick had found a useful tool for his own productivity once he had figured out the interface. A common complaint amongst the mathematics education students was that on the Internet it was hard to find materials appropriate for elementary and secondary education, while materials about university programs and materials for university level mathematics seem to be abundant. Materials appropriate for elementary and secondary mathematics education are becoming more available but they are still harder to find in the 'sea of information' on post-secondary mathematics education.

Allen, unlike the other students, reported success in using search engines to search for information on conic sections.

I was initially discouraged. I thought that I had retrieved a program enabling the construction of the conic sections. Instead I had obtained something that was much more beneficial: a complete listing of sites which contained text files, abstracts, and programs [software] pertaining to conic sections! As the cliché appropriately indicates, I had "found a diamond while mining for coal." I now possess a thorough listing of a myriad of sites containing information on conics [sections] whereby I can directly access the location of the desired software.

Using the sites obtained in the aforementioned search on conic sections, I used FTP to retrieve programs and abstracts on this topic from Osnabrueck [sic], Germany. The programs were compressed, so I downloaded them to a floppy disk and decompressed them on my computer at home. These programs now enable me to easily graph all of the conic sections: circles, ellipses, hyperbolas, and parabolas. This was a problem on the graphic calculator, since it could only graph functions.

Allen also described a problem of access to some servers "due to the limited number of users allowed access at any given time." He indicated that this problem was a personal deterrent to his search activities. He indicated that he kept "geographical location" and "time zones" in mind when searching to try to minimize these problems. By searching places where it was the middle of the night he was sometimes able to get a connection.

Nora described "blind fumbling" in her initial searches of the Internet (as evidenced in her logged files).

> *I realize there is a lot of information to be accessed this way but I think it is more useful if you know exactly what you are looking for since the files can not be viewed until they are downloaded. For me it was like looking for a particular package in a very dark room. You go in, pick-up the first package which remotely feels like what you were looking for and bring it out into the light to open it. Chances are its not what you are looking for so you try again. Needless to say, I found this very frustrating.*

This metaphor for searching for computer software or information resources demonstrates the difficulty of finding what one is looking for on the Internet, especially when it is software or other materials which must be downloaded before it can be viewed. If one can get more information on a web site about the materials before downloading them, that is helpful.

Hindrances to Success

We have seen through this study that some students had difficulties in using the Internet, in particular student use of search techniques seemed to be frustrating. Other hindrances to student success in using the Internet were noted. Jo wrote that

> *I have not worked with computers at all in my studies thus far, and hence this extensive jump into the Internet has been a very traumatic, yet exciting, event for me. My lack of experience with computers is indeed the cause for my anxieties regarding Internet. These anxieties, in turn, have kept me from attempting much exploration of the Internet....My "fears" of computers kept me from attempting to access Internet at various times during the day other than math class.*

If teachers, whether pre-service or in-service, are to be successful in taking advantage of the Internet, then they must be able to become comfortable with it. Jo, with her fear of the computer, was traumatized by the experience. The Internet may well have a similar effect on other teachers.

Michael suggested that his "lack of knowledge concerning how to fully take advantage of it [the Internet] is certainly limiting the benefits that I am able to get from it." Perhaps more information about how to use the Internet for teaching might have been helpful. But then again who has the answers to this question? The field is so new that many educators are just trying to figure out what it is about let alone how to take true advantage of it.

Tracy suggested a third hindrance in her use of the Internet when she suggested that "often I know what I am looking for, in other words, my destination, but the problem is actually getting there." However, she also suggested an interesting use of the Internet in that "even if you are having an off day or feeling a little stressed out, you can go to your computer, get into a navigation tool, choose a site and type jokes. There are endless number of jokes that can set you in a good mood. After all laughter is the best medicine."

Rick described some general search heuristics he used in searching for files on the Internet.

> *I typically use the same heuristics each time I search. Generally, I will go into [the search engine]…and just look at the directory titles related to what I am interested in. Within each sub-directory, this procedure continues until I have narrowed my search to a limited area. Quite often, I end up leaving one server and going to another listed somewhere in one of the sub-directories. Though this may seem a little odd, I find that jumping around from server to server is very helpful.*

Other students also noted that they too had used similar techniques. Their search logs indicate that they had similar experiences once they had become more familiar with search engines and searching. Dean even commented that search engines are "very useful if one doesn't like to explore the 'electronic highway' and very quick and easy in finding the desired information." Once these techniques were clarified and students had been successful in finding sites, this approach became their standard technique. Rick further commented on the nature of these techniques.

> *These searching heuristics are almost algorithmic in nature as searches are narrowed by eliminating the undesired results. This makes using the Internet like a mathematical activity. Note that I do this when doing a general search. If I know what I want from the beginning, I will use [a search engine]...and review the materials found. In the same way, if I know what I want I may use a [navigator]...to get a list of sites. Sometimes, I pick up good site addresses by word of mouth.*

Note that there is a distinction between the times when students know what they want and when they don't. If they know what they are looking for it is more efficient to use a navigator. If not, use the other techniques. This does seem very algorithmic in nature. The interesting thing is that algorithms are equated with mathematics. Rick may be inadvertently suggesting Skemp's (1987) instrumental understanding of mathematics. Allen described a group discussion with several classmates in which the questions of "What is/isn't math?" arose.

> *We eventually resolved that virtually everything can be considered mathematical if reasoned to its basic components. Hence, the Internet can be thought of as math since it exists on a computer which is mathematical in nature. It can also be traced using a flow chart which outlines the logistics which must be followed to execute a function, which is also mathematically oriented.*

The nature of mathematics is algorithmic and traceable in a concrete way using a flowchart. From this description mathematics retains a traditional position in the lives of these mathematics pre-service teachers. The Internet is just an extension of this position by analyzing it to its basic parts. Perceptions of mathematics are not challenged nor are they seen to change in the perceptions of these pre-service teachers.

INTERNET'S IMPACT ON LEARNING AND MATHEMATICS EDUCATION

Terry, a student in the class, described his perception of the Internet's success in "changing the way we conduct searches for information resources and the way we learn." This may seem like an expansive claim but is not unlike the ones heard in popular media. Terry summarized the list of environments which were open to these preservice teachers: "This vast amount of information is made available to us through the use of Gopher, World Wide Web, Telnet, ARCHIE, Veronica, FTP, e-mail, mail lists, and news groups." Terry indicated that access to the Internet on the part of students

> *will probably change the way students gather information and hence greatly affect learning. Students can use the Internet to contact other high schools and Universities around the world and to some extent have access to their resources. This is an exceptionally good feature for schools in a rural setting...where there is limited access to resources. Students can be kept up to date on current events, trends and research in areas of interest to them.*

It is interesting that Terry would feel that the Internet would be so helpful given that he had described difficulties in accessing Internet resources and using searches to find information. However, he indicated that on his plane trip back to campus after his term break, he had been seated next to the provincial Minister of Education who is widely known to express positive views of the use of the Internet. Terry indicated that this conversation with the Minister had some influential effects on his perceptions. Terry suggested that

> *The student...will be the main beneficiary of what the Internet can offer. I can see the Internet used in a co-operative learning context where students help each other learn. There would be less teacher training [of students] and more student learning. The Internet gives students something hands-on to work with and think about; there would be more active rather than passive learning.*

I have to wonder if school students will be the main beneficiary of the Internet? Will students be actively engaged in the process? Will the Internet increase student learning? What will students learn? Will collaboration be fostered by the Internet's presence in classrooms?

Richard, a classmate of Terry's, also indicated that "students using the Internet can discover a whole new kind of learning." He believes that the ability to "interact with students and resources from anywhere" will affect learning.

> *Learning [in an Internet context] would be discovery based. I know from my own experience that once I learned how to use the Internet I didn't want to stop exploring. I think high school students will find searching on the Internet very appealing as well.*

The ability to search for information and to find resources was of sufficient interest for Richard to want to continue. He described the experiences of using the Internet as "search[ing] for information, using ARCHIE, Veronica, Gopher" or the teachers' network. He described his own and his classmates learning about the Internet as learning "as they go." He emphasized exploratory independent learning.

> *I may not get everything right the first time but through trial and error I do eventually get it right. After I put all that work into finding out how to use Internet the information is firmly entrenched in my mind so I won't forget it for awhile. Thus I'm learning as I go.*

Richard suggests that in his own activity he has 'found out' how to use the Internet. As a result of his own engagement he feels he will remember what he has learned. But he uses the word entrenched in his description. It's an interesting choice of words. Has Richard merely learned a set of procedures and processes – algorithms perhaps – which he can replicate and therefore he is 'entrenched'? Goldenberg (1989, p. 1970-71) describes a common perception of mathematics as "the least creative of subjects: A dead unchanged body of facts and techniques...tolerating no room for inquiry, every question bearing one and only one answer, an answer that is already known by someone." Is the Internet in Richard's conception simply another example of an uncreative subject, a dead unchanging set of techniques, a place for instrumental understanding? Or as Goldenberg suggests:

> *Mathematics* can *be the most freeing of subjects, a game in which the player is free to invent any set of playing pieces, rules, and constraints, and then reason out or observe the consequences of these choices. It is a game whose players frequently use the words* elegant *and* beauty, *and whose beauties are both visual and intellectual. Yet we show little or none of this to our students. (Goldenberg, 1989, p. 1970-71)*

Does the Internet in mathematics education capture this sense of playfulness, engagement, elegance, and beauty? Can the Internet be a space for relational understanding?

Richard also suggested that students using the Internet are "learning on their own without the aid of teachers." Is the Internet merely to take on the role of the teacher as 'dispenser' of information? Mathematics teachers were once (and perhaps still are) seen as 'keepers' of the mathematics to be 'dispensed' to students. It is possible that some envision the Internet as assuming this role formerly held by the teacher. As long as we put the 'right' stuff on the Internet for students to 'discover' then the orientation does not necessarily change. Mathematics teaching is just shifted with the Internet assuming the teacher's former role as dispenser of information.

Allen, a classmate of Richard's, provides an alternative image of teaching of mathematics and the potential impact of the Internet in this endeavor.

> *In the past…mathematics was taught as any other subject: with a textbook. However, as technological advances invade virtually all aspects of life, modifications must be made to accommodate and make use of this valuable learning resource. By using the computer, students of all ages can engage in the learning and exploration of mathematical principles through the process of self-discovery.*

Allen's self-discovery approach seems to privilege the students' role in mathematical activities and envisions the Internet as an aid in this endeavor. Students are to be active in the process and perhaps the Internet is to be an environment in which students can take action. Is the Internet in mathematics education to engage participants and encourage mathematical activity? Or is the Internet to be used as 'dispenser' of information and users of the Internet are to be passive recipients? Many questions emerge for education. What is the Internet as a space for mathematics education? What kinds of uses can be made of the Internet in mathematics education? What are the pedagogic underpinnings of such choices?

INTERNET ISSUES FOR EDUCATORS

Many issues arise when considering the Internet and education. Rick suggested that "exploring the Internet is probably the only way to really get an understanding of the Internet." Explorations of the Internet require a considerable time investment. Bruce indicated that "with such a vast, overwhelming amount of resources at one's disposal the possible learning is amazing. But the required learning (in order to use it) is daunting both for myself and my students." Can educators find the time to spend in this pursuit?

Margaret described her attempts to "decode some of the buzz words the net users always toss about. I have been trying to demystify the Internet world and get it to work for me." Discussions of the Internet, like discussions of any other area of computing, is littered with jargon which would be unfamiliar or even daunting to new users. The hype and popular media attention paid to the Internet is amazing. That it needs to be demystified is quite reasonable given the Internet's current position in media and print.

Margaret also commented on her usage of Internet functions, initially "for the purposes of practicing them." However, as her familiarity increased she found herself "automatically turning to the net for ideas and information and found that I 'needed' to use E-mail" and search tools suggesting she was "more concerned with the product than with the process." The Internet has transformed her experiences, amplifying her searching for ideas and information. She has moved toward a requirement for the Internet and its functionality. Is the Internet so powerful in the lives of users that it is "needed" in order to be 'productive?'

Rick wrote, "the Internet is one of the most valuable technological advancements to reach the public domain to date." He seems to be enamored with the Internet and his statement reflects the 'hype' surrounding discussions of the Internet. Is the Internet an "advancement" for education? Rick further suggested that the Internet's "vast information sources and efficient communication modes are expanding the world's knowledge base by shrinking the physical barriers between countries all over the globe." Winner (in Zerzan and Carnes, 1991) ponders information and its relationship to knowledge. "What is the 'information' so cherished as knowledge? It is not understanding, enlightenment, critical thought, timeless wisdom, or the content of a well-educated mind." (p. 166). Rick, in another excerpt, wrote that "The use of the vast stores of information is extremely helpful to both the teacher and the learner. As well, the communication capabilities stimulates the passing of knowledge around the world. These characteristics of the Internet expand the minds of its users and strongly influence the way people view the world around them."

How can knowledge be "passed" around the world? It appears that what Rick is really talking about is information which is distributed via the Internet. But if this is the case, can the Internet "expand the minds of its users?" Simply receiving information does not seem likely to have this effect. However, if we were to consider the social construction of knowledge and that the Internet expands access to people in multiple communities, thereby potentially expanding the images, metaphors, life examples to which one is exposed, then it might be possible for the Internet to impact the lives of its users by extending the experiences through which we produce understandings. This could in turn "affect the way people view the world around them." But that assumes that more than information is being shared on the Internet and that the experiences are rich enough to make a difference. Examples in this study (in the case of the shared understanding of teaching algebra using algebra tiles) were limited in regard to the ability of Internet experiences to transform our understandings.

Another issue which arises in discussions of the Internet is access. Tony reported,

"From a personal view the Internet...is in-accessible for the majority of people (students and teachers). If it were not for the computers at the Education building I would not have been able to access the system as much as I did."

All teachers in this province have the ability to acquire accounts for the teachers' network. Acquiring the equipment and connections to use the accounts is another issue. Some schools have a lot of equipment while others do not. Training and support to use the Internet is another issue. If inequity and lack of access and support are issues for teachers, these certainly are issues for students.

WHAT IS THE INTERNET? STUDENT PERSPECTIVES

This course and study was conducted in a educational setting in which only meager resources for teaching secondary school mathematics were frequently available to teachers. Student-teachers expected to begin their teaching careers in small towns or villages in remote locations where access to resources would be even more limited. As a result the Internet was viewed as a source of information. Student-teachers in the study viewed the Internet as analogous to other sources of information in their lives. Dean suggested that "the Internet is best described as being one large database or information center that can be accessed through a computer and modem." Tony suggested

> *The possibilities [of the Internet] are endless. The Internet, I must admit, even after my bitter defeat at conquering the beast, is a vast and seemingly endless supply of information. The topics which can be investigated are more than mind boggling...As a future educator the sources of information will be useful.*

Tony mentioned that he was defeated in his efforts to use the Internet and its information resources. When the Internet is viewed as an information resource, one expects to be able to find information. Many students, each with a previous university degree, had considerable abilities to search electronic databases for information, including the on-line catalogues of library contents, and ERIC. The Internet, viewed as a database, can be a frustrating place. There are no thesauri or structured subject headings to guide its use. The closest thing might be Yahoo or other such lists available on the World Wide Web (WWW) which provide links to information under broad subject headings.

Mary, another student in the course, described the Internet as acting "like a newspaper: it provides a variety of information for a variety of people" and with this provision as well as the provision of conversations acts as a source of entertainment. It also acts like an answering machine in that it records responses to queries made in news groups.

Winner (in Zerzan and Carnes, 1991, p. 166) also ponders information and its influence in our world.

> *Looking closely at the writings of computer enthusiasts, "information" means enormous quantities of data manipulated by various kind of electronic media, used to facilitate the transactions of large, complex organizations. In this context, the sheer quantity of information presents a formidable challenge. Modern organizations continually face "overload," a flood of data that threatens to become unintelligible.*

The Internet is already creating a situation of overload in our worlds. How is this manifest in the spaces on the Internet?

The Internet as Space for Communications and Information Searching

The Internet, as with all technologies, affects the user and his/her actions and the user affects the Internet. There is an interplay between the two in the generation of any action on the Internet. Consider the Internet's influence and communication. It provides a range of possible interactions through which pre-service teachers may communicate. They could easily send text to friends, family members, and colleagues but the sending of images was more difficult. Pre-service teachers were constrained by particular features of the technology. However, within these possibilities defined by the technology, their activities were facilitated by appropriate tools. For example, consider the use of an electronic mail utility. Pre-service teachers initially used the mail utility to send messages to single e-mail address. Later, they created a mailing list for the class or subsets of it and forwarded messages to the entire list. In an upgrade to the facilities they used was a mail utility which also enabled reading of news groups. Suddenly communicating on the Internet had a new dimension. Communicating via news groups became associated with e-mail communications because they now occurred together in a single utility. These communicative actions were facilitated by the e-mail utility. It affected perception of communication on the Internet by facilitating certain possibilities including text-based communications with single users, groups of users, or through general access news groups. The utility affected perceptions of actions on the Internet. It mediated these actions. This is part of the transforming affects of technology (Ihde, 1979).

The pre-service teacher, by engaging in interaction on the Internet, experiences elements of the Internet context – including groups on the Internet, groups of teachers, friends, family members, and colleagues. These elements are determined by the location on the Internet that is searched, with whom the pre-service teacher communicates, and the forums in which the teacher interacts. Therefore, in considering the impact of the Internet in educational settings, it is important to consider the full range of interactions with the Internet in which pre-service teachers, indeed all educators, engage. To assess this full range requires in-depth study of teachers (in this case pre-service teachers) so that interactions with the Internet become evident.

There is an interplay between teachers, and the Internet. They influence each other through their interactions. As an example of the interaction between the user and Internet and their occasioning of each other, consider the development of new applications/environments for the Internet. World Wide Web (WWW) utilities encompass a point and move interface that capitalizes on user needs and expectations. As users explore this environment, they have a sense of the Internet as 'fluid' because they can move from site to site or file to file by simply pointing to the text or graphics before them. The underlying structures enabling the movement are hidden and not attended to as users navigate. The user experiences the Internet through these links that create the potential for action. The user can point to a new location and the computer will respond by changing the view to this location. The Internet responds to the user as the user responds to the Internet. They mutually specify each other in a coordination of actions.

DISCUSSIONS OF TEACHING, EXPERIENCES AND THE INTERNET

How is being a teacher different given access to the vast "information superhighway?" Students and teachers now have access to both communications and information resources that they have not had before. It is both exciting and intimidating for educators. If they are to be seen as progressive and active in their field, they need to access the Internet. But this requires learning new skills and procedures, as well as spending the time to become experienced with the Internet in order to become capable of using it. These are heavy demands to place on pre-service or in-service teachers already busy in teaching activities.

How does access to the Internet change how we see ourselves as learners and educators? The role of teacher is shifted in educational contexts towards a researcher and facilitator. The roles for students are more active too. But what is the role of information? This seems to be a very important question. The Internet has the potential to be more than an information dispenser; in its current form we may be inclined to focus upon this usage. If this is the case, the Internet may be destined to be another information resource, albeit a large and powerful one, in the lives of teachers. And if this is the case in the ever-increasing role of the Internet, then the role of information seems to be being pushed to the forefront by the technology. As this technology increases its impact in education, there is the potential for information to become (or perhaps to continue to be) the primary focus of education. The Internet, in this capacity, will shift the focus of dispensing the information away from the teacher and toward the Internet to fulfill this role. Bowers (1988, p. 78) suggests that "education for the Information Age fosters an egocentric universe in which decontextualized information is seen as the source of intellectual empowerment and connectedness among individuals." If one thinks of the Internet and its ability to bring us enormous quantities of information, Bowers' comments seem particularly appropriate.

What if we focus upon the expressive possibilities of the Internet and engage distributed populations in education in activities in which collectives of users engage in challenging, constructing, and discussing knowledge? Then the Internet might have greater impacts for education and society at large. It may modify the ways we construct understandings of our worlds and modify images of our worlds. Bowers (1988, p. 78) suggests that information age technology has the potential to foster "an awareness of the self as part of an ecological network of interdependencies and continuities."

We really don't know how the Internet in society, or in education, is being perceived, used, and changed. It is clear that teachers and students, as well as broader society, are challenged by the presence of the Internet in their lives. The Internet is already impacting the lives of educators. This preliminary investigation raises many questions. What is the role of the Internet in education? Dispenser of information? Space for construction of knowledge? What is teaching in the information age? Facilitating of exploration? Upstaged by technology? Dominated by information? Exploring the world?

Acknowledgements

Research reported in this paper was supported in part by the Memorial University of Newfoundland, Vice-President's Research Grant.

REFERENCES

Arias, A. & Bellman, B. (1990). "Computer-mediated Classrooms for Culturally and Linguistically Diverse Learners." *Computers in the Schools, 7*(1-2), 227-242.

Ashley, C. (1992). "Internet Groups Allow for Productive Information Gathering." *Online Review, 16*(3), 157-159.

Basch, R. (1993). *Secrets of the Super Searchers.* Wilton, CT: Eight Bit Books.

Bowers, C.A. (1988). *The Cultural Dimensions of Educational Computing.* New York: Teachers College Press.

Collis, B. (1992a). "Supporting Educational Uses of Telecommunications in the Secondary School: Part I. An Overview of Experiences." *International Journal of Instructional Media, 19*(1), 23-44.

Collis, B. (1992b). "Supporting Educational Uses of Telecommunications in the Secondary School: Part II. Strategies for Improved Implementation." *International Journal of Instructional Media, 19*(2), 97-109.

Flores, M. (1990). "Computer Conferencing: Composing a Feminist Community of Writers." In C. Handa (Ed.), *Computers and Community: Teaching Composition in the Twenty-First Century.* Portsmouth, NH: Boynton/Cook.

Goldenberg, E.P. (1989). "Seeing Beauty in Mathematics: Using Fractal Geometry to Build a Spirit of Mathematical Inquiry." *Journal of Mathematical Behavior, 8*, p. 169-204.

Heim, M. (1987). *Electric Language: A Philosophical Study of Word Processing.* New Haven: Yale University Press.

Heim, M. (1993). *The Metaphysics of Virtual Reality.* Oxford: Oxford University Press.

Ihde, D. (1979). *Technics and Praxis.* Boston: D. Reidel Publishing.

Martel, A. and Peteret, L. (1988) "Feminist Pedagogies: From Pedagogic Romanticism to the Success of Authenticity." In Tancred-Sheriff, Petra, (Ed.), *Feminist Research, Prospect and Retrospect.* Kingston and Montreal: McGill-Queen's University Press, 80-95.

McLaren, P. (1993). "Border Disputes: Multicultural Narrative, Identity Formation, and Critical Pedagogy in Post Modern America." In D. McLaughlin & W. Tierney (Eds.), *Naming Silenced Lives* (pp. 201-235). New York: Routledge.

Millsap, L. & Ferl, T.E. (1993). "Search Patterns of Remote Users: Analysis of OPAC Transaction Logs." *Information Technology & Libraries*, *12*(3), 321-343.

Muffoletto, R. (1994). "Schools and Technology in a Democratic Society: Equity and Social Justice." *Educational Technology*, *34*(2), 52-54.

Myers, J. (1993). "Constructing Community and Intertextuality in Electronic Mail." In *Examining Central Issues in Literacy Research, Theory, and Practice*. Chicago: National Reading Conference, Inc.

Newby, G. (1993). "The Maturation of Norms for Computer-mediated Communication." *Internet Research: Electronic Networking Applications and Policy*, *3*(4), 30-38.

Postman, N. (1992). *Technopoly: The Surrender of Culture to Technology*. New York: Alfred A. Knopf.

Rheingold, H. (1991). *Virtual Reality*. New York: Summit Books.

Shedletsky, L. (1993). "Minding Computer-mediated Communication: CMC as Experiential Learning." *Educational Technology*, *33*(12), 5-10.

Skemp, R. (1987). *The Psychology of Learning Mathematics*. Hillsdale, NJ: L. Erlbaum.

Slatin, J. M. (1990). "Reading Hypertext: Order and Coherence in a New Medium." *College English*, *52*(8), 870-83.

Turoff, M. (1989). "The Anatomy of a Technological Innovation: Computer Mediated Communications." *Journal of Technological Forecasting and Social Change*, *36*, 107-122.

CHAPTER 14
CLASSROOM MANAGEMENT IN THE NETWORKED CLASSROOM
NEW PROBLEMS AND POSSIBILITIES
ELIZABETH MURPHY AND THÉRÈSE LAFERRIÈRE

During class one day, I happened to be by the printer when a jam occurred. I decided that I would handle the problem since I was next to the machine, although, usually students took care of this sort of troubleshooting. One of the students was quite insistent that he take care of the problem. He said he really needed the picture. He was so insistent that I sensed immediately that there was more to this situation than I was being led to believe. I asked the student to return to his seat. He did so reluctantly. There was a real buzz going on throughout the room. All eyes were riveted on me as I pulled the tangled piece of paper from the printer. It was exactly as I suspected; a very explicit centrefold of Pamela Anderson in her birthday suit.

The emergence of new information and communication technologies on the educational horizon brings with it many possibilities as well as many challenges for teachers. Often, it is the technical aspect of learning how to use new electronic tools that is highlighted when we think of these challenges. There's no doubting the fact that learning to use new tools represents the first step, one that encompasses its own challenges for teachers and requires an investment of time, energy and effort. However, we cannot overlook the fact that teachers face other challenges besides technical ones as they integrate new technologies into their existing practices. In many instances, it is not the technical issues that will challenge teachers in their use of emerging information and communication technologies: it is the pedagogical ones. More specifically, teachers will have to grapple with problems related to classroom organization and management as they begin to work in networked classrooms, i.e., classrooms where computers are not only connected to each other, but, as well, to the Internet. Problems like the one faced by the teacher in the excerpt at the beginning of this chapter highlight some of the dilemmas that teachers are facing with technology integration. Yet, the solutions they have devised in the past often don't fit the problems which they face in the new networked classroom. For this reason, we have a situation where relatively experienced classroom teachers are having to face new classroom management issues.

Information overload, multi-tasking, monitoring and control, increased workload, changing roles: these are some of the issues which teachers are facing as they begin to integrate technology. These are some of the issues considered in this chapter that explores new pedagogies in general and classroom management in the networked classroom in particular. The issues are explored in relation to cases which are meant to reflect the lived experience of teachers in the day-to-day organization and management of their networked classes. Different cases are included in order to portray the experiences of teachers from primary to high school in classes where there are only a few computers to situations where there is high access to technology. For each case, the situation of one teacher is described. While the situations represent constructed cases, they were cases constructed in part from the transcripts of a study of teacher beliefs about online learning. They were nonetheless designed to reflect as accurately as possible real individuals in real classrooms. The situations are followed by a "reflection" which is designed to provide some possible problem-solving options. The reflection places the case into a larger context and provides an opportunity to appreciate and understand the case in light of broader pedagogical issues. The situation regarding the centerfold that was described at the beginning of this chapter may be exceptional. Yet, the problem is very real and, perhaps, fairly common. Solutions to classroom management in the past might simply have involved rearranging the class or the seating arrangements. As the cases that follow will illustrate, in the networked classroom, the computer acts as a catalyst for re-organizing instruction, revising roles and, even, rethinking practices. This chapter provides a starting point to begin thinking about why and how the networked classroom can potentially lead to changing instruction, roles and practices.

INFORMATION OVERLOAD SITUATION

Initially, I was delighted to find so much information on the Internet related to the rain forest. Our school's library was not well stocked and our community's library was worse still. For us, certainly, one of the big advantages of having an Internet hook-up was that it provided access to resources that we would never have otherwise because of our geographic isolation and because our school was so small.

When the project first began I showed the students how to use the search engines. We typed in *rain forest* with the quotations just as the learning resource teacher had showed us. If we had just typed in *rain forest* without the quotations, we would have had over 1000 sites. However, even using the quotations, the number of sites returned to us was still a problem because it listed almost 60 sites.

Students started searching through these sites but often turned up dead links, sites that weren't at their level, sites that weren't on the topic, sites that were too long, too short or simply inaccurate. While I had, at first, welcomed access to the Internet, I now felt overwhelmed by the amount of information in front of me, and in front of the students. I also felt quite disoriented while searching. At least when I have a book or a number of books in front of me I don't lose track of where I am or of what materials I am using. I can't say the same for using online resources. It was obvious that we were going to lose a lot of time and that we would not finish the projects as scheduled.

REFLECTION

There's no doubt that the Internet's capacity to provide its users with up-to-date and voluminous information is one of its great advantages. At the same time, ironically, others would argue that it is also one of its greatest disadvantages. Schools are used to dealing with information and knowledge. Information is to schools what money is to a bank. In the past, we have relied frequently on this banking analogy to describe the process of transmitting information from the teacher to the student. The "money" was transferred to the students where it could be invested for later use. The Internet reminds us why this analogy can no longer work. In this information age, schools cannot rely solely on transmitting information. On the one hand, there is simply too much of it. On the other hand, students not only need to be able to process it or use it to build on what they already know, but to apply it to new situations in order to make sense of the world around them. The purpose of schools thus becomes one of providing students with opportunities to build on their existing knowledge through gathering and sharing of information and knowledge. The process of relating and interpreting new information to prior knowledge in order to build more elaborate knowledge constitutes a cornerstone of learning.

In the situation where the teacher felt overwhelmed in trying to find online information on the rain forest, what was needed was not less information, but more emphasis on retrieving and processing the information. As teachers, we have to remember when we are using vast databases such as the Internet that what we are most interested in is not the necessarily the final product but the process itself. For students to search online requires not only that they know certain practical techniques for searching in large databases, but that they be able to define very clearly what it is that they are searching for. More than ever before, we need to plan, evaluate, define and articulate our priorities and our strategies before we even begin to search for new information. We have to ask: *What am I looking for specifically? What do I already know about this subject and what more do I need to find out? What are the key words related to my topic? What information have I found already?*

Students need to be carefully guided through this process, especially if they have been or are used to a mode of learning that favors transmission of information. They may be accustomed to dealing with discreet chunks of information that have already been processed by the teacher or by their textbook. The information found online can be very different in nature. The authentic, real-world quality means that it may not be in the format, length, or depth of treatment expected. It may be far beyond what the student is accustomed to in terms of level of understanding or it may be below their expectations. Making choices about the information, knowing where to search for it, how to search for it, what parts of it to include or exclude: these are some of the aspects of constructing knowledge from information retrieved online. Some of this preplanning can be done in a whole-group setting. Other strategies, such as validating the source of information, may be better accomplished in teams. Finally, some activities and certain parts of the process may be done individually. What is important is that students take ownership of the process, and that they not become too impatient about wanting to have a final product.

In terms of specific search strategies, there is plenty of information available on the Internet. Most search engines allow the user to choose the advanced search option and they then provide numerous suggestions on how to refine the search. As well, there is always the option of working in a smaller database on the Internet. Many sites provide, for example, a search capacity for their site only. Government sites most often offer this option. For younger students, there is the option of using search engines and databases specifically designed with children in mind such as *Ask Jeeves for kids*, *Kid info* or *Kids Click*. There are new search engines being born each day. Some actually cater to educational needs and to specific age groups. Teachers and students need to locate the engine or engines that best suit their particular needs. They also have to preplan, and to use search strategies. By doing a search on a particular topic ahead of his/her students, a teacher gets a sense of what the students may find. He/she may create a webpage with specific links for the students to go to. Most importantly, teachers need to emphasize the process of information retrieval and knowledge construction. When teachers take this type of approach, they will be better able to appreciate the wealth of information that the net provides as well as its value in the entire learning process.

MULTI-TASKING SITUATION

I had been teaching for exactly 20 years so I felt as if I had a lot of experience under my belt. I was confident that the types of learning situations I provided for students were challenging and interesting. During the summer, the school had been fully networked so that my classroom now contained ten state-of-the-art computers to be shared among 25 students. Nothing was lacking: I had high-speed Internet access, all sorts of programs, different peripherals such as a printer, headphones, speakers, scanner, etc. I felt that I was very well equipped – except for one thing: I was not prepared psychologically or, most importantly, pedagogically, for the new type of learning situations that became part of our new networked classroom. I was very open to the use of technology. I had seen what some other teachers had done. I had my own computer with Internet access at home, and I was very impressed by the possibilities and potential offered to me by this new technology. It's a good thing that I was so enthusiastic! Otherwise, I would have given up pretty soon, packed the computers back into their boxes and shipped them off to some other school where the teacher would know what to do with them. It wasn't the technical aspect of it that posed a problem. I felt fairly comfortable and even knew how to create a basic web page. It was more the change in the classroom situation that I found difficult to manage. In the past, although I had made some use of learning centres and used a theme-based approach, I had still relied extensively on whole-group instruction. I was concerned about being efficient, about getting through the curriculum and about making sure that I had covered all the material with all the students.

We were working on our dinosaur unit. I had divided the class up into five teams of five students each. Each team had picked a particular dinosaur and had to research it and then complete a visual and oral presentation. The groups of students were expected to rotate around the different centres which I had set up in the classroom. We were using print and Internet based materials. Using the computers and the Internet made class management a lot more hectic. Working with primary children is challenging at the best of times because they place so many demands on our time and energy and the differences in ability are often so great at that level. I really had to be a jack of all trades and needed to be in all places at one time. There were all kinds of problems to solve: sometimes they were technical ones, like when the students couldn't get the file to print or the problems were social – students were arguing over whose turn it was to use the computer, or students couldn't find what they were looking for online. And everyone was at a different point in the project. Some students had begun their display while others had not managed to locate any material. Those who had completed their display called on me to help them just as much as those who were still searching online.

I felt exhausted and overwhelmed by the whole situation. It seemed like my class had been transformed into a beehive where students were coming and going in what seemed to me to be a disorganized and disruptive way. I didn't know who to give my attention to. Everyone needed me. As well, I had the impression that a few of the students were no longer on task. They had a problem and were waiting for me to come and help them, but I just could not get the time to help them. Some students were constantly asking me questions and soliciting my help whereas others seemed to either have tuned out or to be completely off task. While I was helping one student or team, the others were calling on me so that even I was distracted and I wasn't really helping anyone. I obviously did not have enough eyes or ears to help everyone who needed me. I actually felt for the first time in a long time that I did not have control in the class and wondered what the students were learning.

REFLECTION

There's a wide gulf between a class in which students are all doing the same thing at the same time and one in which students are using technology to complete individual or small group activities and projects. A teacher that engages his students in the latter knows deep inside that he is capable of handling the situation. The beginnings may be difficult, but the competent teacher will quickly learn by doing, and adopt classroom management strategies that suit what she wants students to accomplish. There's no doubt that it's not in this type of environment that a teacher can sit back and remain idle. The teacher must organize the classroom in a way that encourages students to be active learners. No matter how well prepared or organized, he will have to improvise, act spontaneously and immediately in order to respond appropriately during class. The teacher who has chosen to integrate technology by putting the computer in the hands of students, considerably empowers students in their role as learners. Consequently, her role in the class and her management of this role becomes that of a director or a guide who clarifies instructions, draws students back towards the question under inquiry or to the principle objectives of the activity and helps select the appropriate information. To be able to do this, teachers must have a clear idea of the core content to be mastered and of the learning outcomes, especially given that each student does not take the same path in order to achieve them. The first experiences can be trying given the great diversity of interventions and questions that can arise. However, the teacher does not need to know everything.

For example, when it comes to a technical problem related to the computer, the teacher can draw on the expertise of students who have the related aptitudes. This would be especially appropriate in elementary and secondary school classes. In a primary classroom, students can provide some assistance, but to a lesser degree. In this case, teachers may want to rely on assistance from older students in higher grades who may be scheduled to come to the class periodically. Certainly, they too can benefit from such experience. Parent volunteers can also be useful in terms of providing some support to the teacher and students in a primary classroom. Most importantly, as well, the teacher needs to rely on the use of peer learning. Part of the expertise of the teacher that comes into play involves making decisions about grouping students into teams that will allow for an appropriate balance of skills, abilities and knowledge. Students will require some instruction and guidelines related to working in teams to ensure that these teams form a supportive and cohesive group. Preplanning, organizing, clear guidelines and directions, appropriate groupings: these are some of the prerequisites for the teacher in the networked classroom. These may not be new elements to some teachers, but they will find them especially necessary in classrooms where students are empowered by computers. For others, the networked classroom will provide teachers with an opportunity to practice what they learned during professional development activities. Another important asset to rely on is that of spontaneity. The teacher in the networked classroom knows from the start that, unlike in the traditional classroom, he cannot always expect that the lesson will go as planned. Not only will technical problems or glitches result in unforeseeable occurrences, but the mere fact that the class is more student-centered will result in a greater diversity of needs, activities and problems which will require the teacher to make quick decisions and to problem-solve on the spot. An important principle of working in a networked classroom is that the teacher must be "omnipresent." The teacher has to circulate constantly throughout the classroom. Students will call on her frequently and continually.

Obviously too, the teacher must foster a class climate which is well suited to learning. From the beginning, the teacher must accept that he will not have control of everything at all times. This is probably one of the most difficult realizations that the teacher will encounter. In terms of managing students' behaviors, this context of decentralized control has the advantage of allowing the teacher to quickly know each student and to determine which ones are likely to exhibit divergent or inappropriate behaviors. Knowing students in this way, the teacher can more easily act proactively rather than reactively. However, the context of learning in the networked classroom is not only accompanied by difficulties. The very nature of using technology affects the motivation of students and, consequently, mitigates certain undesirable behaviors. When students are engaged and actively pursing their learning goals, they are more likely to remain on task and to exercise internal control and discipline. In a class where technology is used frequently, students have to be encouraged to first try to solve the problem or answer their question before coming to the teacher for help. They need to be encouraged to draw on the knowledge and skill expertise in their group. Before the teacher takes on another task, he has to ask: "Can this wait until later?" or "Can someone else in the room carry out this task for me?" The teacher has to expect unforeseeable occurrences. However, being well prepared before each class can reduce the number of interventions and tasks required during class time. At the same time, multi-tasking should not interrupt the flow of the lesson, and student rotation around class centres should proceed smoothly. Some groups may have to wait until another time to move to another task when it becomes important to avoid breaks in concentration for other groups and to ensure a smooth, coherent, pattern of interaction, of communication and of involvement. In some cases it may help for teachers to keep a log or record of their activity during class. Frequent analysis of the log will allow teachers to determine where they are spending most of their time. They may need to look at ways of introducing greater efficiency by cutting down on some tasks. Pre-assigning certain responsibilities to students on a rotating basis can help alleviate some of the burden. For example, certain students can be responsible for distributing any handouts, for clearing jams in the printer, for troubleshooting, etc. The use of technological tools can also help in the completion of tasks. The teacher needs to ask: "Is there a way that the computer or copier or some other tool can do this more efficiently?" In general, the old adage of "killing two birds with one stone" is a central one when it comes to multi-tasking. For those new to this type of learning situation or context, multi-tasking is not easy. When all students are working on the same task with the teacher in front of the class, controlling everything that goes on is easier – or, at least, it appears this way. It is also difficult for teachers to accept that they cannot control everything.

Monitoring and Control Situation

Before we had access to the computer lab, students typically went to the Resource Centre to access the materials they needed in order to do their paper/research project. The advantage provided by the computer lab is that students were able to access more current and more varied materials. As well, they could add images in order to provide a more polished look to their project. One of the important aims in their course was that of individualizing the process and the product. The computer lab certainly helped us to achieve this goal. Our lab was state-of-the-art. We had high-speed access as well as computers with fast processors. Downloading images, sound clips, and video files was easy on such powerful machines. Students often remarked that they would have liked to have such machines at home so that they could download images and videos. I too was pleased with and proud of our new computer lab and felt that I had all the tools I needed to deliver a great course.

However, this new computer lab, along with the sophisticated tools it offered, also brought with it a whole new set of problems that I had never dealt with before and which made me feel very uncomfortable. During class one day, I happened to be by the printer when a jam occurred. I decided that I would handle the problem since I was next to the machine, although students usually took care of this sort of troubleshooting. One of the students was quite insistent that he take care of the problem. He said he really needed the picture. He was so insistent that I sensed immediately that there was more to this situation than I was being led to believe. I asked the student to return to his seat. He did so reluctantly. There was a real buzz going on throughout the room. All eyes were riveted on me as I pulled the tangled piece of paper from the printer. It was exactly as I had expected; a very explicit centrefold of Pamela Anderson in her birthday suit.

In spite of the protestations of students, I required them to return to their classrooms. I told them to immediately take their hands off the keyboards. The students were making all kinds of excuses, complaining that they had to leave, that they had not finished their work, etc. I didn't know how to deal with this right away. I just wanted everyone to go back to class so that, as a group, we could discuss what had happened and what the implications might be. As we were leaving the lab, I checked a few of the students' computers. While some of them had obviously been on sites related to their projects, others had, I discovered, been visiting sites of a sexual nature, sites with computer games, or sites of their favorite rock groups.

REFLECTION

What happened in this situation is not surprising. One of the great advantages of having a networked classroom also represents one of its disadvantages. Networked computers provide students with access to a very wide array of authentic, real-world materials. Students can access everything they need in order to complete projects on almost any topic. Some of this material might never be found in a school's resource centre or in a public library. With this wide access to authentic, real-world materials comes as well access to information and materials that we normally would not want students to access in school. Not only might viewing some of this material be inappropriate, but it could as well be illegal especially in cases where students may be downloading pornography. So, in this case, the teacher had good reason to be alarmed, upset, disappointed, discouraged and concerned.

However, the presence of such materials on the Net and the ease of access afforded students to such materials should not discourage teachers from making use of the medium. Controlling and monitoring the activities of students to avoid such incidents can be fairly easily accomplished. First of all, ensuring that students are on task, doing work and visiting sites related to their assignments can be accomplished to a certain degree by a well-planned and co-ordinated pedagogical approach. The arrangement of the computers in the lab may help or hinder: preferably, the teacher must be able to see the screens, and it is actually easier to do this when computers are not aligned in traditional rows.

Students need to be afforded opportunities to choose their own learning paths. Restricting them to certain sites may actually backfire, resulting in a situation where students are even more tempted to wander outside of the boundaries set by the teacher. However, as indicated earlier, the teacher can provide a certain range in the form of suggested sites which may be bookmarked before the lesson or provided to students in a handout. The motivation and determination that accompanies opportunities to set one's own learning path can often provide students with the drive they require to remain on task for most of the lesson. Timeframes need to be clearly established and closely monitored and adhered to. Students can be evaluated during the process and not on the final product. Thus, the teacher can require students to complete a log sheet at the end of each session in the lab. Students should indicate on this sheet what they accomplished during the lesson and what sites they visited. It's harder to be off-task when you have strict time limits to which you must adhere. There always needs to be a backup plan or alternate route for students who are near the end of the class and who may finish their project before the end of the class. These students may be more inclined than others "to wander off" to sites where they should not go.

In spite of the best pedagogical planning, there will always be those students who will nonetheless test the limits. That is one of the reasons why students have to be made aware of the school's expectations and consequences related to online use. These expectations and consequences usually take the form of an Acceptable Use Policy. Many schools now require students of all ages to sign an Acceptable Use Policy in which expectations for computer use are clearly delineated. Consequences for infringement of the policy can include revoking a student's computer privilege, suspension, expulsion and, even, criminal charges. Teachers also have to be very watchful in a networked classroom. If students are aware that the teacher can quickly check, control and monitor students' recent navigation history, they will no doubt be more cautious about straying from the paths they should be on. There will always be students who will nonetheless push the limits and try to get away with what they can. However, these students can lose their computer privileges and the teacher will no longer have to worry about their online behavior. A final solution to preventing students from accessing such sites would be to install a program on the school's server that would block access. One of the problems, however, with blocking software is that schools have a responsibility to instruct students about safe and ethical computing. Using such filters does not provide this opportunity. These programs can also provide a false sense of security since computer-savvy kids will often find ways around the filters. In this case, sound pedagogical intervention may ultimately prove more effective than a quick technological fix.

WORKLOAD SITUATION

Working with primary children is demanding even at the best of times. One thing that makes it so demanding is that there are often such great differences between students at this age. Their reading levels can vary greatly. Some may be a few grades ahead, while others may be a few grades behind. Some are very mature socially, while others are not. Some have long attention spans, while others are not able to attend to a task except for very short periods. As a teacher, I had the responsibility of trying to meet the needs of all of these students at the one time. I managed as well as I could. Having taught for 15 years, I had built up a supply of materials to suit all levels. I had readers for all levels as well as supplementary materials for the more advanced students. My filing cabinet was filled with all sorts of activities and lesson plans, which I had developed, for use with primary students of all levels. In the regular classroom, it seemed like all students were able to follow along when I was teaching the class or when students were doing an activity.

When we were working in the computer lab, the situation was very different. There were lots of resources available online for the theme that we were doing. We even managed to find a site that was designed especially for primary. The problem, however, was that the reading level of a lot of the material was just too difficult. I needed to take a number of these students aside to work with them and to help them read the material. I also bookmarked a large number of sites and added them to my space on our school's site so that students could access them more directly. This approach seemed to work better, but I had to ask myself if all this extra work was really making a difference in the end. I had little preparation time as it was and a lot of that was being spent on committee work. I wanted to use a more student-centered approach and take advantage of the possibilities offered by technology, but there just didn't seem to be enough hours in the day.

REFLECTION

Working in a networked classroom requires that the teacher be willing to accept a change in classroom roles. But the new roles and activities should not result in an increase in the workload of the teacher, at least, not once new routines are installed. On the contrary, the teacher as facilitator shifts a considerable portion of her delivery time to the students, who become actively engaged in problem-based and inquiry-based learning. Thus, if there is to be an increase in workload, it is the students who will bear the burden as learning becomes a more active endeavor and as the student is called upon to plan, implement and evaluate tasks. The teacher in the conventional classroom must be constantly directing, talking, organizing. He is constantly "on the stage" competing for the attention of students, maintaining their interest and motivation. The teacher is always visible, always central, always called on to make decisions, to explain and to solve problems.

In the networked classroom, the teacher remains a central figure in terms of guiding the students and providing the necessary supports, assistance, and prompting at the necessary moment. However, the student takes more active responsibility for her learning, and it is not the teacher who must be relied on to conduct activities, to make all the decisions and to maintain students' attention. In the networked classroom, students play a more active role in planning and organizing, and conducting activities. They must actively and energetically solve problems, apply knowledge and skills, communicate, collaborate, design and deliberate. The teacher has the responsibility to help students engage in these types of activities. This responsibility makes her role more complex and challenging, but does not imply more work in the end.

Students do not necessarily work with didactic materials or artefacts, which have been brought into the classroom or prepared by the teacher. Instead, other teachers' materials may be accessed, as well as authentic and real-world materials, to solve real-world problems and do real-world tasks. In the conventional classroom, the pattern of interaction of teacher to students places tremendous strain on teachers' time and energy, obliging them to be on centre stage at all times. The patterns of interaction in the networked classroom are often decentered, diversified and more collaborative. Not only does integration of technology require a more student-centred approach but it may often include outside interaction through collaboration and communication with individuals in other classrooms, with teachers of the same subject matter, and with experts from the near-by or extended community.

For many teachers, technology integration may place an initial strain on their time and energy. There are new skills to learn, new patterns of interaction to get used to, and of course, there is some getting used to and defining one's role in a networked classroom. For the teacher who has built up a repertoire and a base of materials and activities, this changing context may mean abandoning use of many of these materials and activities. Shifting approaches or strategies may also require that the teacher abandon certain ideas about the nature and needs of the learner. For example, beliefs in the need for students to be in possession of prerequisite reading skills in order to access authentic materials may not be compatible with working in the networked classroom. Instead, the teacher may need to shift his attention to the needs of the learner in the authentic learning situation who is working with whole materials in real contexts.

Indeed, new skills and new ways of thinking and of interacting will be required of the teacher. While such role transformation may appear to increase the workload of the teacher, in the end it will actually make the teacher's job, not only easier, but more rewarding. As students take greater ownership of the learning process, the teacher becomes more of a partner in learning. Each year, there may be new projects, new collaborators, and new ways of solving problems, of planning, organizing and implementing. Teaching responsibilities shift from preparing didactic materials and transmitting information, to planning projects, finding solutions to problems, providing support, and guiding. The issue of workload should gradually shift as the teacher becomes accustomed to the new responsibilities and abandons some of the tasks that she previously took responsibility for and which proved no doubt onerous. All of this will take some time, adjusting, initial headaches, and ways of dealing with uncertainties. In the end, the teacher should find his load lightened. More importantly, she will discover many opportunities to, not only share knowledge and skills with others, but to learn new skills and build new knowledge along with the students. For many teachers, such an opportunity will represent time and energy well spent.

TEACHER AS FACILITATOR SITUATION

At the high school level, we had come to depend on lectures as the principal mode of instruction. This was especially true in Social Studies' classes, where students spent considerable time taking notes. Students were expected to complete projects, but these were largely done individually and outside of class time. In many ways, these projects were peripheral and not an integral part of the learning process. Towards the latter part of the 90s, a number of factors combined to result in a shift in focus throughout our school in general and in the Social Studies' Department in particular. Our school had become fully networked and we now had computer labs which were available, not only for computer classes, but for all subject areas. The introduction of all this new equipment had resulted in somewhat of a re-evaluation of teaching methods, with a greater focus now being given to promoting student-centered and resource and project-based approaches to learning. In addition to these changes, there seemed to be a bit of a curriculum renewal taking place. A lot of our textbooks and curriculum guides were being replaced, new courses were being introduced and there was more inservice time available. Our Social Studies' Department Head was really advocating the adoption of a more technology-based approach, particularly in the World History course in grade 12 where students were mature enough to handle being given a lot of responsibility. Also, we agreed that, of all the courses in the Department, the World History course lent itself very well to extensive use of the Internet in terms of accessing information and resources and, as well, in terms of sharing information with other schools and getting information from experts in the field.

I personally felt comfortable with this new approach, even if for me it did mean a lot of new planning and some rethinking of the ways I had done things in the past. I felt that I had the support of the school and of my colleagues and that we were all working together in order to infuse the school with new pedagogical approaches. Unfortunately, there was one group whose support I needed in all of this, but who I didn't seem to be able to count on: the students. They had been accustomed throughout their student careers at being fairly passive most of the time. They were used to taking notes. Many of them felt reassured that they had actually learned something if they could open up their exercise books and find pages and pages of notes that they had copied down and which they were expected to memorize. This was their last year of school and many had plans to go off to university. They had become very conscientious and very concerned about having the skills and knowledge necessary to be able to do well at the post-secondary level. The school was evolving its conception of learning and so was I, but the students were not. They resisted my attempts at being a facilitator. They wanted me to be the holder/dispenser-of-all-knowledge type of teacher. They wanted to pack their notebooks with as much information as they could and they wanted me to test them so that they could prove that they could learn the material off by heart.

Their resistance to my role of facilitator took various forms. Some students were very direct in their disapproval and made comments to the effect that I wasn't doing my job. During parent-teacher interviews, a few parents complained that their children felt that, instead of teaching, I spent more time walking around the room watching what others were doing. Some students went to the Guidance Counsellor to complain that "they weren't learning anything." He sent them back to me, but it seemed as if I could not convince them of the validity of these new ways of knowing and of learning and the new roles that were required. Other students complained that they "had to do all the work." That was the other problem with the approach. Students were accustomed to being fairly passive in the past. In this new approach, there was a lot more expected of the students in terms of planning and then following through on their plan to completion of the project. There was more demanded of them cognitively and socially. They had to learn to work with each other and to determine answers to questions which they themselves posed. Sometimes, I heard them comment behind my back when I answered their question with a question, things like "we need a teacher who knows the answer", or "how are we supposed to find the answer if she doesn't know it?"

I just could not seem to get their co-operation. The projects were not going as I had planned, which made it even harder to convince the students of the validity of the approach. At one point, I even began to doubt my role and wondered if I shouldn't resort to just lecturing and giving notes. Looking back on the situation, I think that I was just as frustrated as they were. Yet I was still convinced that my role as a teacher was to assist the students, to be a facilitator, a "guide on the side" and not the "sage on the stage." But how could I possibly convince students of that?

REFLECTION

There are many underlying issues related to the teacher being in the role of facilitator. One of these is that it automatically implies that students must take on a different role. The other important issue related to the teacher as facilitator is that it is premised on a particular conception of knowing and of learning. Students' resistance to the teacher in the role of facilitator was likely symptomatic of an underlying lack of acceptance of their new role and with a lack of acceptance of or understanding of the new conception of learning and its related benefits. The students in this situation are not unlike many others who are transitioning to new forms of learning. We cannot expect that students will simply adopt new ways of learning and of knowing without educating them in those new ways. Providing them with some guidance and some explanation is a minimum in this respect. Students need to know what their role is. They need to know what is expected of them. Many will also need guidance in time-management, in working in teams, and in many other areas such as planning, organizing, and evaluating.

It's not surprising that students might initially resist a more learner-centred approach. Sitting passively taking notes and listening to the teacher is far less demanding on students than being responsible for learning. Often, it is less demanding to work individually than it is to work collaboratively. From the point of view of students, if they don't see any added advantage to such an approach, they will likely not want to take on what they will interpret as extra work. Students accustomed to a more teacher-centred approach will not necessarily have the skills for or understand alternate approaches. They will need to be carefully guided through the process initially. Those accustomed to information transmission will need to learn how to construct their understanding starting from their prior knowledge and to determine the desired learning paths in order build further knowledge. Furthermore, they will need to learn how to share knowledge and build it collaboratively. Students should gradually come to see that the teacher facilitator is actively modelling skills and methods, using questioning to foster deeper levels of student inquiry, monitoring progress, and coaching with feedback and refocusing. They will not see the teacher as someone who is simply standing in the sidelines but as someone who intervenes where necessary to respond to student inquiries, moderate discussions, identify problems, guide students, and to provide encouragement and examples.

We often focus on the need to evolve teachers' conceptions of learning, but we forget sometimes that students too need to adopt new perspectives and understandings. This is especially true in the case of older students who, like those in this situation, might be inclined to reflect on and to question the change in teaching approach. This is where a specific focus on metacognitive skills will prove useful to both the students and the teacher. Use of metacognitive strategies by students will help them plan, attend to the task, and evaluate the achievement of outcomes. Some of the planning strategies will include selecting the learning paths, preparing, determining the difficulty of tasks, and the time frames required. In order to attend to the task, students will need to learn to focus on materials, search for, locate, relate, contrast, validate, and relate information to what they know already. In order to evaluate the achievement of outcomes, they will need to review, repeat, revise, test, and judge.

The teacher as facilitator has a dual role to play. She is responsible for teaching but also for helping the students learn how to learn. Depending on the students' past experiences in learning, their age, their enthusiasm, this role may be more or less challenging. At the primary levels, students may be more accustomed to a more active learning situation and will likely transition more easily to a more learner-centred approach with teacher as facilitator. It is at the secondary level where the challenge may be more heightened. Students at this age are more conscious of demands placed on them and are more likely to reflect on and question teaching practices. As well, if these students have a prior history of learning through a transmission mode, they will likely have to be coached more specifically in order to be able to transition to a mode that requires them to participate more actively in the learning process.

Roles and responsibilities will need to be clearly defined for and with students. Students must be aware of the teacher's expectations for their performance and involvement. The teacher can model instructional behaviors, which the students can copy for use in their interactions with other students. The teacher can also solicit feedback from students on what works and what does not work. Adopting new approaches in education will require changing ways of thinking. Both teachers and students have established mindsets and paradigms that will need to evolve and shift gradually in order to allow room for new beliefs and behaviours. The teacher as facilitator has an important role to play in teaching students about these new paradigms and new ways of learning.

CONCLUSION

For many teachers, working in networked classrooms can be frustrating at the outset. All the techniques they had down pat, the lesson plans they had been successfully using for years, the approaches they took: many of these will have to change in order to ensure an effective transition to the networked classroom. For this reason, teachers need to be very committed to working with technology. They must have faith in their ability, not only to improve education, but also to transform it by setting up conditions that actually require students to adopt new learning strategies. Working in the networked classroom also requires teachers to shift some of their beliefs about the role of the teacher, the role of the student and, most importantly, about learning.

Classroom management will be redefined in the networked classroom in a way that is coherent with new conceptions of teaching and learning. There will be new approaches to interacting and collaborating as well as new ways of knowing. There will be a different locus of control and an interchange of roles. These changes should not be surprising. In all areas, be it in education, health care, or engineering: as the tools evolve, so too do our practices. However, in education, we have been somewhat slower to embrace use of the new tools. Seymour Papert, (1993) in his seminal book, *The Children's Machine,* recounts the anecdote of the group of surgeons and teachers who have travelled 100 years into the future in order to see what has changed in their profession. While the surgeons witness an operating room where practices and procedures have been transformed as new technology was adopted, the teachers find themselves in familiar territory where little has changed in the past one hundred years. Papert's lesson is a startling one. It reminds us that, as educators, we have to keep pace, that we have some catching up to do, and that, perhaps, too, we have not tapped the full potential of education as we venture into the new millennium. There are new issues and roles, as well as challenges and changes awaiting teachers in the networked classroom. At the same time, for those who are willing to rethink their role, practices and beliefs, there are also new possibilities and potential.

REFERENCES

Papert, S. (1993). *The Children's Machine.* New York: Basic Books.